ART

JOE AND AZAT

JOE AND AZAT

by Jesse Lonergan

ISBN: 978-1-56163-570-2
© 2009 Jesse Lonergan
Library of Congress Control Number: 2009935676

3 2 1

Comicslit is an imprint
and trademark of

NANTIER · BEALL · MINOUSTCHINE
Publishing inc.
new york

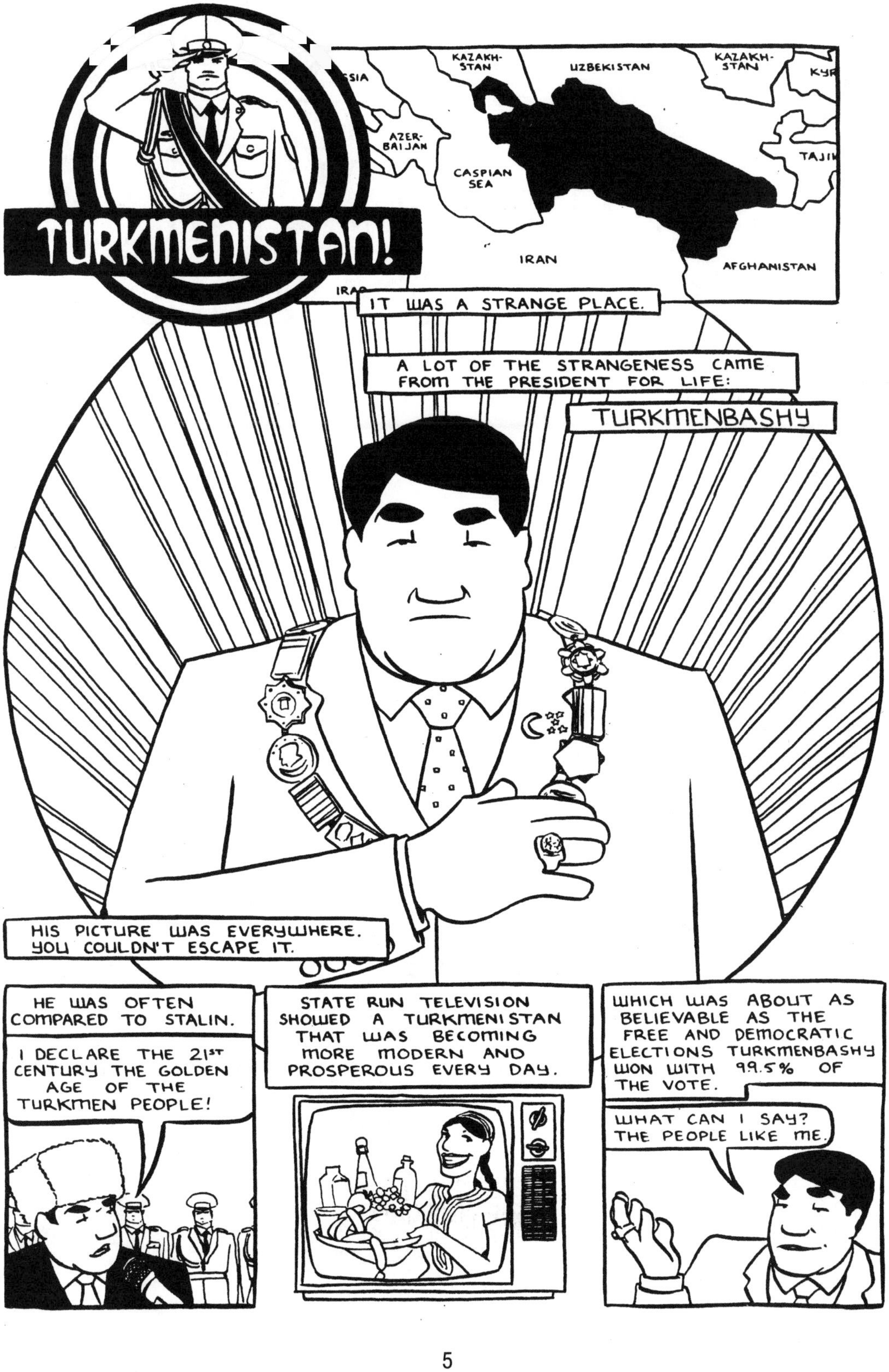

TURKMENISTAN!
KAZAKH-STAN
UZBEKISTAN
KAZAKH-STAN
AZER-BAIJAN
CASPIAN SEA
IRAN
AFGHANISTAN
IT WAS A STRANGE PLACE.
A LOT OF THE STRANGENESS CAME FROM THE PRESIDENT FOR LIFE:
TURKMENBASHY
HIS PICTURE WAS EVERYWHERE. YOU COULDN'T ESCAPE IT.
HE WAS OFTEN COMPARED TO STALIN.
I DECLARE THE 21ST CENTURY THE GOLDEN AGE OF THE TURKMEN PEOPLE!
STATE RUN TELEVISION SHOWED A TURKMENISTAN THAT WAS BECOMING MORE MODERN AND PROSPEROUS EVERY DAY.
WHICH WAS ABOUT AS BELIEVABLE AS THE FREE AND DEMOCRATIC ELECTIONS TURKMENBASHY WON WITH 99.5% OF THE VOTE.
WHAT CAN I SAY? THE PEOPLE LIKE ME.

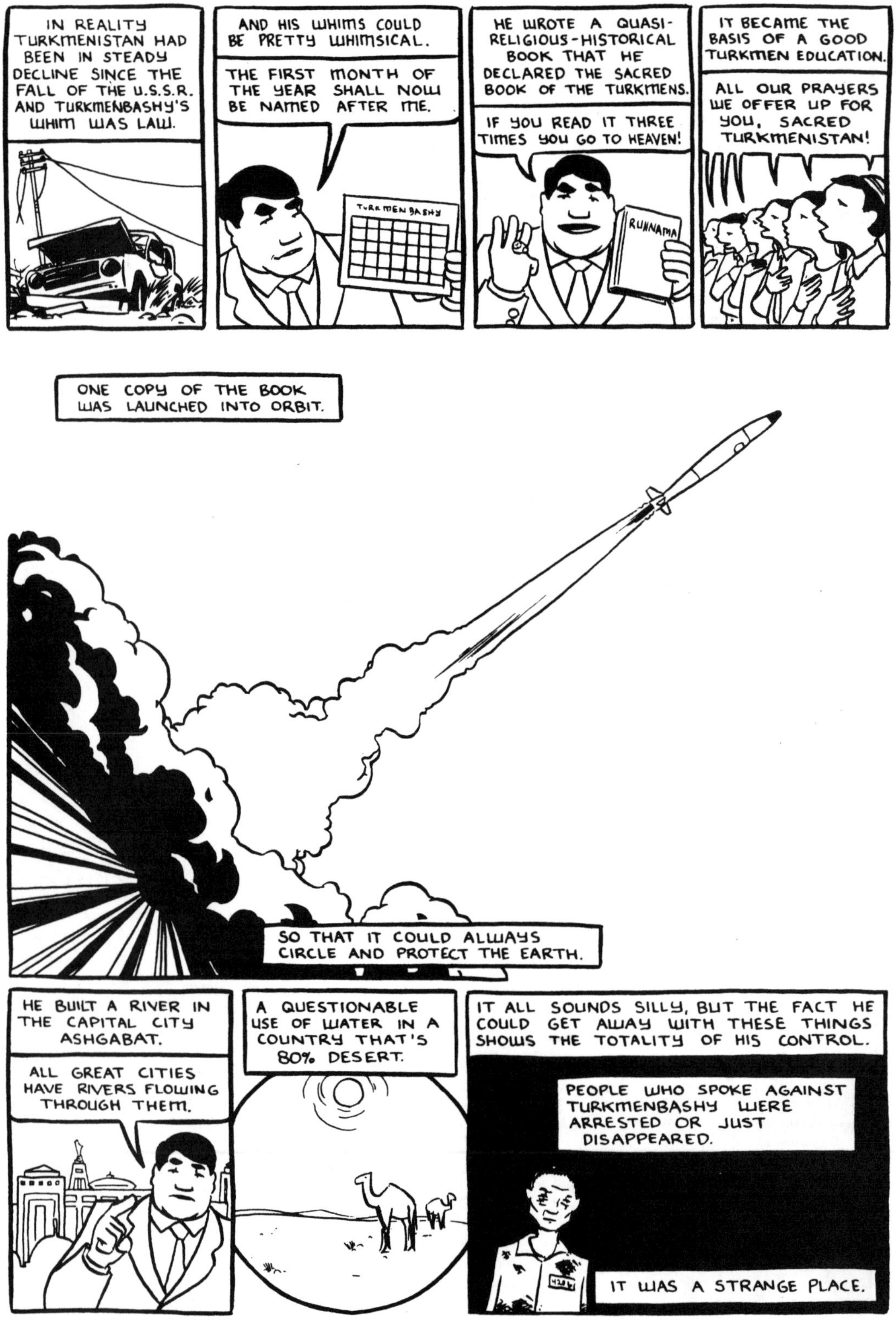
IN REALITY TURKMENISTAN HAD BEEN IN STEADY DECLINE SINCE THE FALL OF THE U.S.S.R. AND TURKMENBASHY'S WHIM WAS LAW.
AND HIS WHIMS COULD BE PRETTY WHIMSICAL.
THE FIRST MONTH OF THE YEAR SHALL NOW BE NAMED AFTER ME.
TURKMENBASHY
HE WROTE A QUASI-RELIGIOUS-HISTORICAL BOOK THAT HE DECLARED THE SACRED BOOK OF THE TURKMENS.
IF YOU READ IT THREE TIMES YOU GO TO HEAVEN!
RUHNAMA
IT BECAME THE BASIS OF A GOOD TURKMEN EDUCATION.
ALL OUR PRAYERS WE OFFER UP FOR YOU, SACRED TURKMENISTAN!
ONE COPY OF THE BOOK WAS LAUNCHED INTO ORBIT.
SO THAT IT COULD ALWAYS CIRCLE AND PROTECT THE EARTH.
HE BUILT A RIVER IN THE CAPITAL CITY ASHGABAT.
ALL GREAT CITIES HAVE RIVERS FLOWING THROUGH THEM.
A QUESTIONABLE USE OF WATER IN A COUNTRY THAT'S 80% DESERT.
IT ALL SOUNDS SILLY, BUT THE FACT HE COULD GET AWAY WITH THESE THINGS SHOWS THE TOTALITY OF HIS CONTROL.
PEOPLE WHO SPOKE AGAINST TURKMENBASHY WERE ARRESTED OR JUST DISAPPEARED.
IT WAS A STRANGE PLACE.

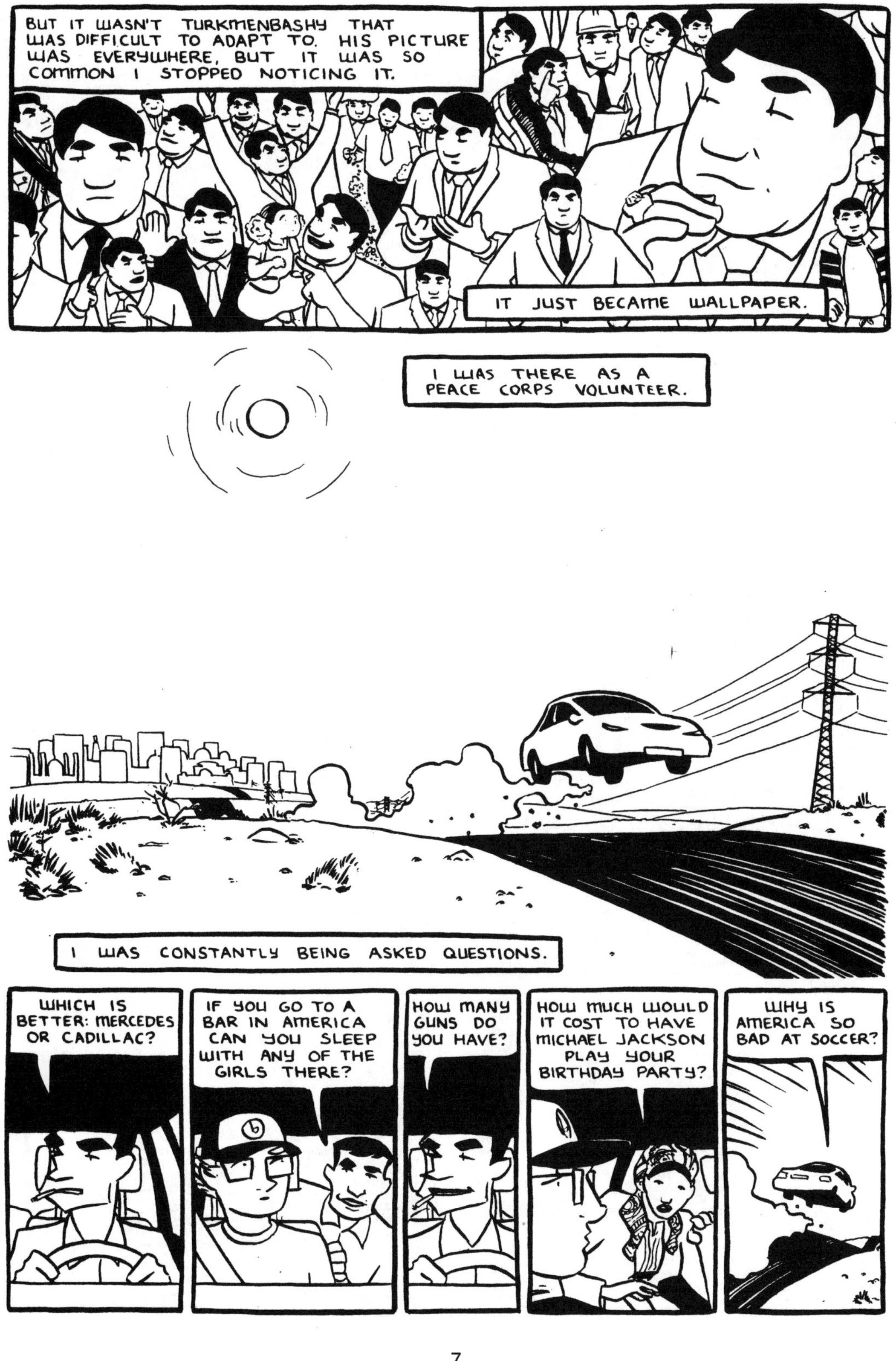
BUT IT WASN'T TURKMENBASHY THAT WAS DIFFICULT TO ADAPT TO. HIS PICTURE WAS EVERYWHERE, BUT IT WAS SO COMMON I STOPPED NOTICING IT.
IT JUST BECAME WALLPAPER.
I WAS THERE AS A PEACE CORPS VOLUNTEER.
I WAS CONSTANTLY BEING ASKED QUESTIONS.
WHICH IS BETTER: MERCEDES OR CADILLAC?
IF YOU GO TO A BAR IN AMERICA CAN YOU SLEEP WITH ANY OF THE GIRLS THERE?
HOW MANY GUNS DO YOU HAVE?
HOW MUCH WOULD IT COST TO HAVE MICHAEL JACKSON PLAY YOUR BIRTHDAY PARTY?
WHY IS AMERICA SO BAD AT SOCCER?

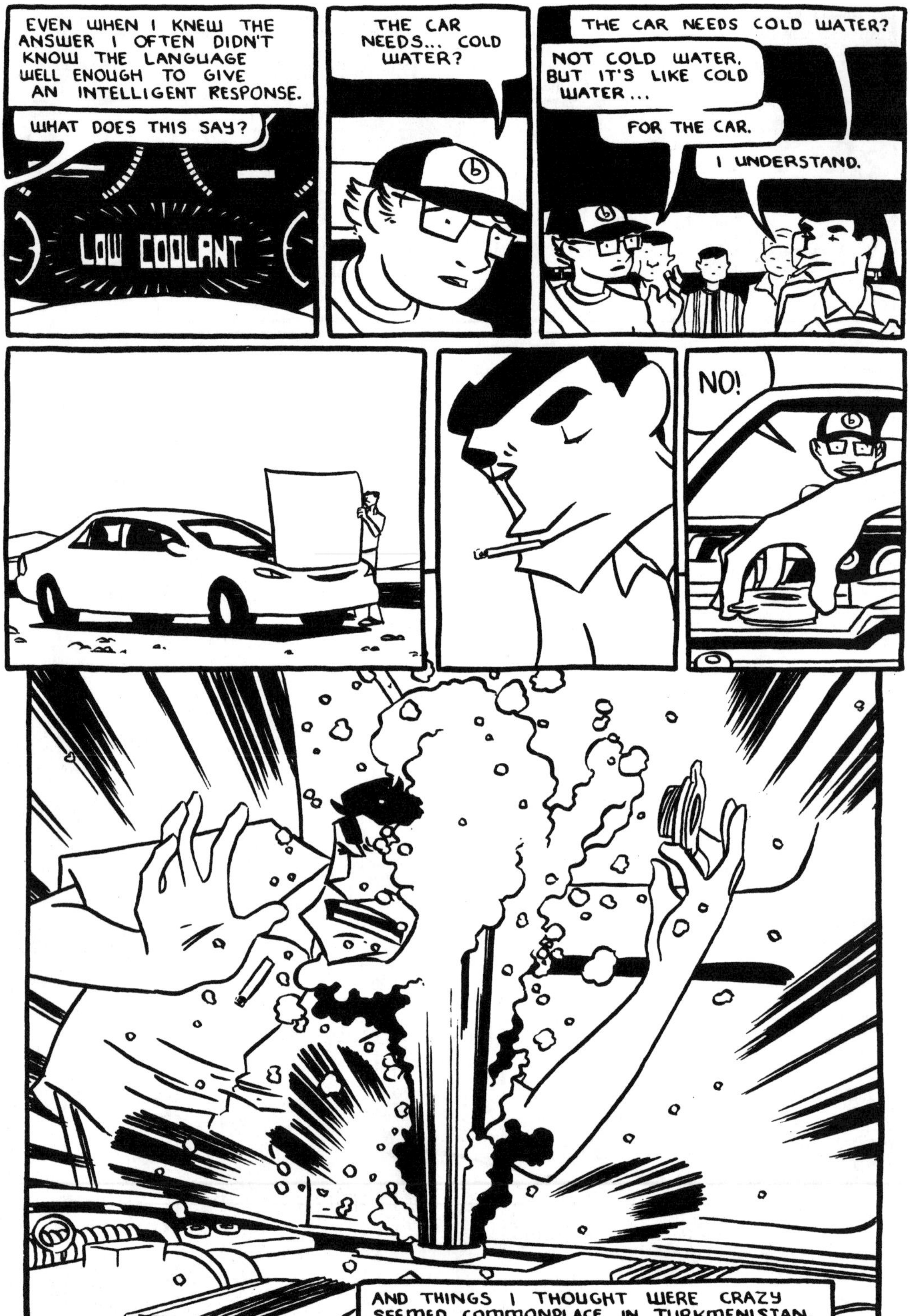
EVEN WHEN I KNEW THE ANSWER I OFTEN DIDN'T KNOW THE LANGUAGE WELL ENOUGH TO GIVE AN INTELLIGENT RESPONSE.
WHAT DOES THIS SAY?
LOW COOLANT
THE CAR NEEDS... COLD WATER?
THE CAR NEEDS COLD WATER?
NOT COLD WATER, BUT IT'S LIKE COLD WATER...
FOR THE CAR.
I UNDERSTAND.
NO!
AND THINGS I THOUGHT WERE CRAZY SEEMED COMMONPLACE IN TURKMENISTAN.

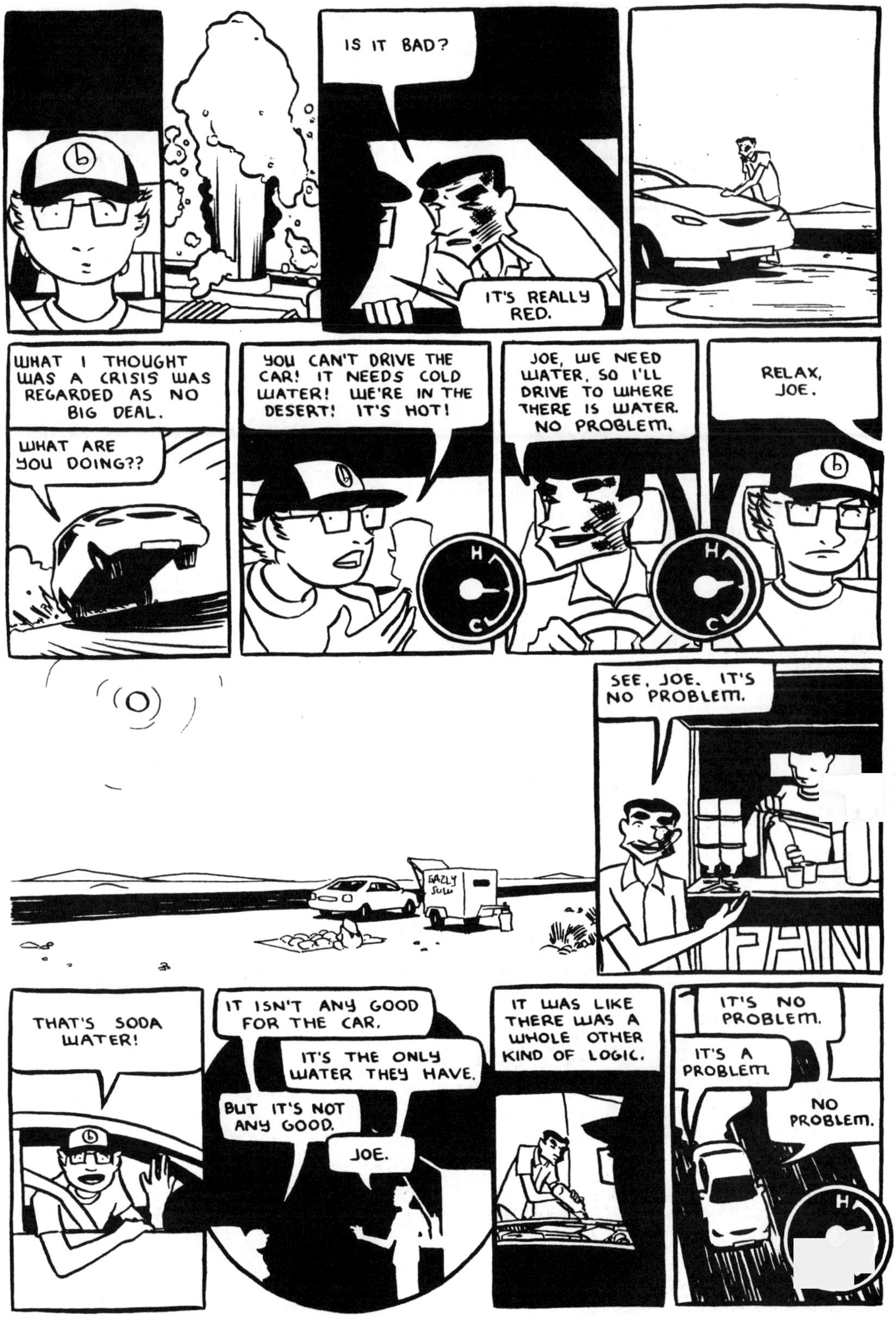
IS IT BAD?
IT'S REALLY RED.
WHAT I THOUGHT WAS A CRISIS WAS REGARDED AS NO BIG DEAL.
WHAT ARE YOU DOING??
YOU CAN'T DRIVE THE CAR! IT NEEDS COLD WATER! WE'RE IN THE DESERT! IT'S HOT!
H
C
JOE, WE NEED WATER, SO I'LL DRIVE TO WHERE THERE IS WATER. NO PROBLEM.
H
C
RELAX, JOE.
SEE, JOE. IT'S NO PROBLEM.
THAT'S SODA WATER!
IT ISN'T ANY GOOD FOR THE CAR.
IT'S THE ONLY WATER THEY HAVE.
BUT IT'S NOT ANY GOOD.
JOE.
IT WAS LIKE THERE WAS A WHOLE OTHER KIND OF LOGIC.
IT'S NO PROBLEM.
IT'S A PROBLEM.
NO PROBLEM.
H

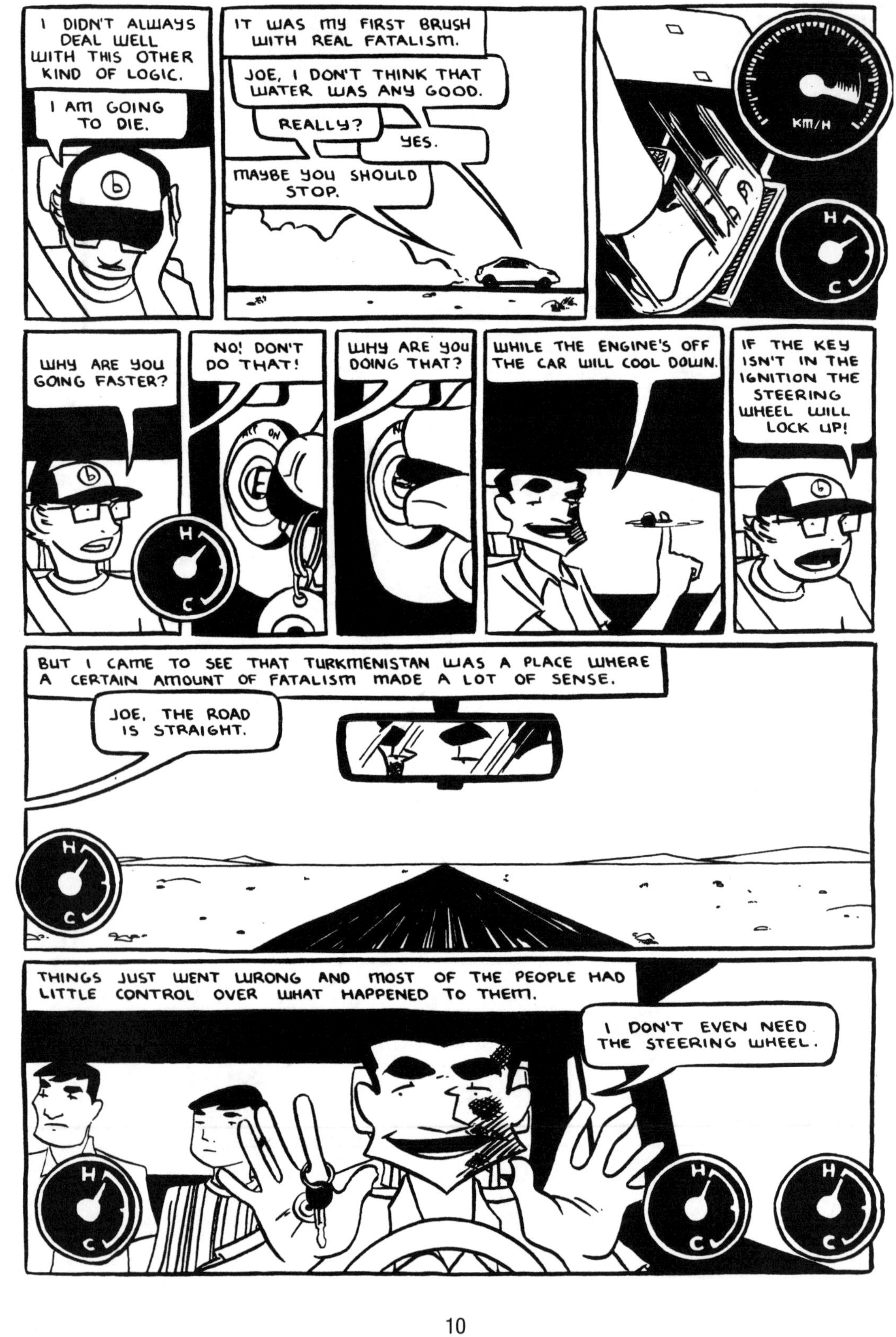

I DIDN'T ALWAYS DEAL WELL WITH THIS OTHER KIND OF LOGIC.
I AM GOING TO DIE.
IT WAS MY FIRST BRUSH WITH REAL FATALISM.
JOE, I DON'T THINK THAT WATER WAS ANY GOOD.
REALLY?
YES.
MAYBE YOU SHOULD STOP.
KM/H
H
C
WHY ARE YOU GOING FASTER?
NO! DON'T DO THAT!
WHY ARE YOU DOING THAT?
WHILE THE ENGINE'S OFF THE CAR WILL COOL DOWN.
IF THE KEY ISN'T IN THE IGNITION THE STEERING WHEEL WILL LOCK UP!
BUT I CAME TO SEE THAT TURKMENISTAN WAS A PLACE WHERE A CERTAIN AMOUNT OF FATALISM MADE A LOT OF SENSE.
JOE, THE ROAD IS STRAIGHT.
THINGS JUST WENT WRONG AND MOST OF THE PEOPLE HAD LITTLE CONTROL OVER WHAT HAPPENED TO THEM.
I DON'T EVEN NEED THE STEERING WHEEL.

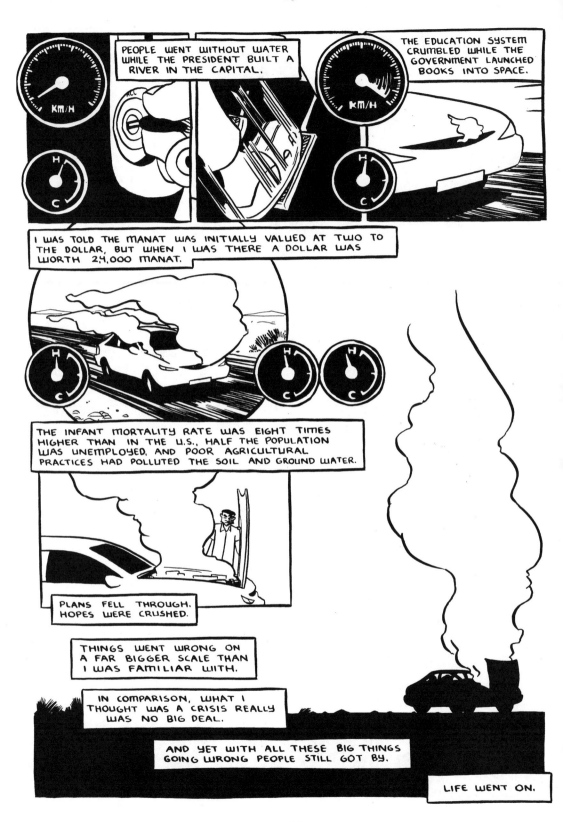

PEOPLE WENT WITHOUT WATER WHILE THE PRESIDENT BUILT A RIVER IN THE CAPITAL.

THE EDUCATION SYSTEM CRUMBLED WHILE THE GOVERNMENT LAUNCHED BOOKS INTO SPACE.

I WAS TOLD THE MANAT WAS INITIALLY VALUED AT TWO TO THE DOLLAR, BUT WHEN I WAS THERE A DOLLAR WAS WORTH 24,000 MANAT.

THE INFANT MORTALITY RATE WAS EIGHT TIMES HIGHER THAN IN THE U.S., HALF THE POPULATION WAS UNEMPLOYED, AND POOR AGRICULTURAL PRACTICES HAD POLLUTED THE SOIL AND GROUND WATER.

PLANS FELL THROUGH. HOPES WERE CRUSHED.

THINGS WENT WRONG ON A FAR BIGGER SCALE THAN I WAS FAMILIAR WITH.

IN COMPARISON, WHAT I THOUGHT WAS A CRISIS REALLY WAS NO BIG DEAL.

AND YET WITH ALL THESE BIG THINGS GOING WRONG PEOPLE STILL GOT BY.

LIFE WENT ON.

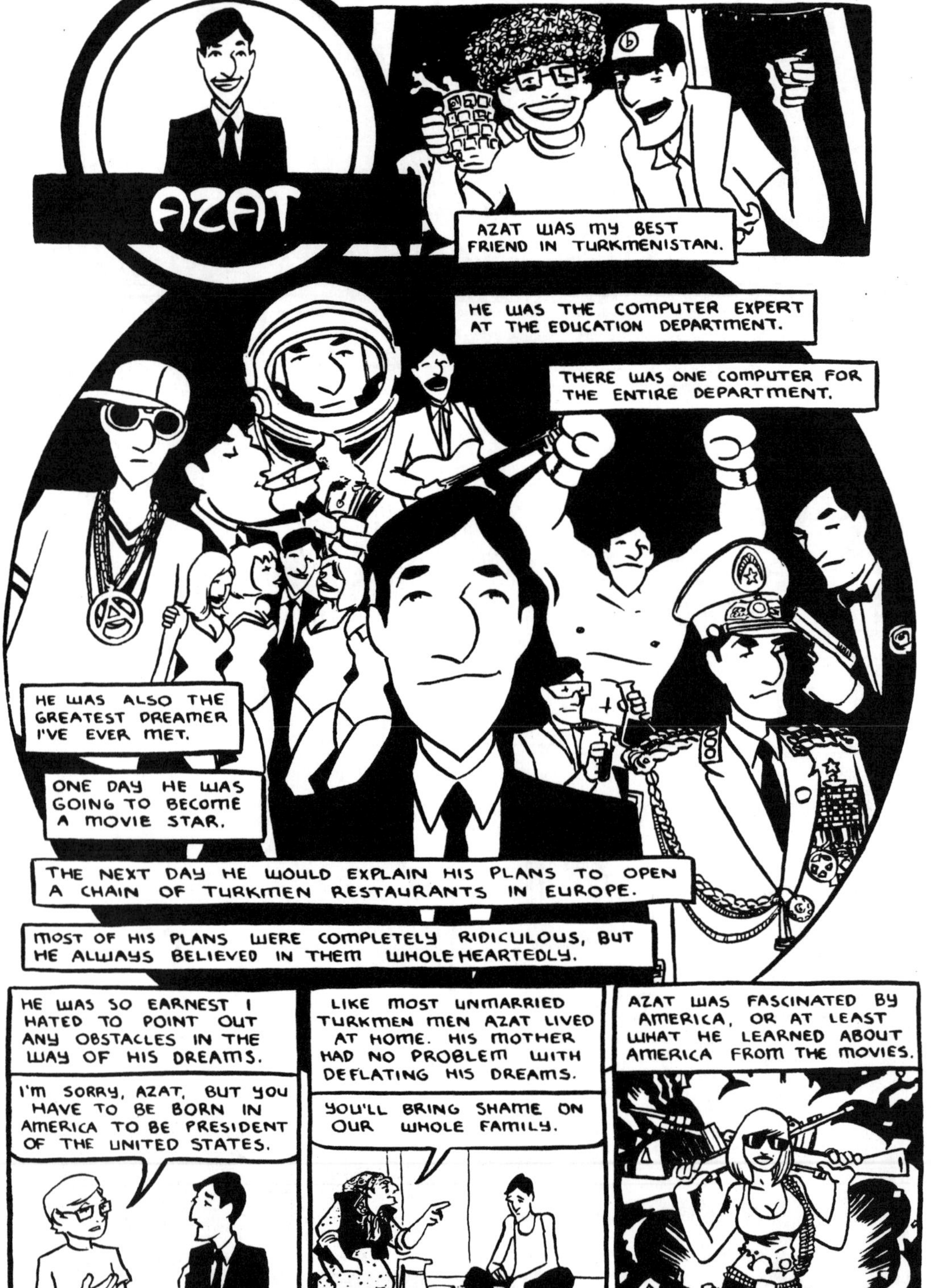
AZAT
AZAT WAS MY BEST FRIEND IN TURKMENISTAN.
HE WAS THE COMPUTER EXPERT AT THE EDUCATION DEPARTMENT.
THERE WAS ONE COMPUTER FOR THE ENTIRE DEPARTMENT.
HE WAS ALSO THE GREATEST DREAMER I'VE EVER MET.
ONE DAY HE WAS GOING TO BECOME A MOVIE STAR.
THE NEXT DAY HE WOULD EXPLAIN HIS PLANS TO OPEN A CHAIN OF TURKMEN RESTAURANTS IN EUROPE.
MOST OF HIS PLANS WERE COMPLETELY RIDICULOUS, BUT HE ALWAYS BELIEVED IN THEM WHOLEHEARTEDLY.
HE WAS SO EARNEST I HATED TO POINT OUT ANY OBSTACLES IN THE WAY OF HIS DREAMS.
I'M SORRY, AZAT, BUT YOU HAVE TO BE BORN IN AMERICA TO BE PRESIDENT OF THE UNITED STATES.
LIKE MOST UNMARRIED TURKMEN MEN AZAT LIVED AT HOME. HIS MOTHER HAD NO PROBLEM WITH DEFLATING HIS DREAMS.
YOU'LL BRING SHAME ON OUR WHOLE FAMILY.
AZAT WAS FASCINATED BY AMERICA, OR AT LEAST WHAT HE LEARNED ABOUT AMERICA FROM THE MOVIES.

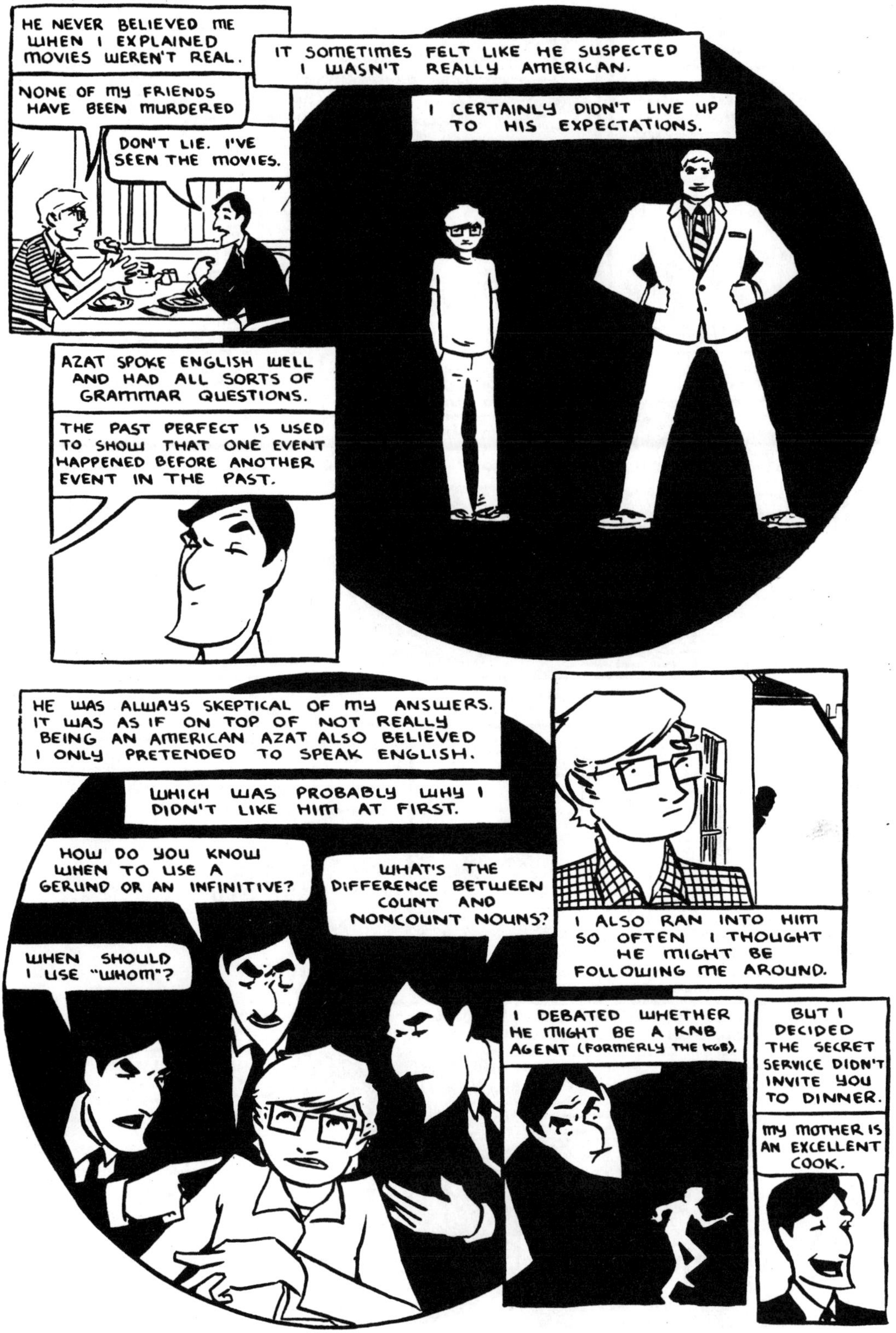
HE NEVER BELIEVED ME WHEN I EXPLAINED MOVIES WEREN'T REAL.
IT SOMETIMES FELT LIKE HE SUSPECTED I WASN'T REALLY AMERICAN.
NONE OF MY FRIENDS HAVE BEEN MURDERED
DON'T LIE. I'VE SEEN THE MOVIES.
I CERTAINLY DIDN'T LIVE UP TO HIS EXPECTATIONS.
AZAT SPOKE ENGLISH WELL AND HAD ALL SORTS OF GRAMMAR QUESTIONS.
THE PAST PERFECT IS USED TO SHOW THAT ONE EVENT HAPPENED BEFORE ANOTHER EVENT IN THE PAST.
HE WAS ALWAYS SKEPTICAL OF MY ANSWERS. IT WAS AS IF ON TOP OF NOT REALLY BEING AN AMERICAN AZAT ALSO BELIEVED I ONLY PRETENDED TO SPEAK ENGLISH.
WHICH WAS PROBABLY WHY I DIDN'T LIKE HIM AT FIRST.
HOW DO YOU KNOW WHEN TO USE A GERUND OR AN INFINITIVE?
WHAT'S THE DIFFERENCE BETWEEN COUNT AND NONCOUNT NOUNS?
WHEN SHOULD I USE "WHOM"?
I ALSO RAN INTO HIM SO OFTEN I THOUGHT HE MIGHT BE FOLLOWING ME AROUND.
I DEBATED WHETHER HE MIGHT BE A KNB AGENT (FORMERLY THE KGB).
BUT I DECIDED THE SECRET SERVICE DIDN'T INVITE YOU TO DINNER.
MY MOTHER IS AN EXCELLENT COOK.

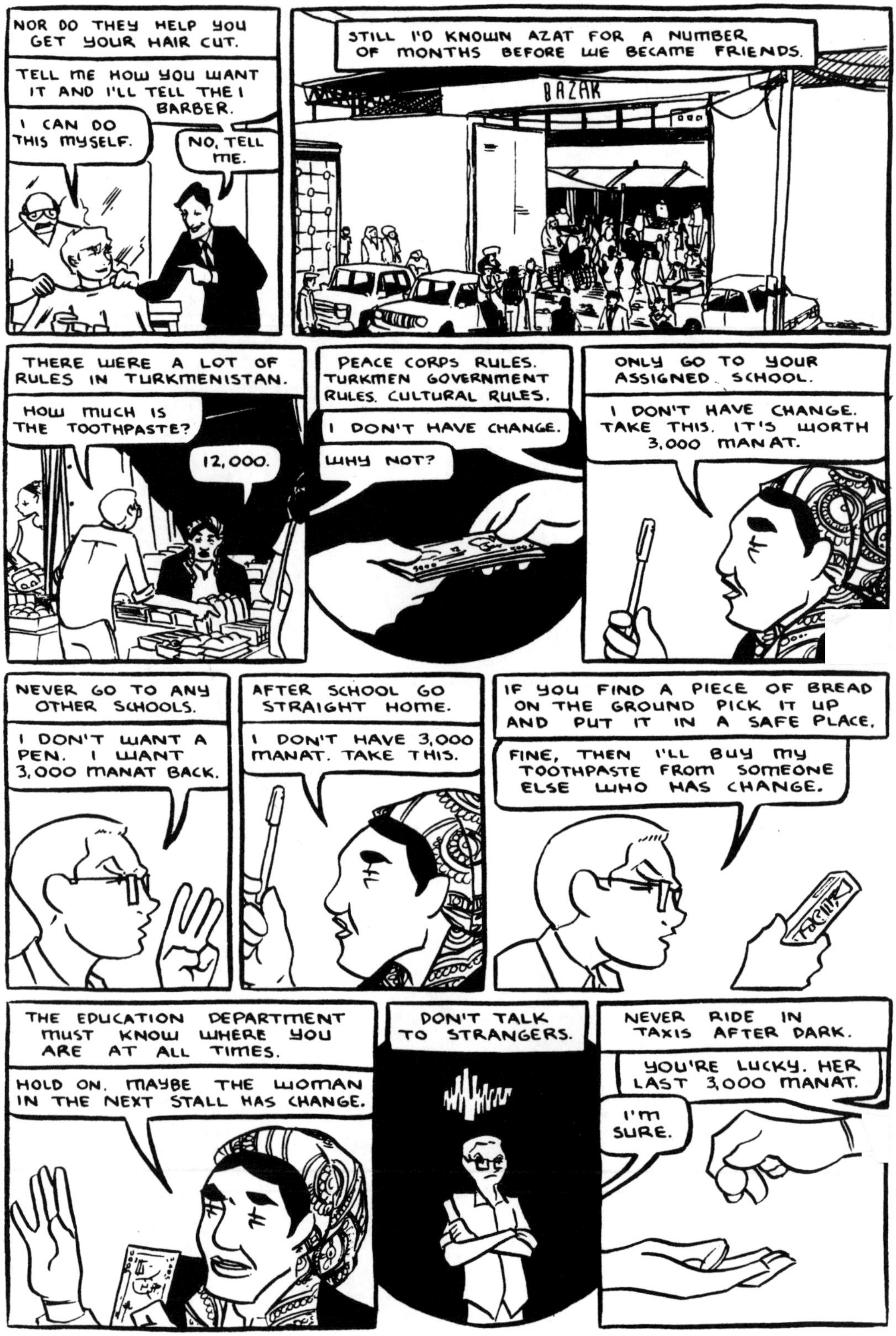

NOR DO THEY HELP YOU GET YOUR HAIR CUT.
TELL ME HOW YOU WANT IT AND I'LL TELL THE BARBER.
I CAN DO THIS MYSELF.
NO, TELL ME.
STILL I'D KNOWN AZAT FOR A NUMBER OF MONTHS BEFORE WE BECAME FRIENDS.
BAZAR
THERE WERE A LOT OF RULES IN TURKMENISTAN.
HOW MUCH IS THE TOOTHPASTE?
12,000.
PEACE CORPS RULES. TURKMEN GOVERNMENT RULES. CULTURAL RULES.
I DON'T HAVE CHANGE.
WHY NOT?
ONLY GO TO YOUR ASSIGNED SCHOOL.
I DON'T HAVE CHANGE. TAKE THIS. IT'S WORTH 3,000 MANAT.
NEVER GO TO ANY OTHER SCHOOLS.
I DON'T WANT A PEN. I WANT 3,000 MANAT BACK.
AFTER SCHOOL GO STRAIGHT HOME.
I DON'T HAVE 3,000 MANAT. TAKE THIS.
IF YOU FIND A PIECE OF BREAD ON THE GROUND PICK IT UP AND PUT IT IN A SAFE PLACE.
FINE, THEN I'LL BUY MY TOOTHPASTE FROM SOMEONE ELSE WHO HAS CHANGE.
THE EDUCATION DEPARTMENT MUST KNOW WHERE YOU ARE AT ALL TIMES.
HOLD ON. MAYBE THE WOMAN IN THE NEXT STALL HAS CHANGE.
DON'T TALK TO STRANGERS.
NEVER RIDE IN TAXIS AFTER DARK.
YOU'RE LUCKY. HER LAST 3,000 MANAT.
I'M SURE.

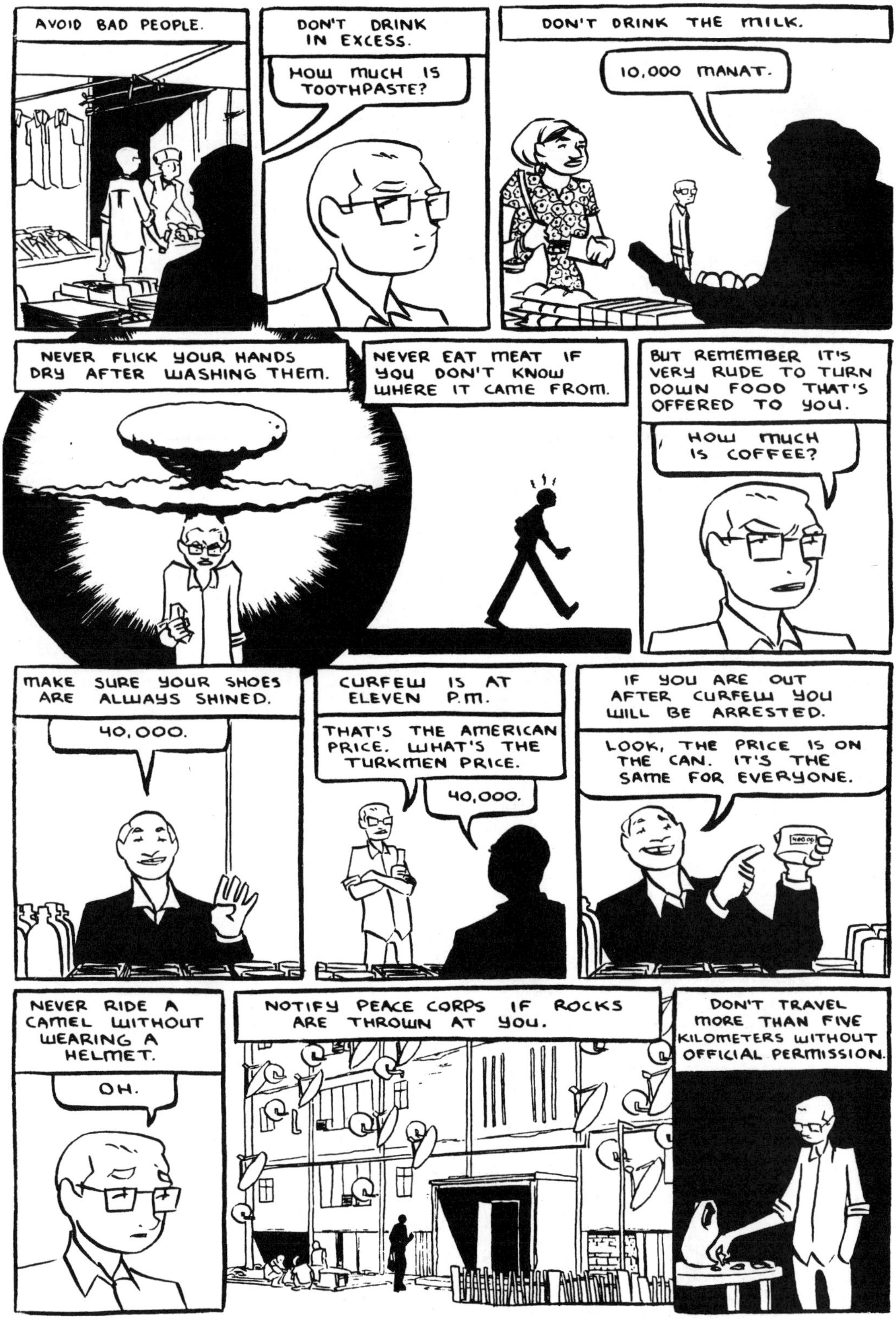
AVOID BAD PEOPLE.
DON'T DRINK IN EXCESS.
HOW MUCH IS TOOTHPASTE?
DON'T DRINK THE MILK.
10,000 MANAT.
NEVER FLICK YOUR HANDS DRY AFTER WASHING THEM.
NEVER EAT MEAT IF YOU DON'T KNOW WHERE IT CAME FROM.
BUT REMEMBER IT'S VERY RUDE TO TURN DOWN FOOD THAT'S OFFERED TO YOU.
HOW MUCH IS COFFEE?
MAKE SURE YOUR SHOES ARE ALWAYS SHINED.
40,000.
CURFEW IS AT ELEVEN P.M.
THAT'S THE AMERICAN PRICE. WHAT'S THE TURKMEN PRICE.
40,000.
IF YOU ARE OUT AFTER CURFEW YOU WILL BE ARRESTED.
LOOK, THE PRICE IS ON THE CAN. IT'S THE SAME FOR EVERYONE.
NEVER RIDE A CAMEL WITHOUT WEARING A HELMET.
OH.
NOTIFY PEACE CORPS IF ROCKS ARE THROWN AT YOU.
DON'T TRAVEL MORE THAN FIVE KILOMETERS WITHOUT OFFICIAL PERMISSION.

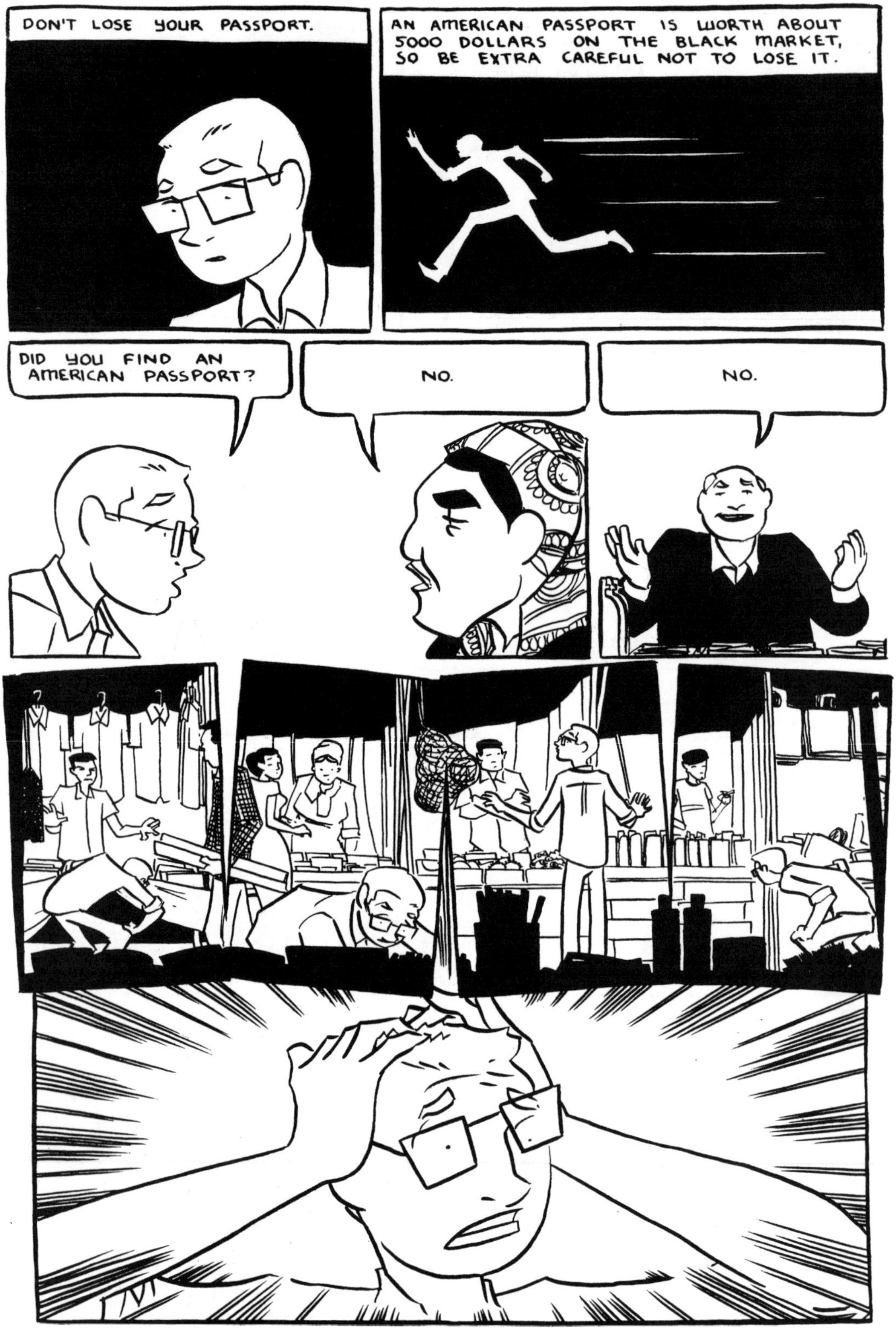
DON'T LOSE YOUR PASSPORT.
AN AMERICAN PASSPORT IS WORTH ABOUT 5000 DOLLARS ON THE BLACK MARKET, SO BE EXTRA CAREFUL NOT TO LOSE IT.
DID YOU FIND AN AMERICAN PASSPORT?
NO.
NO.

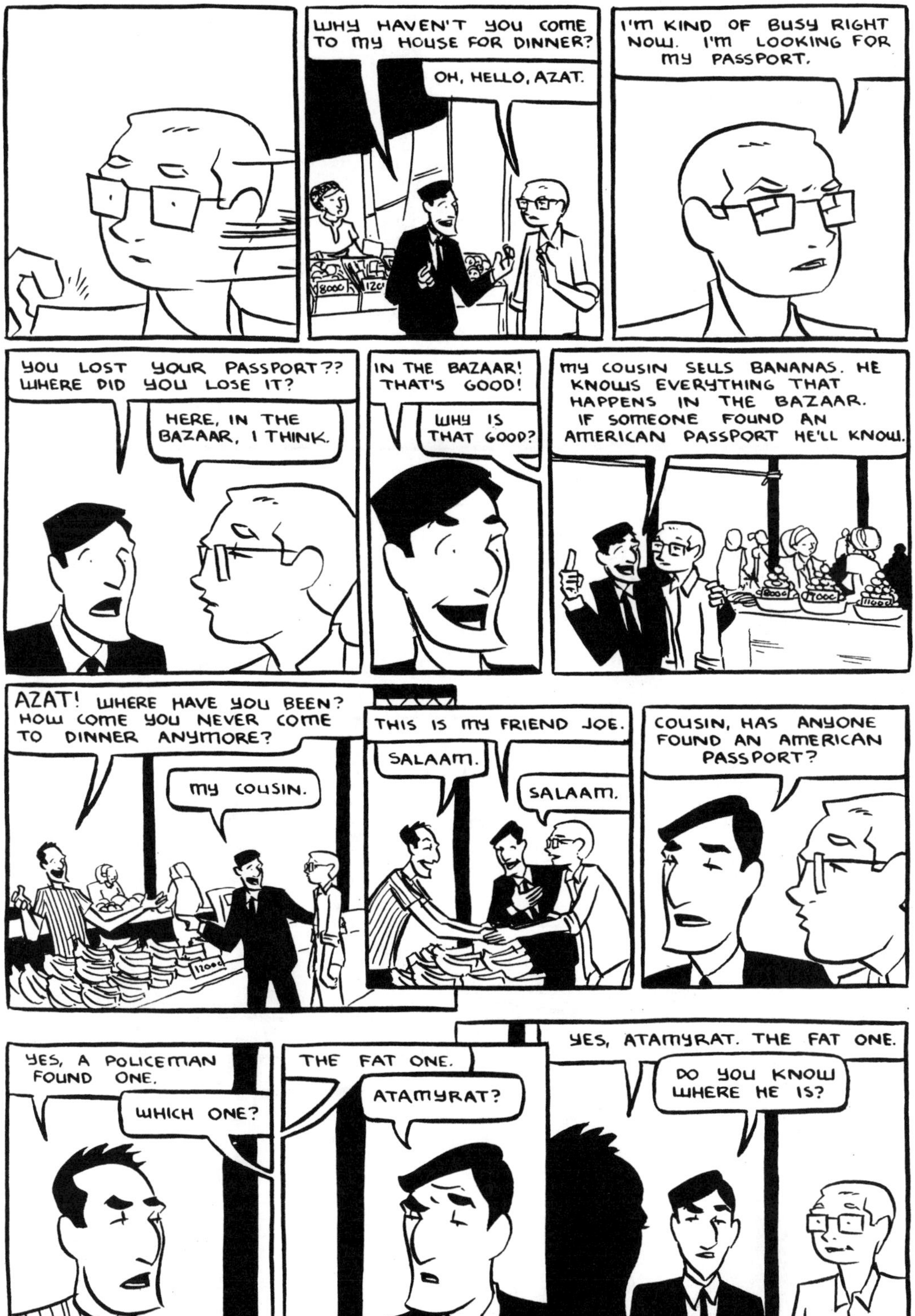
WHY HAVEN'T YOU COME TO MY HOUSE FOR DINNER?
OH, HELLO, AZAT.
I'M KIND OF BUSY RIGHT NOW. I'M LOOKING FOR MY PASSPORT.
YOU LOST YOUR PASSPORT?? WHERE DID YOU LOSE IT?
HERE, IN THE BAZAAR, I THINK.
IN THE BAZAAR! THAT'S GOOD!
WHY IS THAT GOOD?
MY COUSIN SELLS BANANAS. HE KNOWS EVERYTHING THAT HAPPENS IN THE BAZAAR. IF SOMEONE FOUND AN AMERICAN PASSPORT HE'LL KNOW.
AZAT! WHERE HAVE YOU BEEN? HOW COME YOU NEVER COME TO DINNER ANYMORE?
MY COUSIN.
THIS IS MY FRIEND JOE.
SALAAM.
SALAAM.
COUSIN, HAS ANYONE FOUND AN AMERICAN PASSPORT?
YES, A POLICEMAN FOUND ONE.
WHICH ONE?
THE FAT ONE.
ATAMYRAT?
YES, ATAMYRAT. THE FAT ONE.
DO YOU KNOW WHERE HE IS?

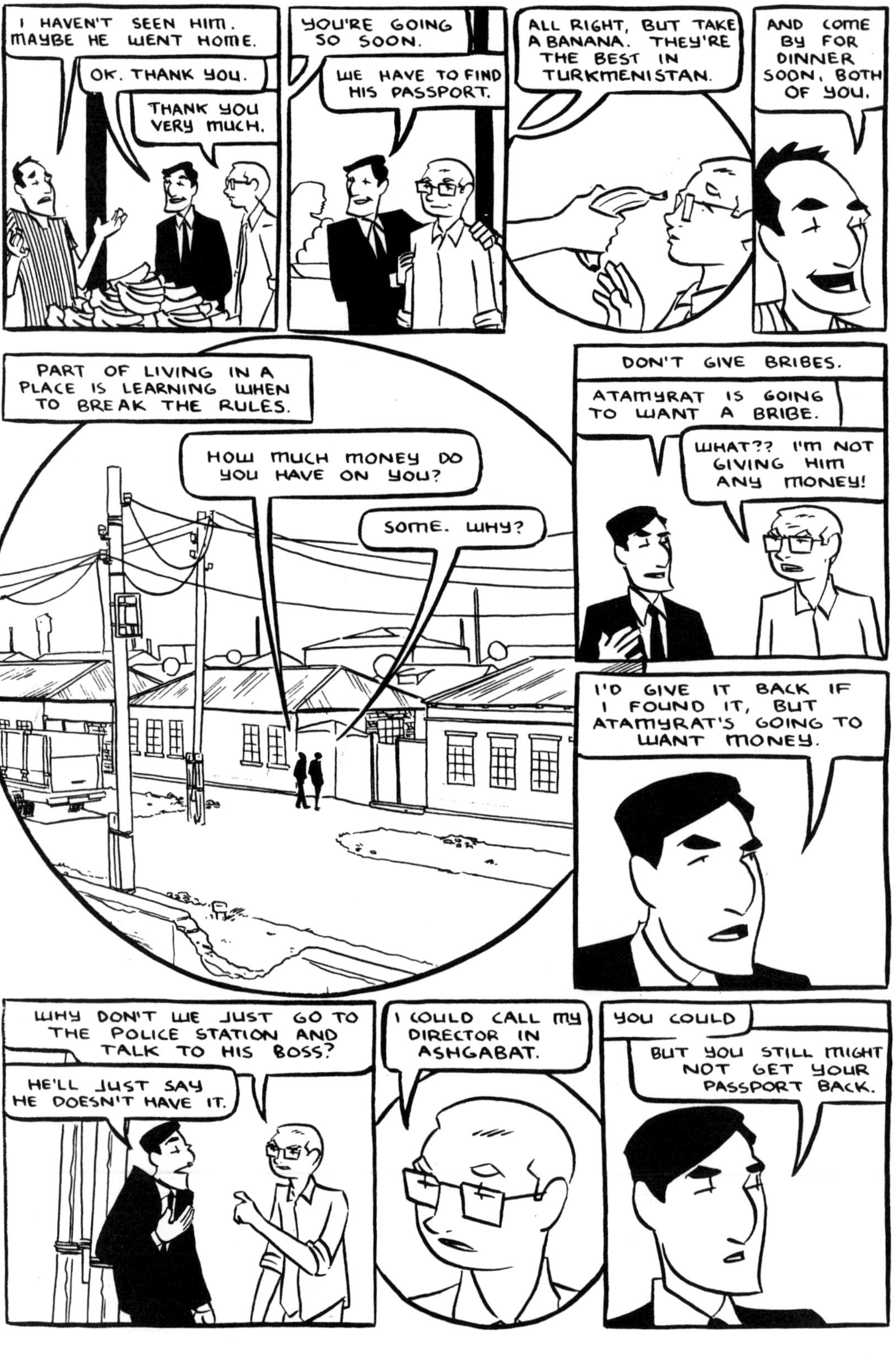
I HAVEN'T SEEN HIM. MAYBE HE WENT HOME.
OK. THANK YOU.
THANK YOU VERY MUCH.
YOU'RE GOING SO SOON.
WE HAVE TO FIND HIS PASSPORT.
ALL RIGHT, BUT TAKE A BANANA. THEY'RE THE BEST IN TURKMENISTAN.
AND COME BY FOR DINNER SOON, BOTH OF YOU.
PART OF LIVING IN A PLACE IS LEARNING WHEN TO BREAK THE RULES.
HOW MUCH MONEY DO YOU HAVE ON YOU?
SOME. WHY?
DON'T GIVE BRIBES.
ATAMYRAT IS GOING TO WANT A BRIBE.
WHAT?? I'M NOT GIVING HIM ANY MONEY!
I'D GIVE IT BACK IF I FOUND IT, BUT ATAMYRAT'S GOING TO WANT MONEY.
WHY DON'T WE JUST GO TO THE POLICE STATION AND TALK TO HIS BOSS?
HE'LL JUST SAY HE DOESN'T HAVE IT.
I COULD CALL MY DIRECTOR IN ASHGABAT.
YOU COULD
BUT YOU STILL MIGHT NOT GET YOUR PASSPORT BACK.

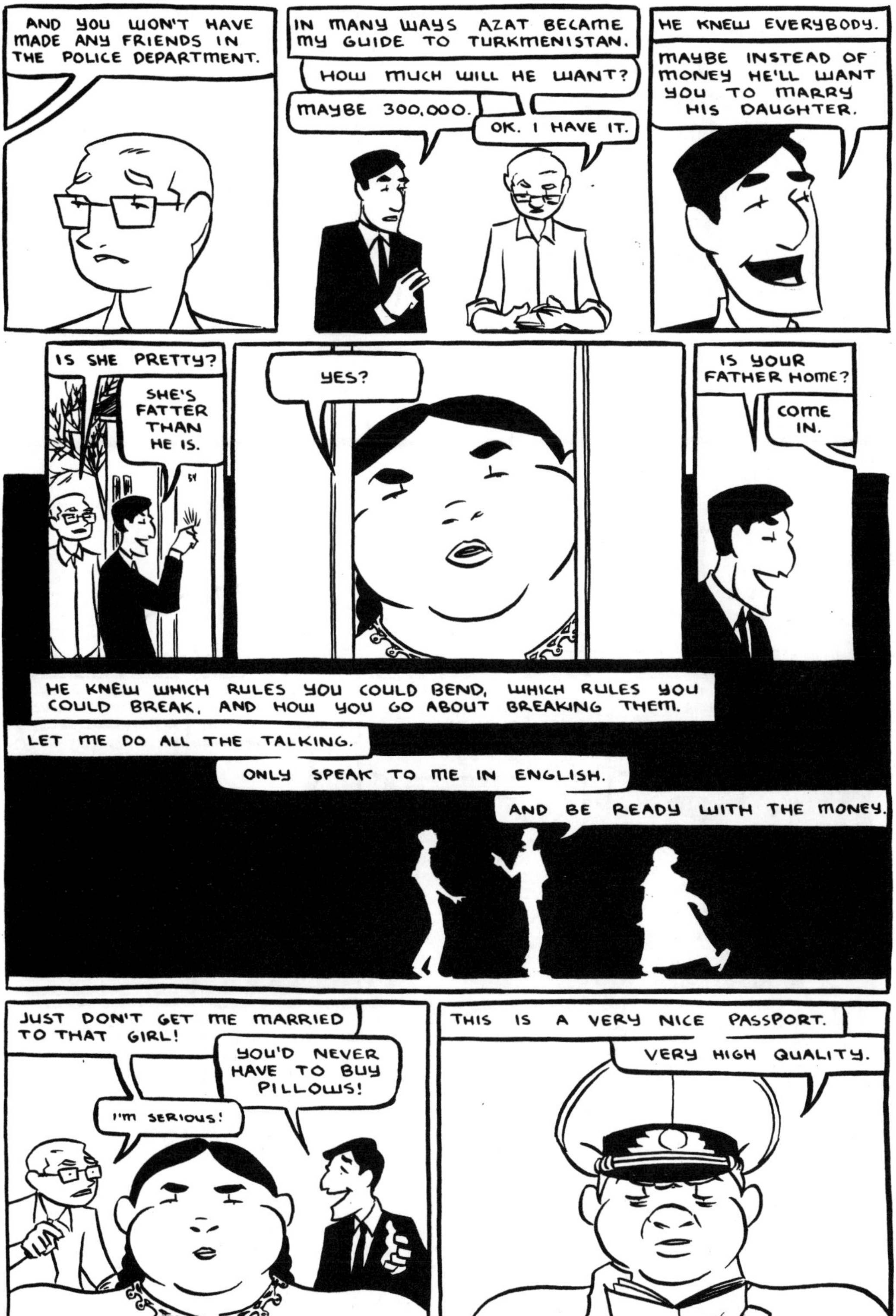
AND YOU WON'T HAVE MADE ANY FRIENDS IN THE POLICE DEPARTMENT.
IN MANY WAYS AZAT BECAME MY GUIDE TO TURKMENISTAN.
HOW MUCH WILL HE WANT?
MAYBE 300,000.
OK. I HAVE IT.
HE KNEW EVERYBODY.
MAYBE INSTEAD OF MONEY HE'LL WANT YOU TO MARRY HIS DAUGHTER.
IS SHE PRETTY?
SHE'S FATTER THAN HE IS.
YES?
IS YOUR FATHER HOME?
COME IN.
HE KNEW WHICH RULES YOU COULD BEND, WHICH RULES YOU COULD BREAK, AND HOW YOU GO ABOUT BREAKING THEM.
LET ME DO ALL THE TALKING.
ONLY SPEAK TO ME IN ENGLISH.
AND BE READY WITH THE MONEY.
JUST DON'T GET ME MARRIED TO THAT GIRL!
YOU'D NEVER HAVE TO BUY PILLOWS!
I'M SERIOUS!
THIS IS A VERY NICE PASSPORT.
VERY HIGH QUALITY.

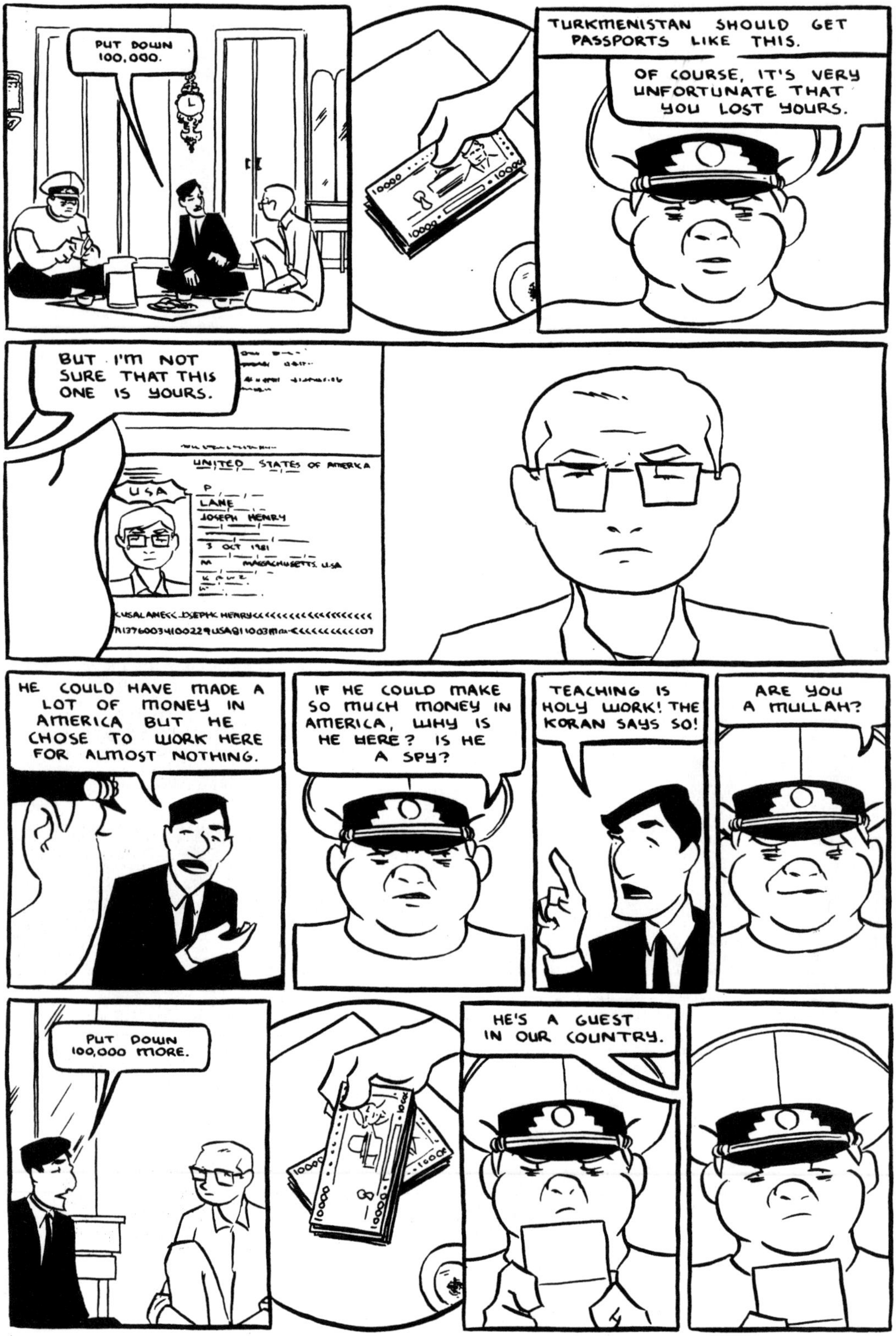
PUT DOWN 100,000.
TURKMENISTAN SHOULD GET PASSPORTS LIKE THIS.
OF COURSE, IT'S VERY UNFORTUNATE THAT YOU LOST YOURS.
BUT I'M NOT SURE THAT THIS ONE IS YOURS.
UNITED STATES OF AMERICA
USA
LANE
JOSEPH HENRY
3 OCT 1981
MASSACHUSETTS, USA
HE COULD HAVE MADE A LOT OF MONEY IN AMERICA BUT HE CHOSE TO WORK HERE FOR ALMOST NOTHING.
IF HE COULD MAKE SO MUCH MONEY IN AMERICA, WHY IS HE HERE? IS HE A SPY?
TEACHING IS HOLY WORK! THE KORAN SAYS SO!
ARE YOU A MULLAH?
PUT DOWN 100,000 MORE.
HE'S A GUEST IN OUR COUNTRY.

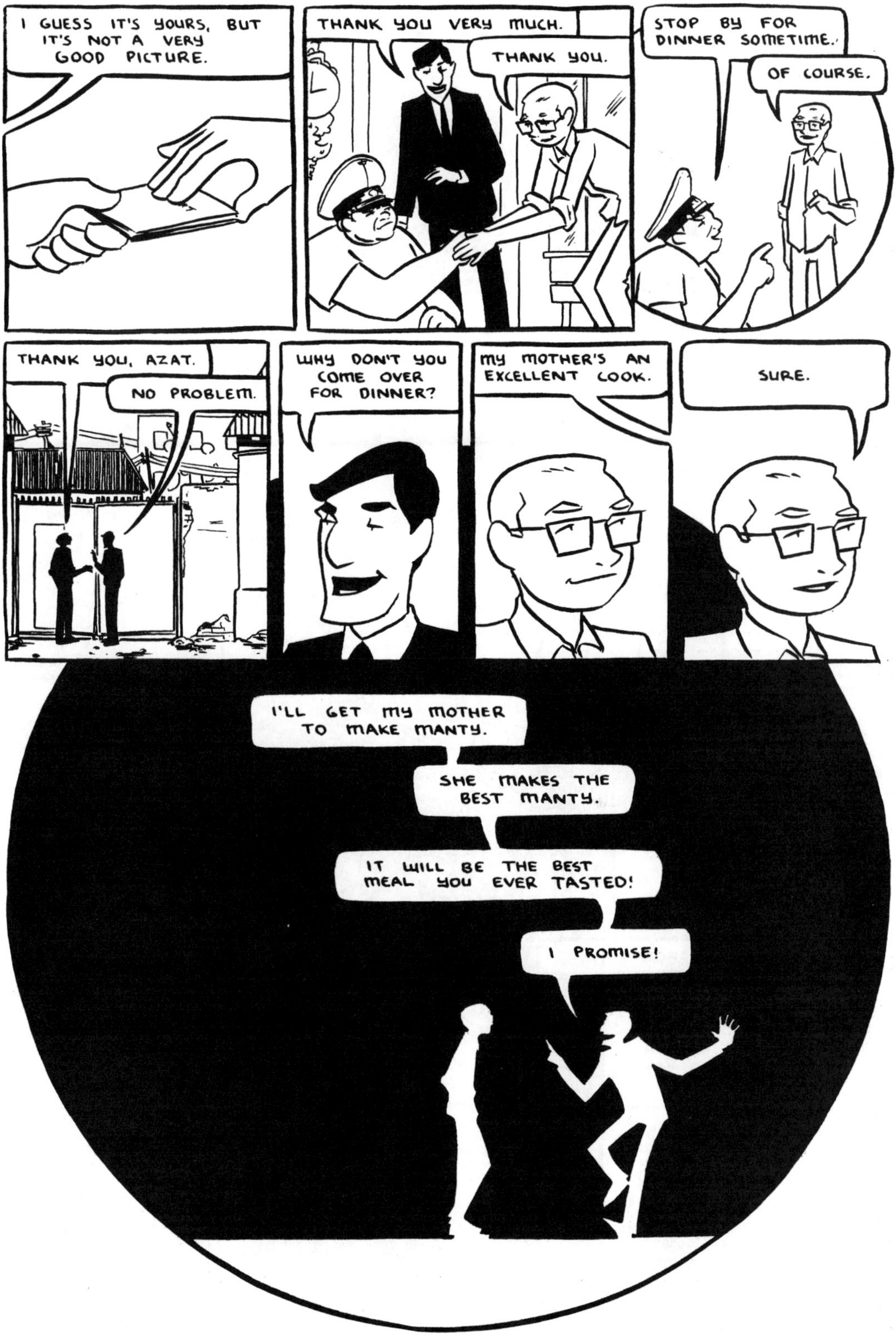
I GUESS IT'S YOURS, BUT IT'S NOT A VERY GOOD PICTURE.
THANK YOU VERY MUCH.
THANK YOU.
STOP BY FOR DINNER SOMETIME.
OF COURSE.
THANK YOU, AZAT.
NO PROBLEM.
WHY DON'T YOU COME OVER FOR DINNER?
MY MOTHER'S AN EXCELLENT COOK.
SURE.
I'LL GET MY MOTHER TO MAKE MANTY.
SHE MAKES THE BEST MANTY.
IT WILL BE THE BEST MEAL YOU EVER TASTED!
I PROMISE!

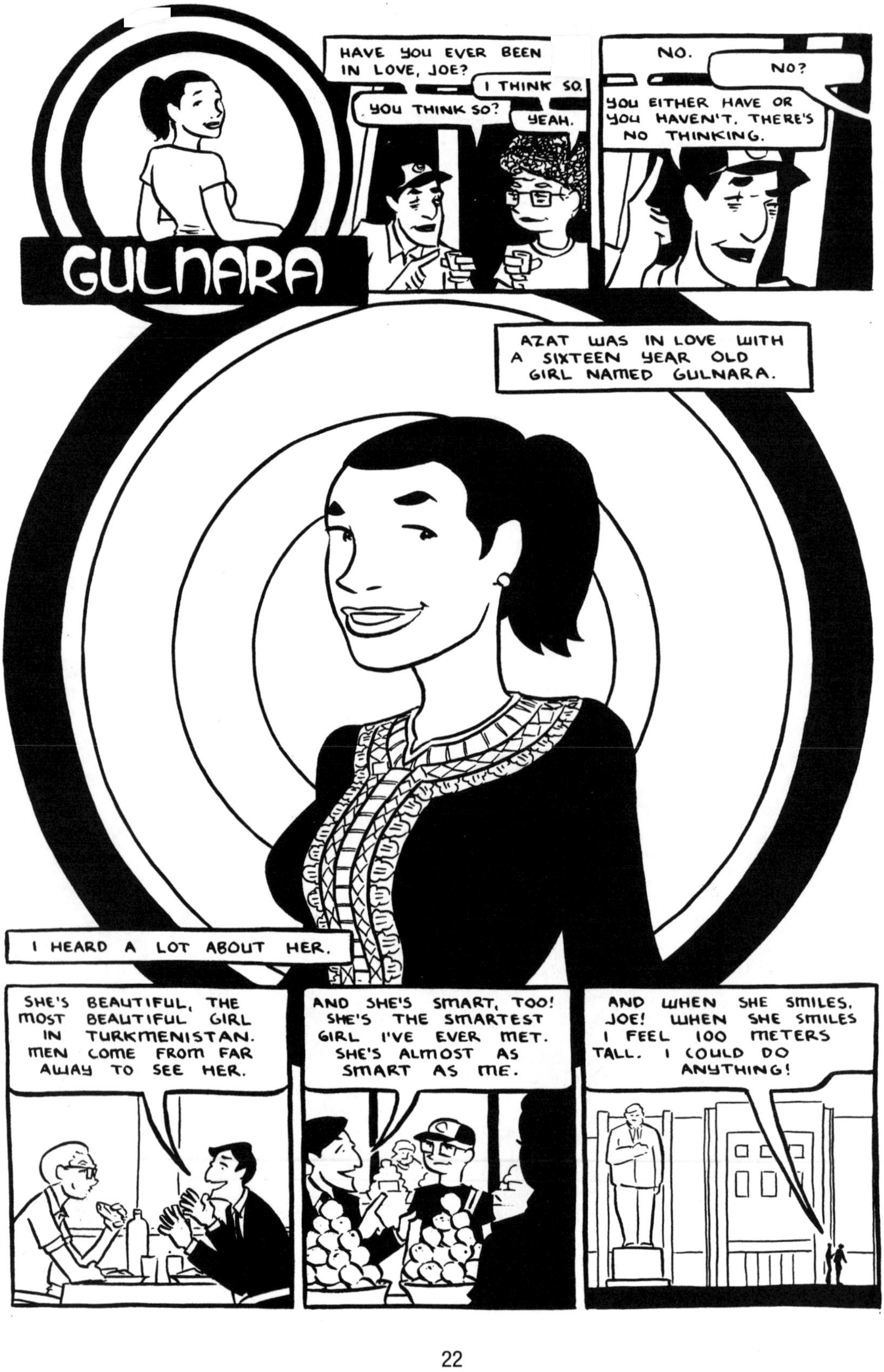
GULNARA
HAVE YOU EVER BEEN IN LOVE, JOE?
I THINK SO.
YOU THINK SO?
YEAH.
NO.
NO?
YOU EITHER HAVE OR YOU HAVEN'T. THERE'S NO THINKING.
AZAT WAS IN LOVE WITH A SIXTEEN YEAR OLD GIRL NAMED GULNARA.
I HEARD A LOT ABOUT HER.
SHE'S BEAUTIFUL, THE MOST BEAUTIFUL GIRL IN TURKMENISTAN. MEN COME FROM FAR AWAY TO SEE HER.
AND SHE'S SMART, TOO! SHE'S THE SMARTEST GIRL I'VE EVER MET. SHE'S ALMOST AS SMART AS ME.
AND WHEN SHE SMILES, JOE! WHEN SHE SMILES I FEEL 100 METERS TALL. I COULD DO ANYTHING!

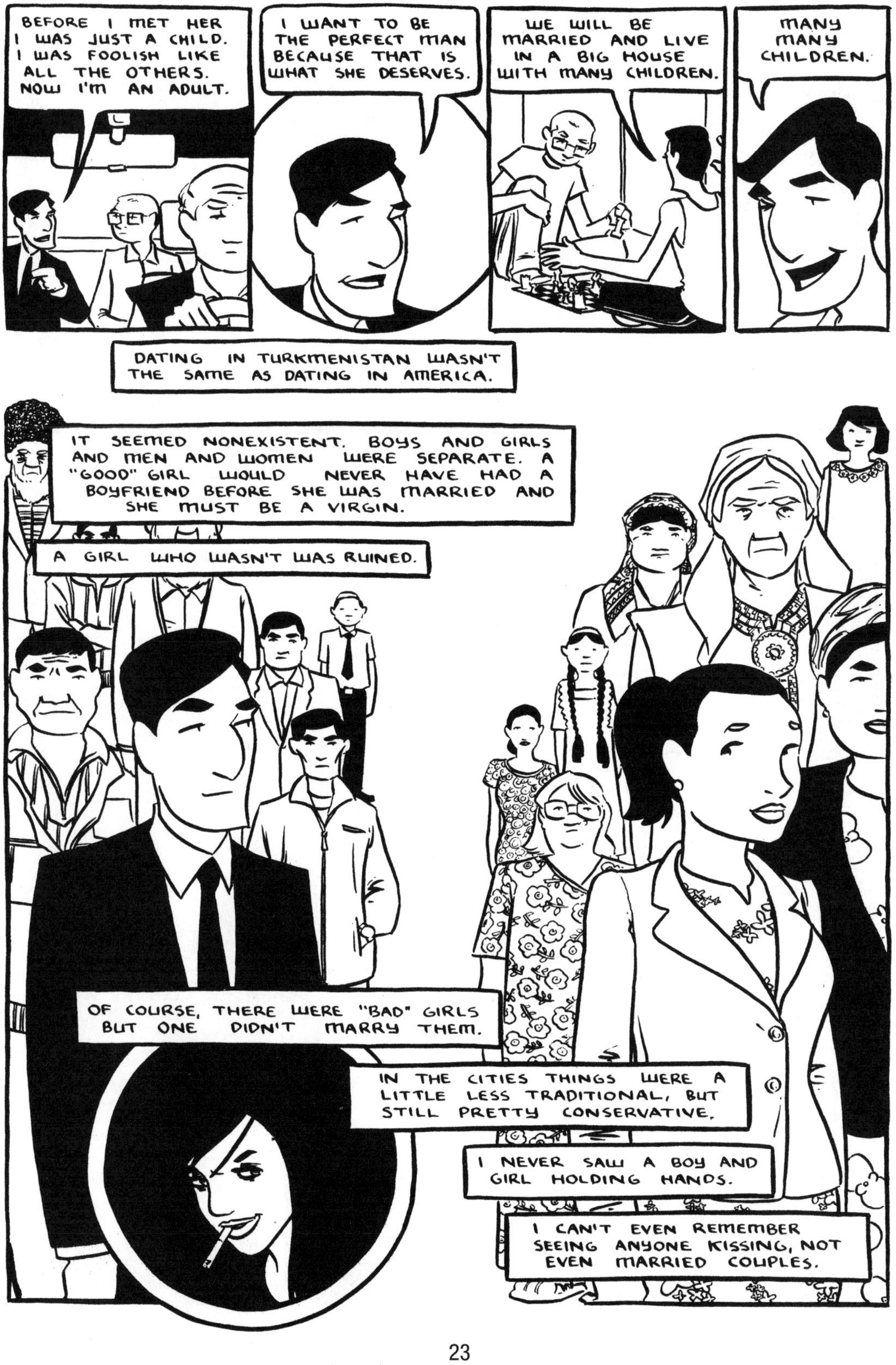
BEFORE I MET HER I WAS JUST A CHILD. I WAS FOOLISH LIKE ALL THE OTHERS. NOW I'M AN ADULT.
I WANT TO BE THE PERFECT MAN BECAUSE THAT IS WHAT SHE DESERVES.
WE WILL BE MARRIED AND LIVE IN A BIG HOUSE WITH MANY CHILDREN.
MANY MANY CHILDREN.
DATING IN TURKMENISTAN WASN'T THE SAME AS DATING IN AMERICA.
IT SEEMED NONEXISTENT. BOYS AND GIRLS AND MEN AND WOMEN WERE SEPARATE. A "GOOD" GIRL WOULD NEVER HAVE HAD A BOYFRIEND BEFORE SHE WAS MARRIED AND SHE MUST BE A VIRGIN.
A GIRL WHO WASN'T WAS RUINED.
OF COURSE, THERE WERE "BAD" GIRLS BUT ONE DIDN'T MARRY THEM.
IN THE CITIES THINGS WERE A LITTLE LESS TRADITIONAL, BUT STILL PRETTY CONSERVATIVE.
I NEVER SAW A BOY AND GIRL HOLDING HANDS.
I CAN'T EVEN REMEMBER SEEING ANYONE KISSING, NOT EVEN MARRIED COUPLES.

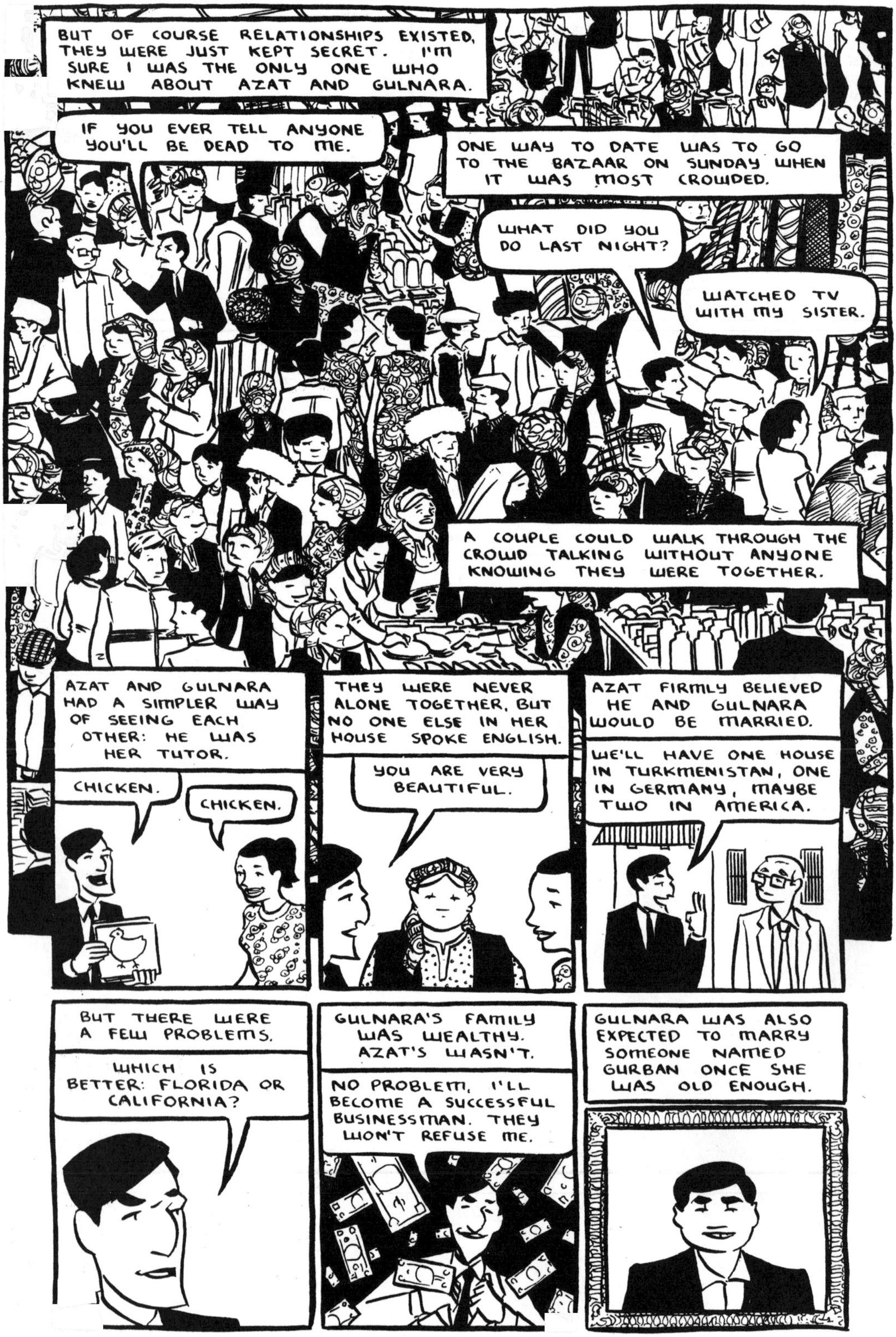
BUT OF COURSE RELATIONSHIPS EXISTED, THEY WERE JUST KEPT SECRET. I'M SURE I WAS THE ONLY ONE WHO KNEW ABOUT AZAT AND GULNARA.
IF YOU EVER TELL ANYONE YOU'LL BE DEAD TO ME.
ONE WAY TO DATE WAS TO GO TO THE BAZAAR ON SUNDAY WHEN IT WAS MOST CROWDED.
WHAT DID YOU DO LAST NIGHT?
WATCHED TV WITH MY SISTER.
A COUPLE COULD WALK THROUGH THE CROWD TALKING WITHOUT ANYONE KNOWING THEY WERE TOGETHER.
AZAT AND GULNARA HAD A SIMPLER WAY OF SEEING EACH OTHER: HE WAS HER TUTOR.
CHICKEN.
CHICKEN.
THEY WERE NEVER ALONE TOGETHER, BUT NO ONE ELSE IN HER HOUSE SPOKE ENGLISH.
YOU ARE VERY BEAUTIFUL.
AZAT FIRMLY BELIEVED HE AND GULNARA WOULD BE MARRIED.
WE'LL HAVE ONE HOUSE IN TURKMENISTAN, ONE IN GERMANY, MAYBE TWO IN AMERICA.
BUT THERE WERE A FEW PROBLEMS.
WHICH IS BETTER: FLORIDA OR CALIFORNIA?
GULNARA'S FAMILY WAS WEALTHY. AZAT'S WASN'T.
NO PROBLEM, I'LL BECOME A SUCCESSFUL BUSINESSMAN. THEY WON'T REFUSE ME.
GULNARA WAS ALSO EXPECTED TO MARRY SOMEONE NAMED GURBAN ONCE SHE WAS OLD ENOUGH.

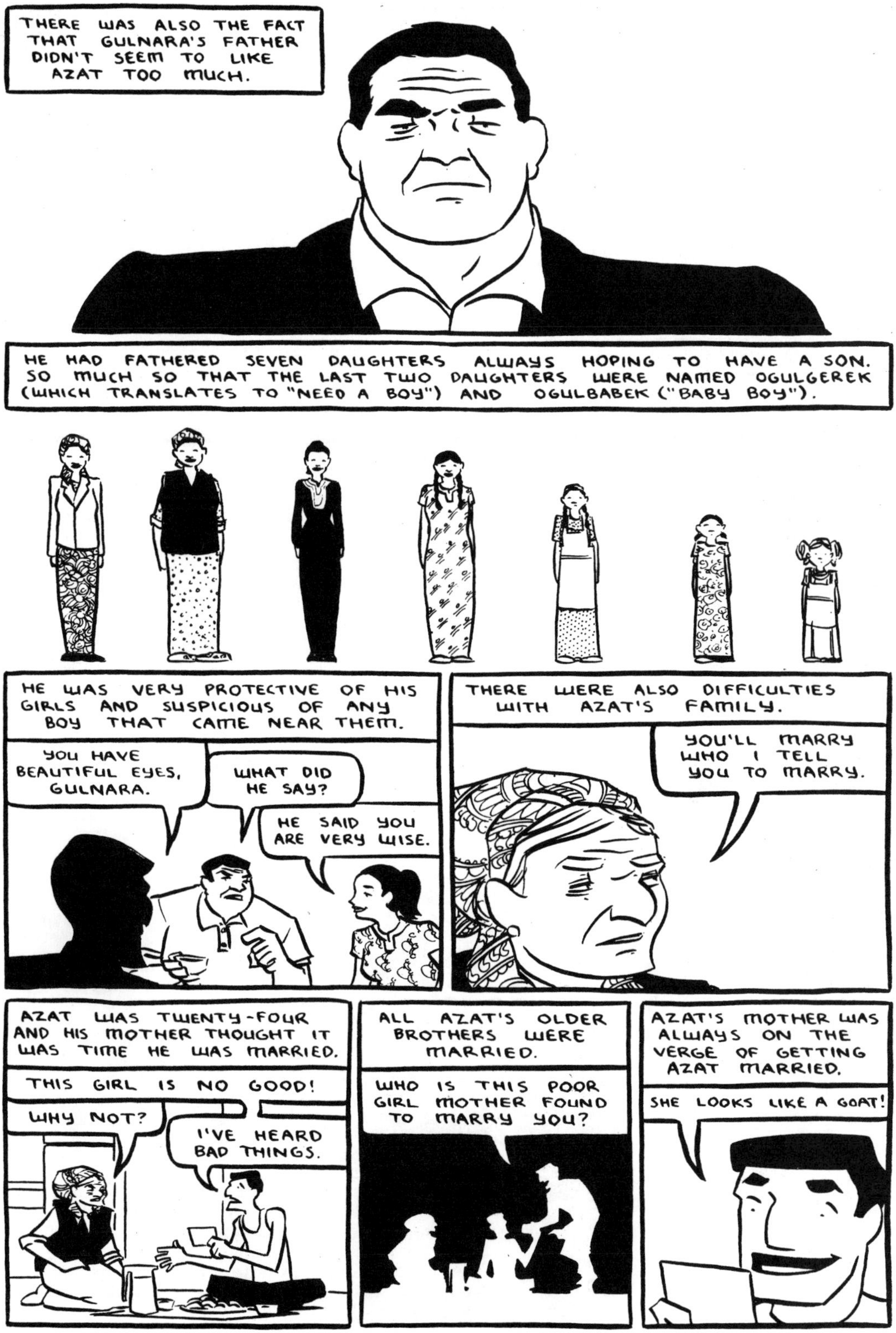
THERE WAS ALSO THE FACT THAT GULNARA'S FATHER DIDN'T SEEM TO LIKE AZAT TOO MUCH.
HE HAD FATHERED SEVEN DAUGHTERS ALWAYS HOPING TO HAVE A SON. SO MUCH SO THAT THE LAST TWO DAUGHTERS WERE NAMED OGULGEREK (WHICH TRANSLATES TO "NEED A BOY") AND OGULBABEK ("BABY BOY").
HE WAS VERY PROTECTIVE OF HIS GIRLS AND SUSPICIOUS OF ANY BOY THAT CAME NEAR THEM.
YOU HAVE BEAUTIFUL EYES, GULNARA.
WHAT DID HE SAY?
HE SAID YOU ARE VERY WISE.
THERE WERE ALSO DIFFICULTIES WITH AZAT'S FAMILY.
YOU'LL MARRY WHO I TELL YOU TO MARRY.
AZAT WAS TWENTY-FOUR AND HIS MOTHER THOUGHT IT WAS TIME HE WAS MARRIED.
THIS GIRL IS NO GOOD!
WHY NOT?
I'VE HEARD BAD THINGS.
ALL AZAT'S OLDER BROTHERS WERE MARRIED.
WHO IS THIS POOR GIRL MOTHER FOUND TO MARRY YOU?
AZAT'S MOTHER WAS ALWAYS ON THE VERGE OF GETTING AZAT MARRIED.
SHE LOOKS LIKE A GOAT!

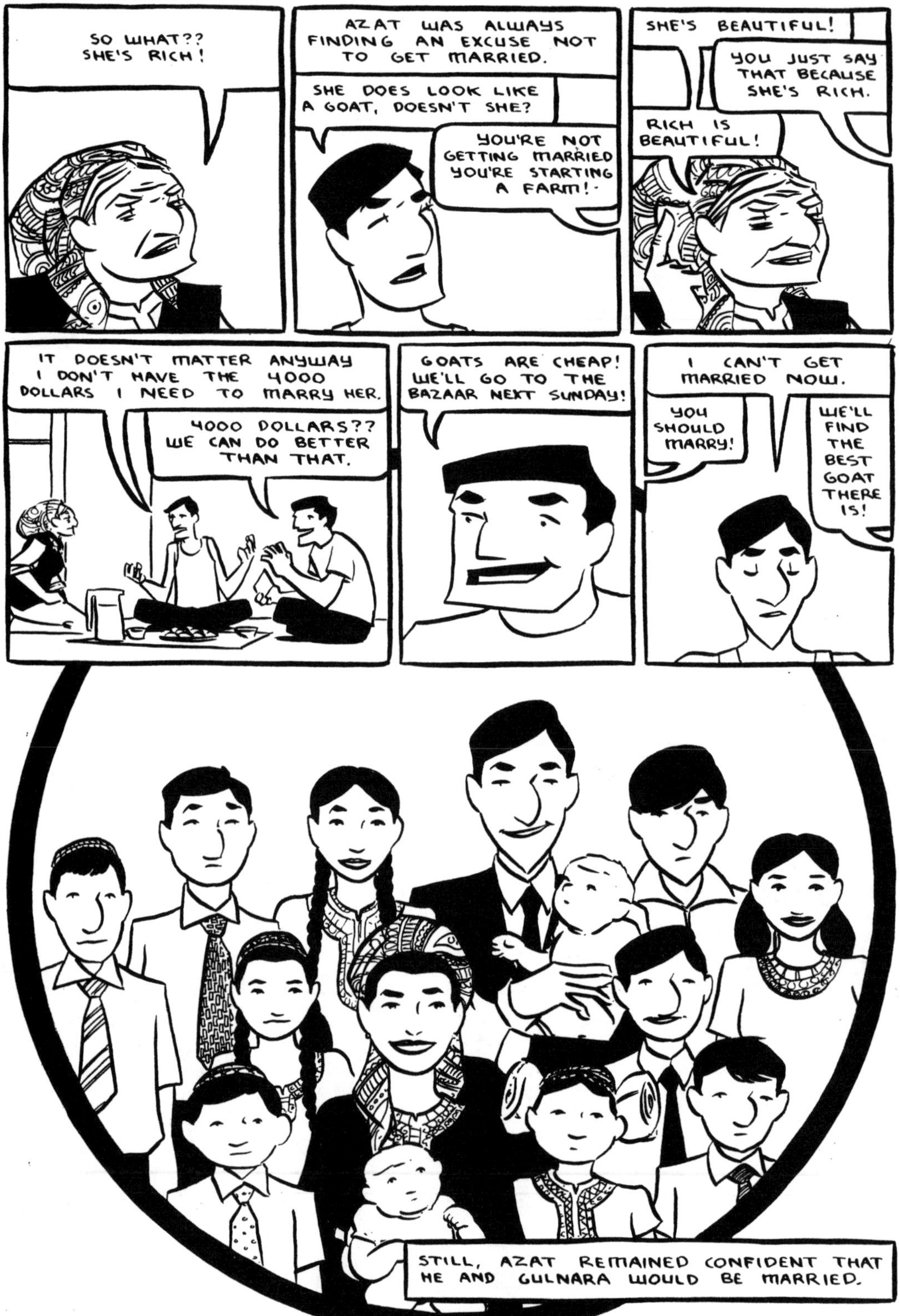
SO WHAT?? SHE'S RICH!
AZAT WAS ALWAYS FINDING AN EXCUSE NOT TO GET MARRIED.
SHE DOES LOOK LIKE A GOAT, DOESN'T SHE?
YOU'RE NOT GETTING MARRIED YOU'RE STARTING A FARM!
SHE'S BEAUTIFUL!
YOU JUST SAY THAT BECAUSE SHE'S RICH.
RICH IS BEAUTIFUL!
IT DOESN'T MATTER ANYWAY I DON'T HAVE THE 4000 DOLLARS I NEED TO MARRY HER.
4000 DOLLARS?? WE CAN DO BETTER THAN THAT.
GOATS ARE CHEAP! WE'LL GO TO THE BAZAAR NEXT SUNDAY!
I CAN'T GET MARRIED NOW.
YOU SHOULD MARRY!
WE'LL FIND THE BEST GOAT THERE IS!
STILL, AZAT REMAINED CONFIDENT THAT HE AND GULNARA WOULD BE MARRIED.

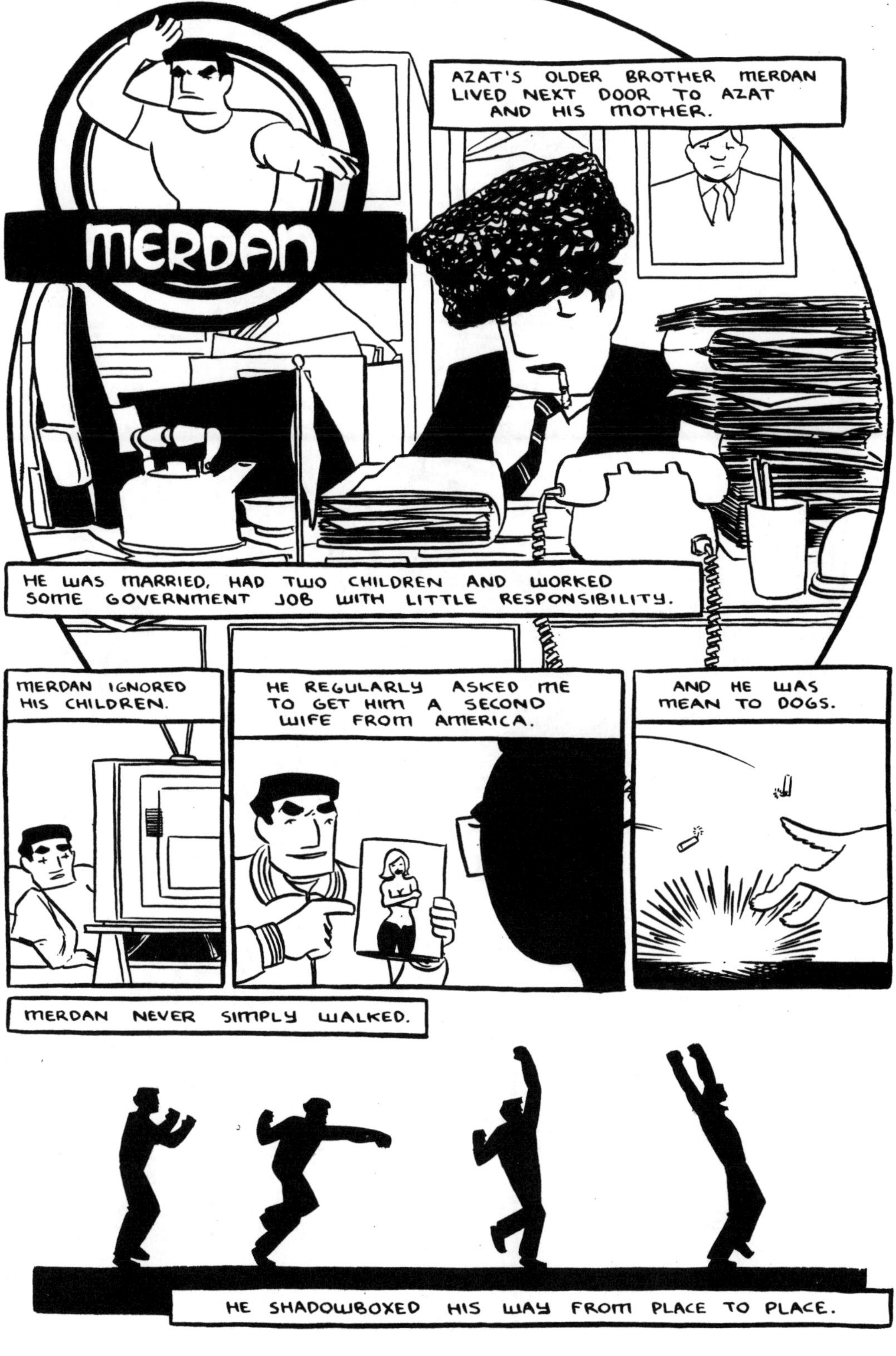
MERDAN
AZAT'S OLDER BROTHER MERDAN LIVED NEXT DOOR TO AZAT AND HIS MOTHER.
HE WAS MARRIED, HAD TWO CHILDREN AND WORKED SOME GOVERNMENT JOB WITH LITTLE RESPONSIBILITY.
MERDAN IGNORED HIS CHILDREN.
HE REGULARLY ASKED ME TO GET HIM A SECOND WIFE FROM AMERICA.
AND HE WAS MEAN TO DOGS.
MERDAN NEVER SIMPLY WALKED.
HE SHADOWBOXED HIS WAY FROM PLACE TO PLACE.

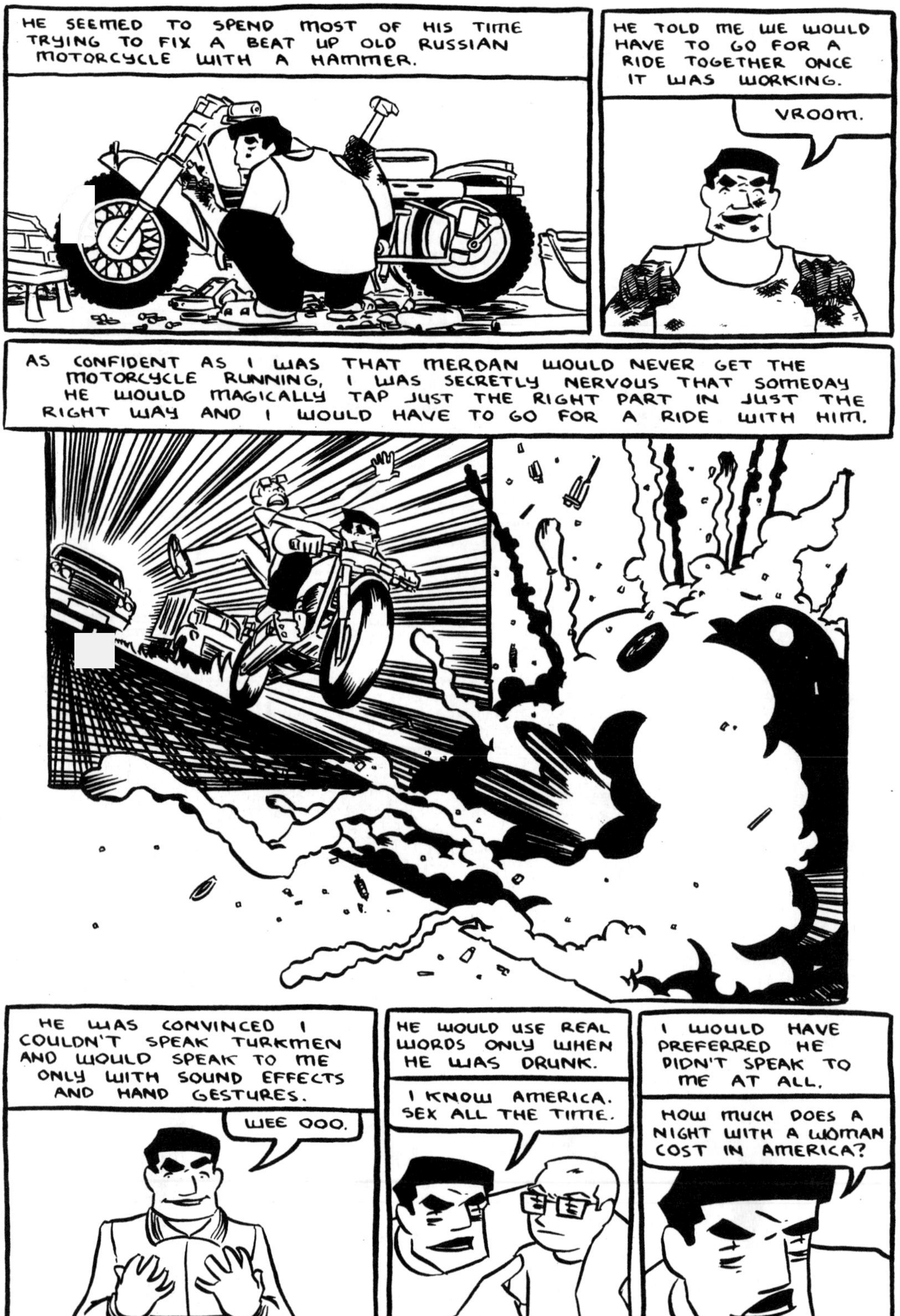

HE SEEMED TO SPEND MOST OF HIS TIME TRYING TO FIX A BEAT UP OLD RUSSIAN MOTORCYCLE WITH A HAMMER.
HE TOLD ME WE WOULD HAVE TO GO FOR A RIDE TOGETHER ONCE IT WAS WORKING.
VROOM.
AS CONFIDENT AS I WAS THAT MERDAN WOULD NEVER GET THE MOTORCYCLE RUNNING, I WAS SECRETLY NERVOUS THAT SOMEDAY HE WOULD MAGICALLY TAP JUST THE RIGHT PART IN JUST THE RIGHT WAY AND I WOULD HAVE TO GO FOR A RIDE WITH HIM.
HE WAS CONVINCED I COULDN'T SPEAK TURKMEN AND WOULD SPEAK TO ME ONLY WITH SOUND EFFECTS AND HAND GESTURES.
WEE OOO.
HE WOULD USE REAL WORDS ONLY WHEN HE WAS DRUNK.
I KNOW AMERICA. SEX ALL THE TIME.
I WOULD HAVE PREFERRED HE DIDN'T SPEAK TO ME AT ALL.
HOW MUCH DOES A NIGHT WITH A WOMAN COST IN AMERICA?

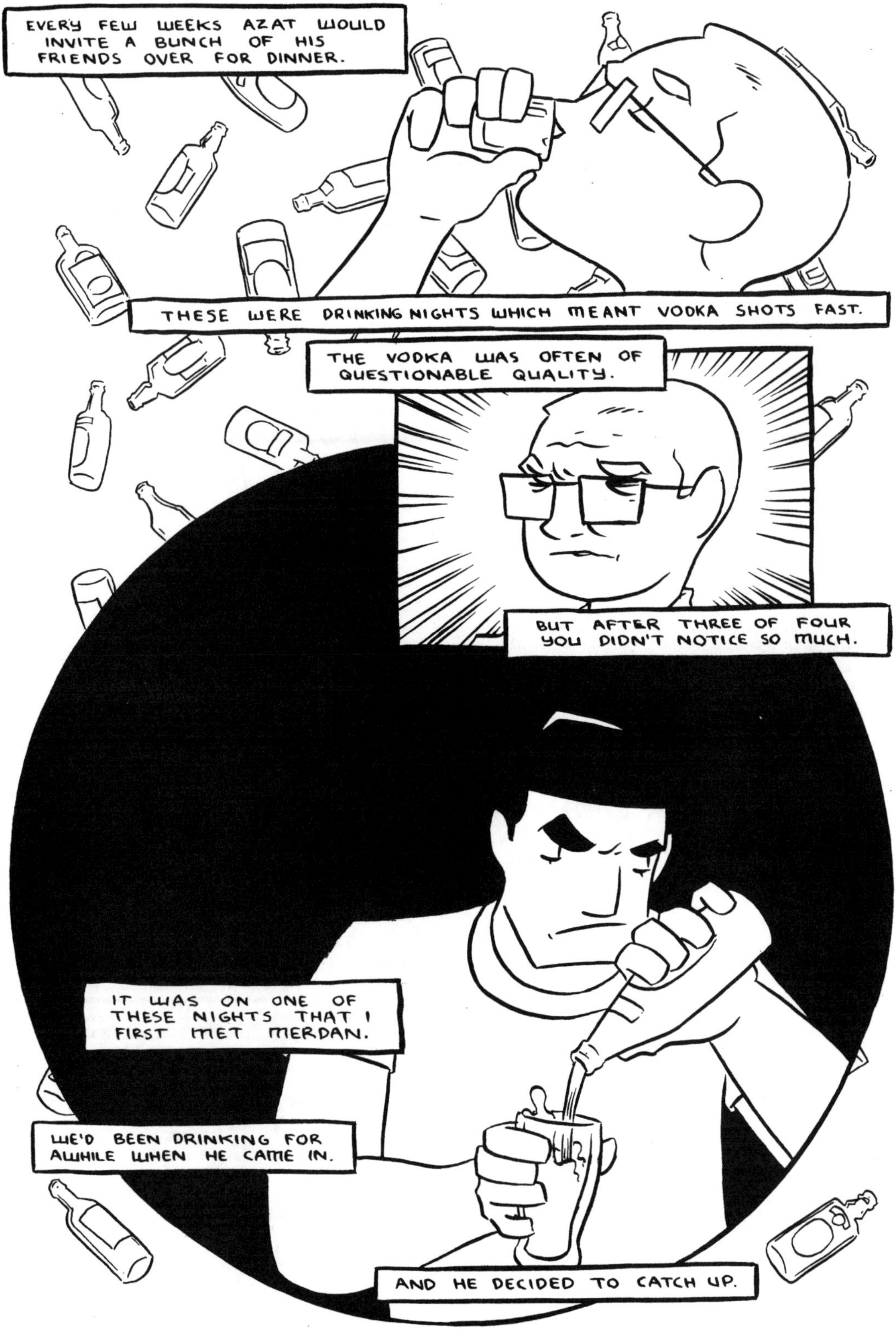
EVERY FEW WEEKS AZAT WOULD INVITE A BUNCH OF HIS FRIENDS OVER FOR DINNER.
THESE WERE DRINKING NIGHTS WHICH MEANT VODKA SHOTS FAST.
THE VODKA WAS OFTEN OF QUESTIONABLE QUALITY.
BUT AFTER THREE OF FOUR YOU DIDN'T NOTICE SO MUCH.
IT WAS ON ONE OF THESE NIGHTS THAT I FIRST MET MERDAN.
WE'D BEEN DRINKING FOR AWHILE WHEN HE CAME IN.
AND HE DECIDED TO CATCH UP.

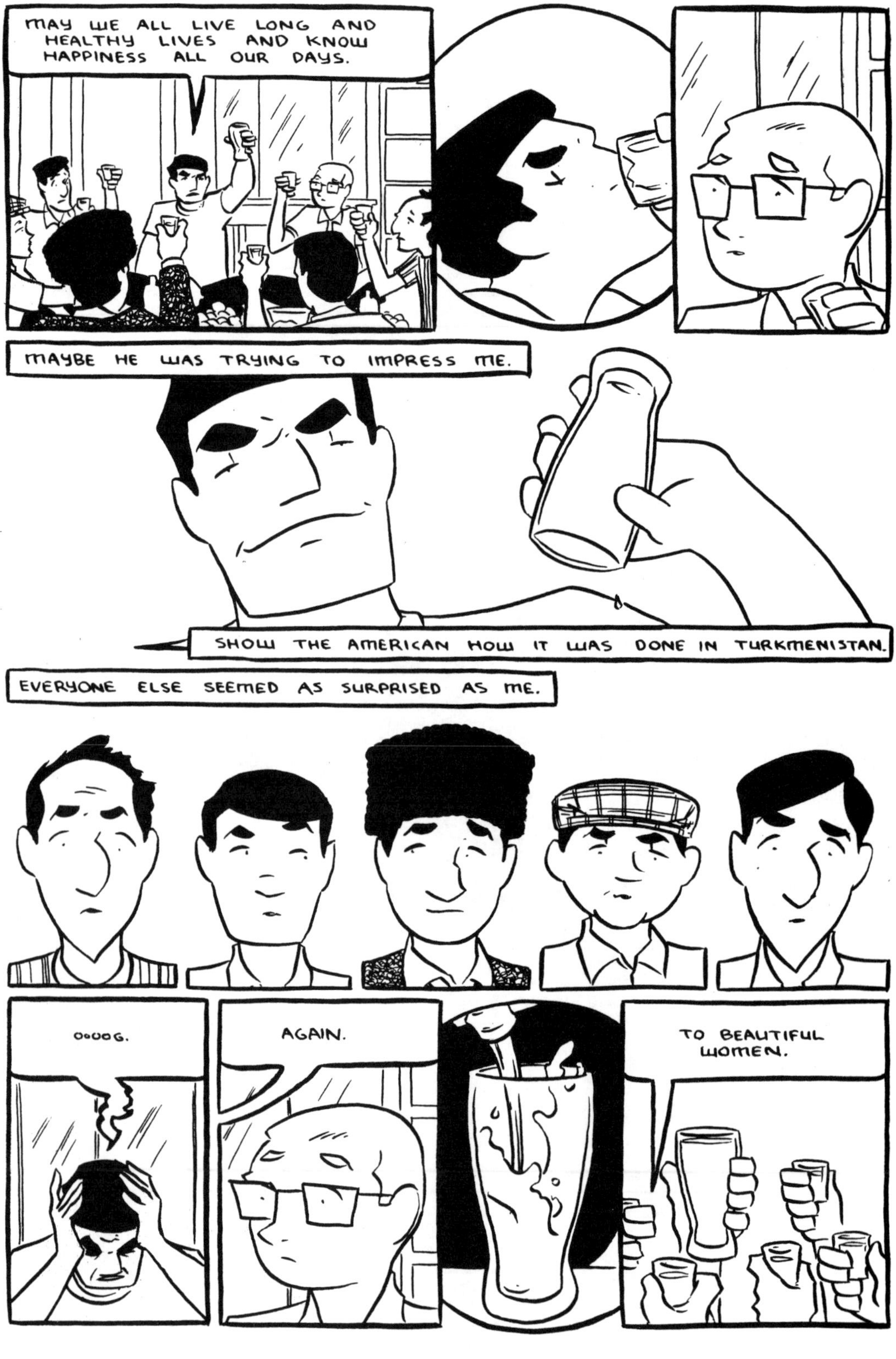
MAY WE ALL LIVE LONG AND HEALTHY LIVES AND KNOW HAPPINESS ALL OUR DAYS.
MAYBE HE WAS TRYING TO IMPRESS ME.
SHOW THE AMERICAN HOW IT WAS DONE IN TURKMENISTAN.
EVERYONE ELSE SEEMED AS SURPRISED AS ME.
OOUUG.
AGAIN.
TO BEAUTIFUL WOMEN.

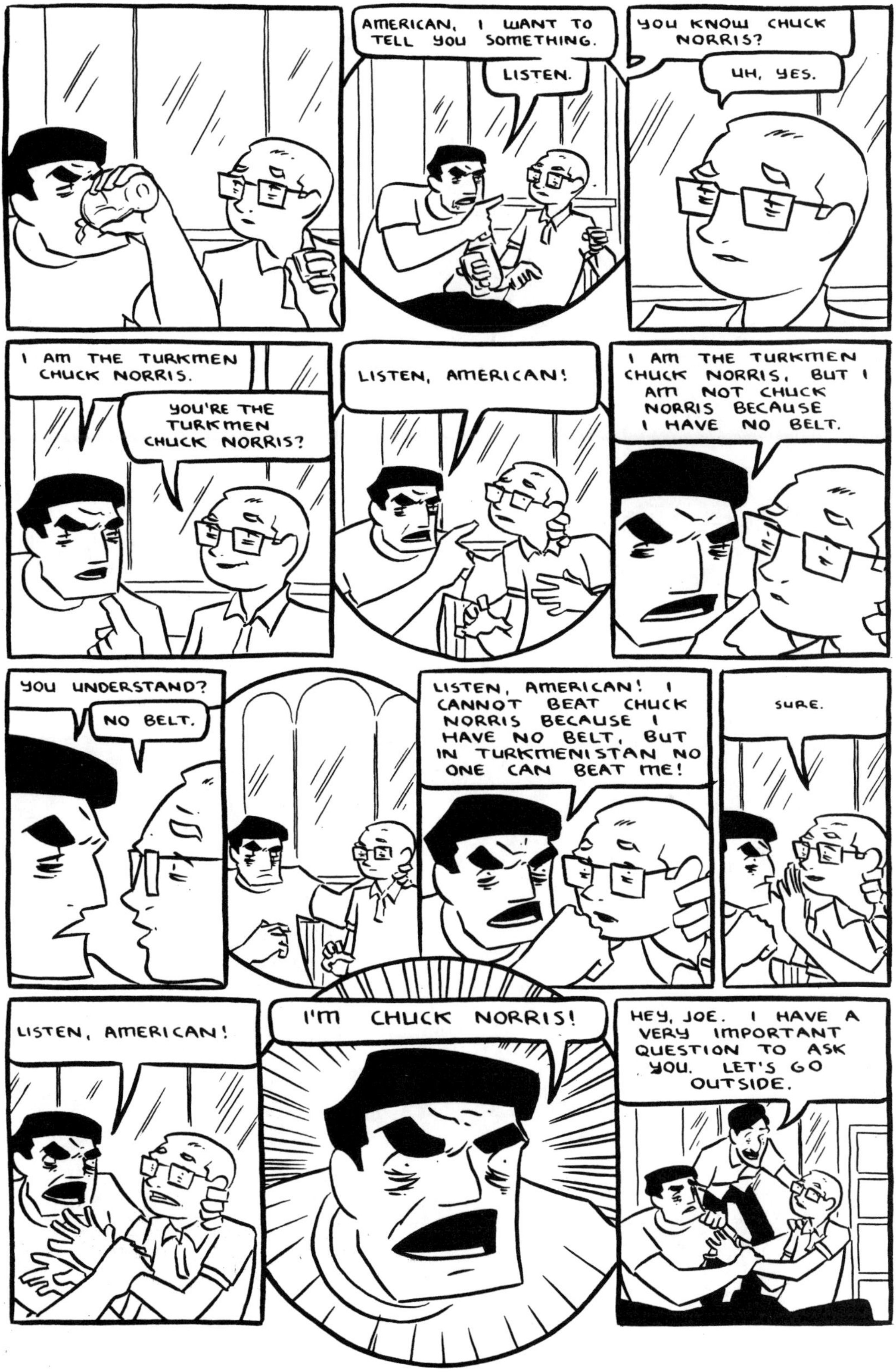
AMERICAN, I WANT TO TELL YOU SOMETHING.
LISTEN.
YOU KNOW CHUCK NORRIS?
UH, YES.
I AM THE TURKMEN CHUCK NORRIS.
YOU'RE THE TURKMEN CHUCK NORRIS?
LISTEN, AMERICAN!
I AM THE TURKMEN CHUCK NORRIS, BUT I AM NOT CHUCK NORRIS BECAUSE I HAVE NO BELT.
YOU UNDERSTAND?
NO BELT.
LISTEN, AMERICAN! I CANNOT BEAT CHUCK NORRIS BECAUSE I HAVE NO BELT, BUT IN TURKMENISTAN NO ONE CAN BEAT ME!
SURE.
LISTEN, AMERICAN!
I'M CHUCK NORRIS!
HEY, JOE. I HAVE A VERY IMPORTANT QUESTION TO ASK YOU. LET'S GO OUTSIDE.

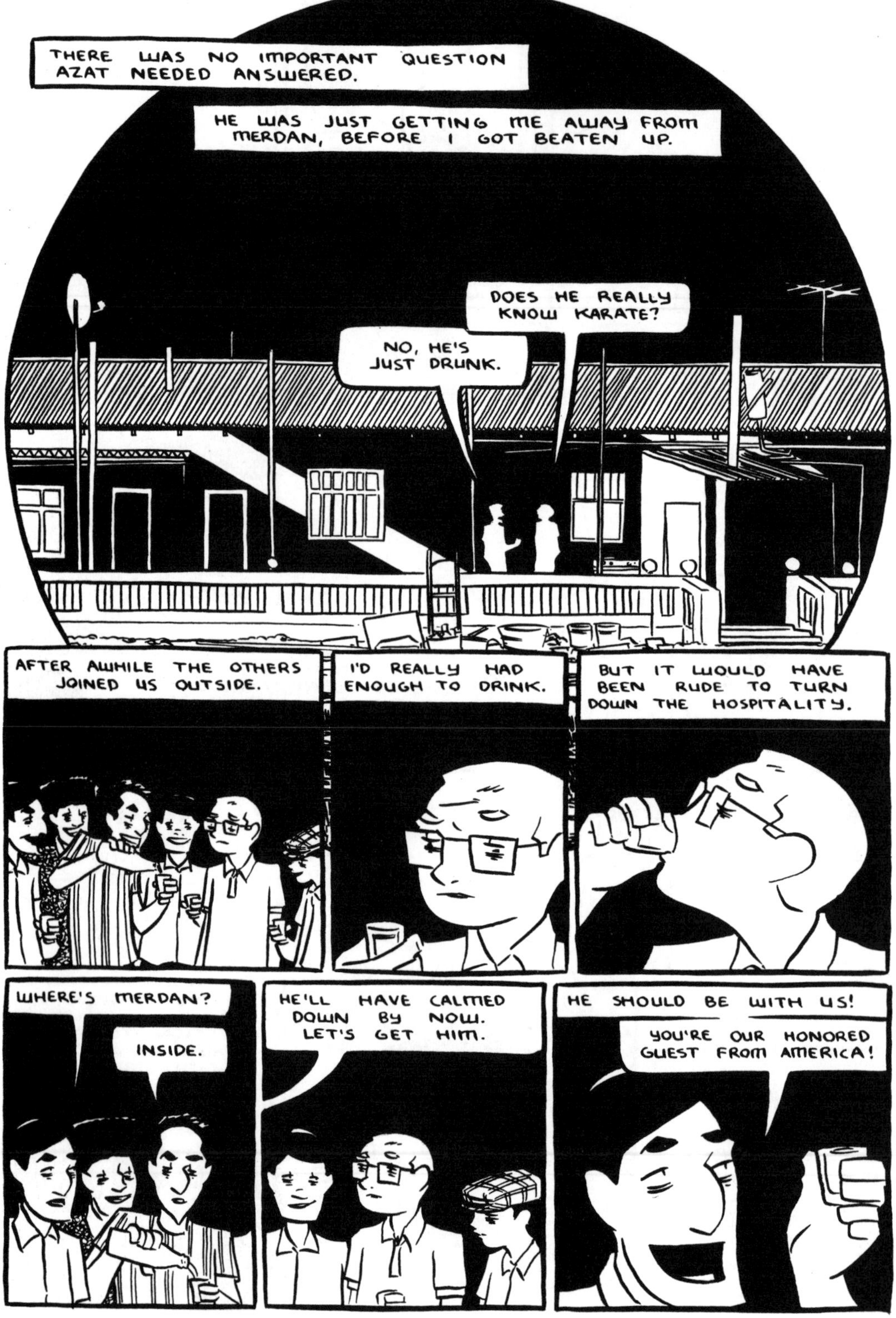
THERE WAS NO IMPORTANT QUESTION AZAT NEEDED ANSWERED.
HE WAS JUST GETTING ME AWAY FROM MERDAN, BEFORE I GOT BEATEN UP.
DOES HE REALLY KNOW KARATE?
NO, HE'S JUST DRUNK.
AFTER AWHILE THE OTHERS JOINED US OUTSIDE.
I'D REALLY HAD ENOUGH TO DRINK.
BUT IT WOULD HAVE BEEN RUDE TO TURN DOWN THE HOSPITALITY.
WHERE'S MERDAN?
INSIDE.
HE'LL HAVE CALMED DOWN BY NOW. LET'S GET HIM.
HE SHOULD BE WITH US!
YOU'RE OUR HONORED GUEST FROM AMERICA!

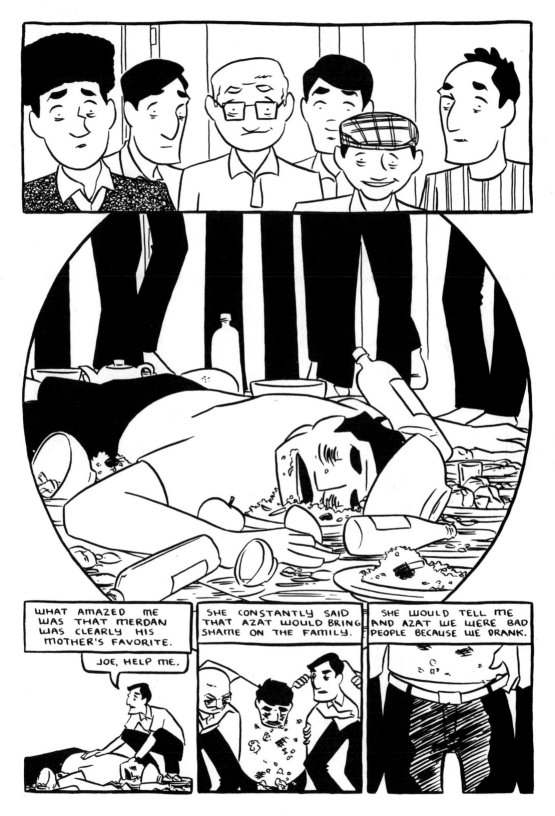

WHAT AMAZED ME WAS THAT MERDAN WAS CLEARLY HIS MOTHER'S FAVORITE.

JOE, HELP ME.

SHE CONSTANTLY SAID THAT AZAT WOULD BRING SHAME ON THE FAMILY.

SHE WOULD TELL ME AND AZAT WE WERE BAD PEOPLE BECAUSE WE DRANK.

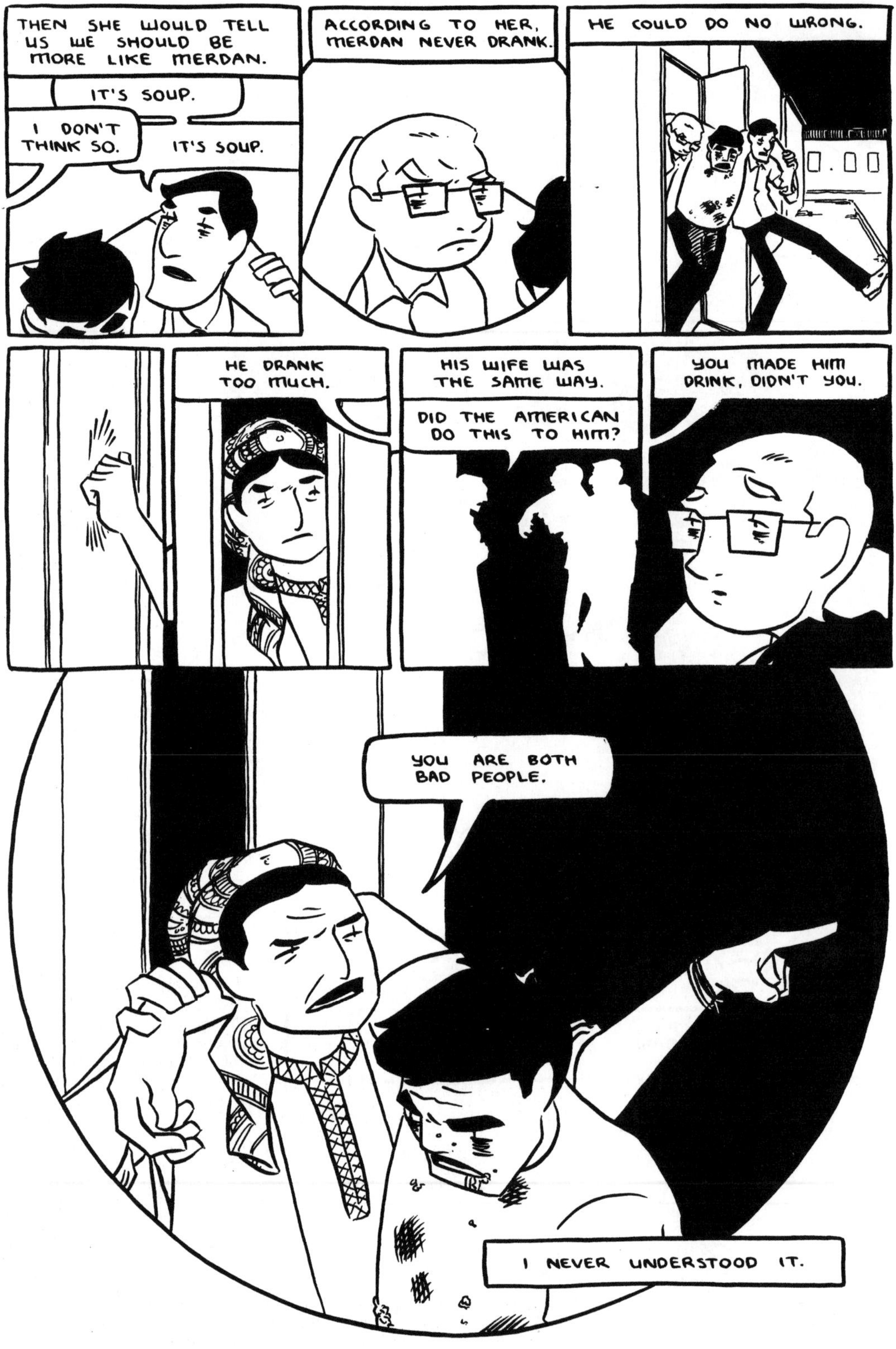
THEN SHE WOULD TELL US WE SHOULD BE MORE LIKE MERDAN.
IT'S SOUP.
I DON'T THINK SO.
IT'S SOUP.
ACCORDING TO HER, MERDAN NEVER DRANK.
HE COULD DO NO WRONG.
HE DRANK TOO MUCH.
HIS WIFE WAS THE SAME WAY.
DID THE AMERICAN DO THIS TO HIM?
YOU MADE HIM DRINK, DIDN'T YOU.
YOU ARE BOTH BAD PEOPLE.
I NEVER UNDERSTOOD IT.

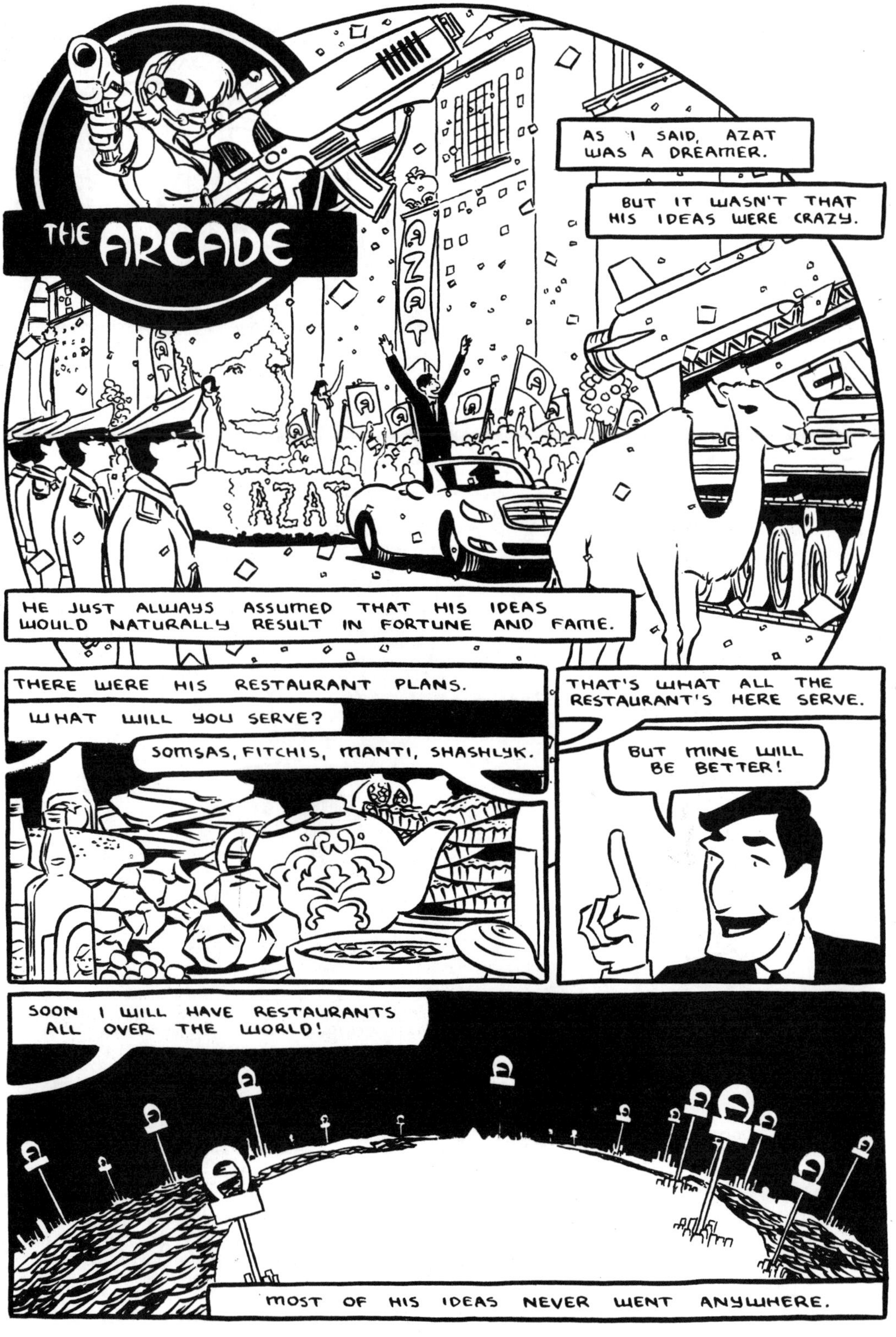
THE ARCADE
AS I SAID, AZAT WAS A DREAMER.
BUT IT WASN'T THAT HIS IDEAS WERE CRAZY.
AZAT
HE JUST ALWAYS ASSUMED THAT HIS IDEAS WOULD NATURALLY RESULT IN FORTUNE AND FAME.
THERE WERE HIS RESTAURANT PLANS.
WHAT WILL YOU SERVE?
SOMSAS, FITCHIS, MANTI, SHASHLYK.
THAT'S WHAT ALL THE RESTAURANT'S HERE SERVE.
BUT MINE WILL BE BETTER!
SOON I WILL HAVE RESTAURANTS ALL OVER THE WORLD!
MOST OF HIS IDEAS NEVER WENT ANYWHERE.

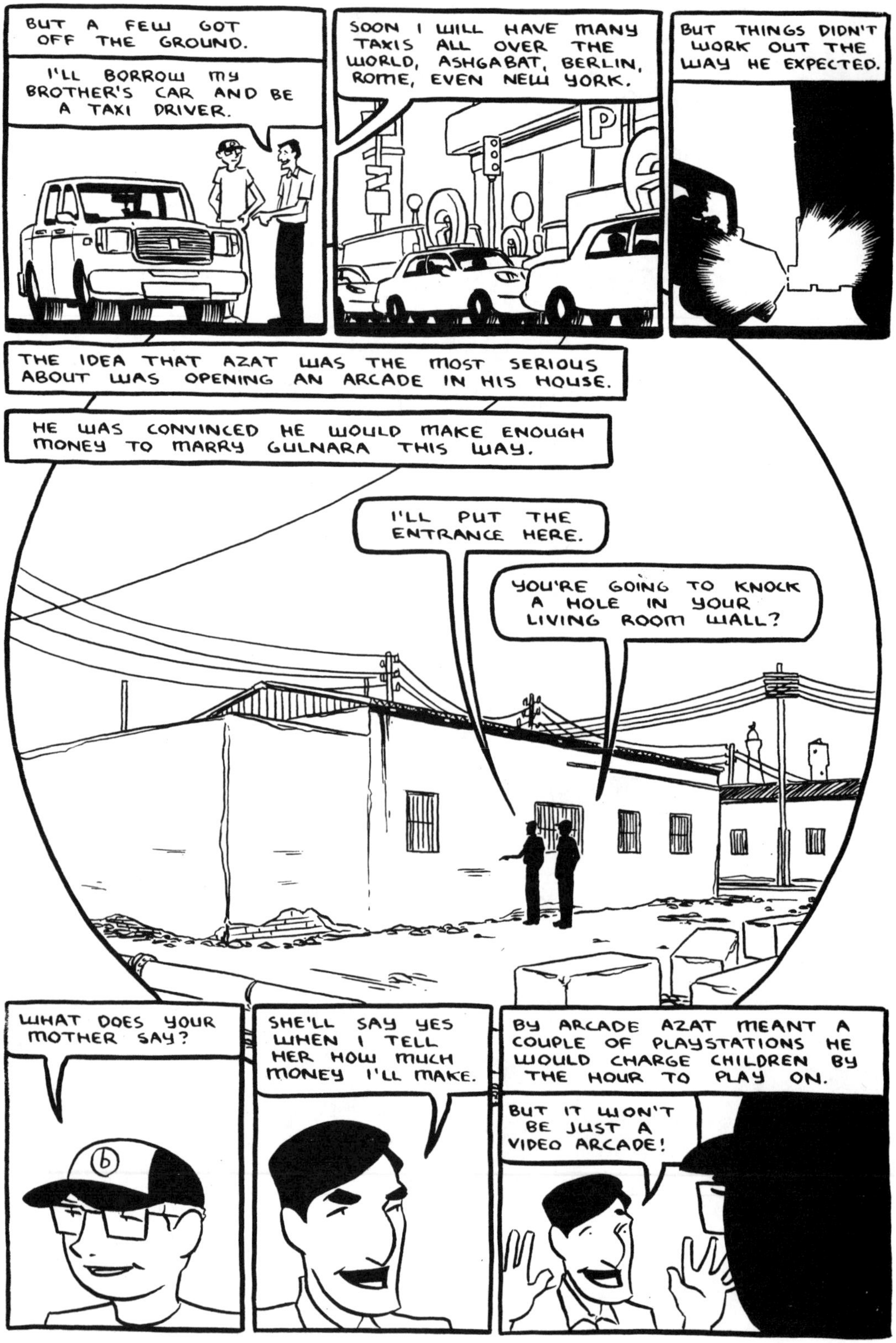

BUT A FEW GOT OFF THE GROUND.
I'LL BORROW MY BROTHER'S CAR AND BE A TAXI DRIVER.
SOON I WILL HAVE MANY TAXIS ALL OVER THE WORLD, ASHGABAT, BERLIN, ROME, EVEN NEW YORK.
P
BUT THINGS DIDN'T WORK OUT THE WAY HE EXPECTED.
THE IDEA THAT AZAT WAS THE MOST SERIOUS ABOUT WAS OPENING AN ARCADE IN HIS HOUSE.
HE WAS CONVINCED HE WOULD MAKE ENOUGH MONEY TO MARRY GULNARA THIS WAY.
I'LL PUT THE ENTRANCE HERE.
YOU'RE GOING TO KNOCK A HOLE IN YOUR LIVING ROOM WALL?
WHAT DOES YOUR MOTHER SAY?
SHE'LL SAY YES WHEN I TELL HER HOW MUCH MONEY I'LL MAKE.
BY ARCADE AZAT MEANT A COUPLE OF PLAYSTATIONS HE WOULD CHARGE CHILDREN BY THE HOUR TO PLAY ON.
BUT IT WON'T BE JUST A VIDEO ARCADE!

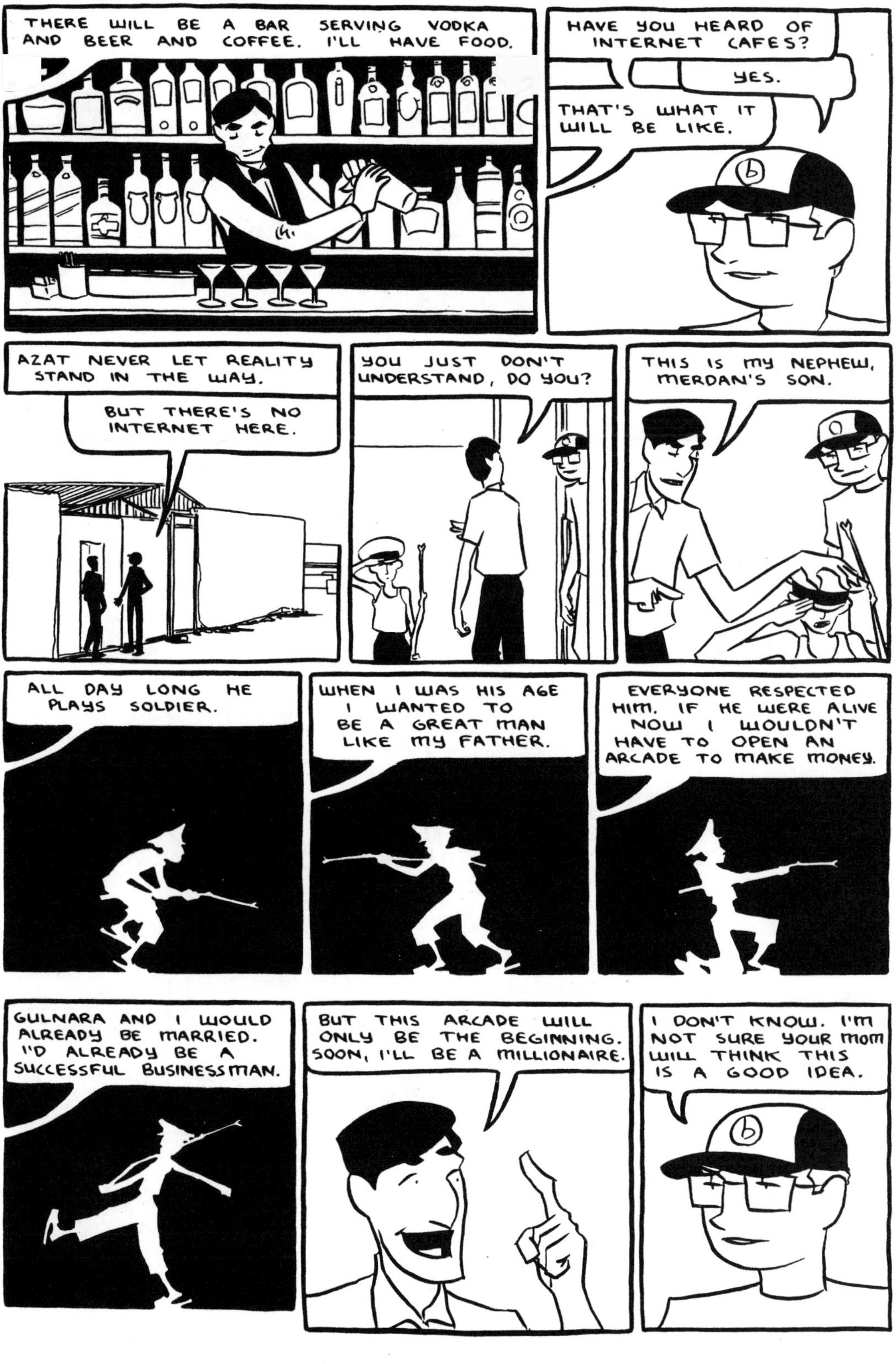
THERE WILL BE A BAR SERVING VODKA AND BEER AND COFFEE. I'LL HAVE FOOD.
HAVE YOU HEARD OF INTERNET CAFES?
YES.
THAT'S WHAT IT WILL BE LIKE.
AZAT NEVER LET REALITY STAND IN THE WAY.
BUT THERE'S NO INTERNET HERE.
YOU JUST DON'T UNDERSTAND, DO YOU?
THIS IS MY NEPHEW, MERDAN'S SON.
ALL DAY LONG HE PLAYS SOLDIER.
WHEN I WAS HIS AGE I WANTED TO BE A GREAT MAN LIKE MY FATHER.
EVERYONE RESPECTED HIM. IF HE WERE ALIVE NOW I WOULDN'T HAVE TO OPEN AN ARCADE TO MAKE MONEY.
GULNARA AND I WOULD ALREADY BE MARRIED. I'D ALREADY BE A SUCCESSFUL BUSINESSMAN.
BUT THIS ARCADE WILL ONLY BE THE BEGINNING. SOON, I'LL BE A MILLIONAIRE.
I DON'T KNOW. I'M NOT SURE YOUR MOM WILL THINK THIS IS A GOOD IDEA.

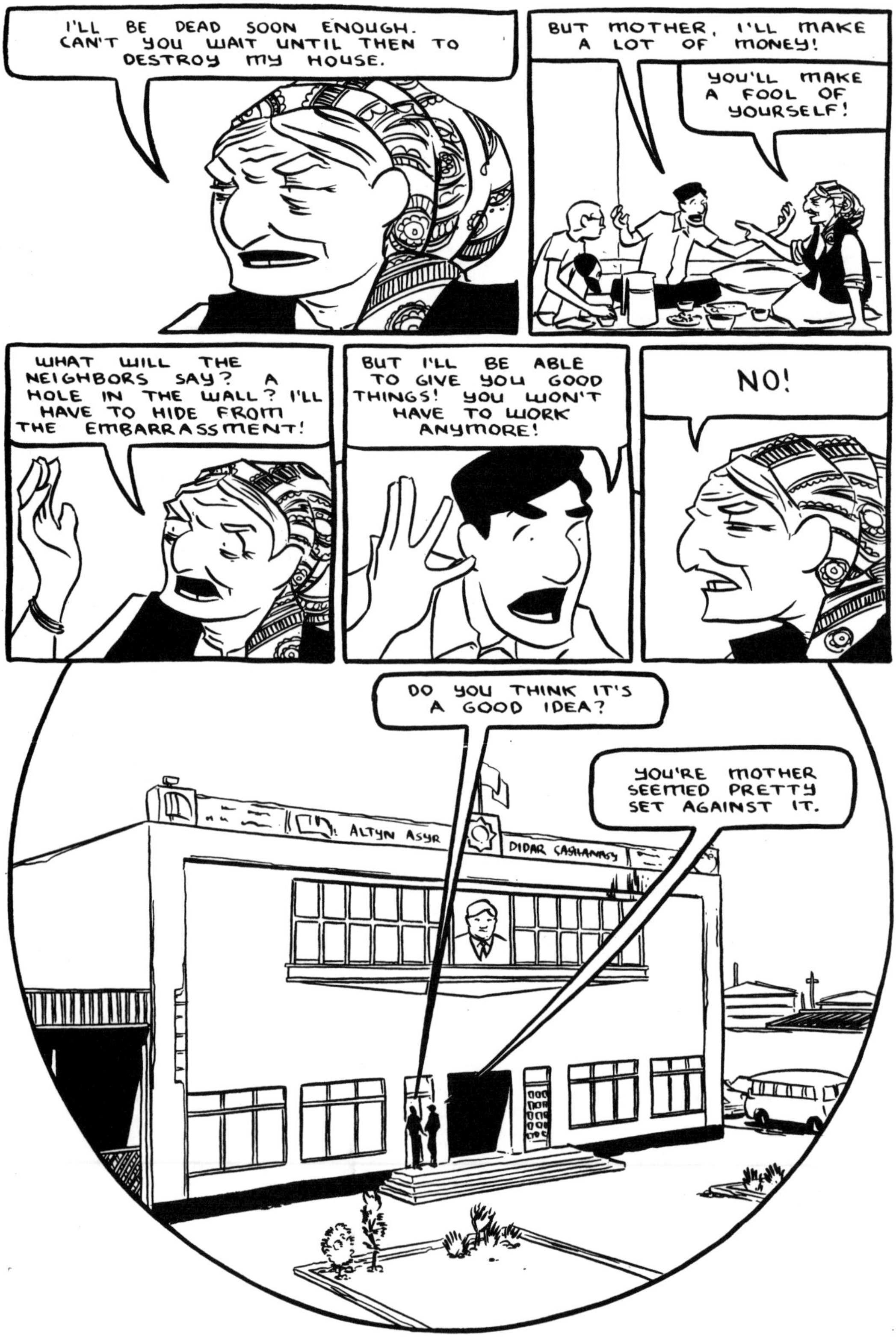
I'LL BE DEAD SOON ENOUGH. CAN'T YOU WAIT UNTIL THEN TO DESTROY MY HOUSE.
BUT MOTHER, I'LL MAKE A LOT OF MONEY!
YOU'LL MAKE A FOOL OF YOURSELF!
WHAT WILL THE NEIGHBORS SAY? A HOLE IN THE WALL? I'LL HAVE TO HIDE FROM THE EMBARRASSMENT!
BUT I'LL BE ABLE TO GIVE YOU GOOD THINGS! YOU WON'T HAVE TO WORK ANYMORE!
NO!
ALTYN ASYR
DIDAR CASHANASY
DO YOU THINK IT'S A GOOD IDEA?
YOU'RE MOTHER SEEMED PRETTY SET AGAINST IT.

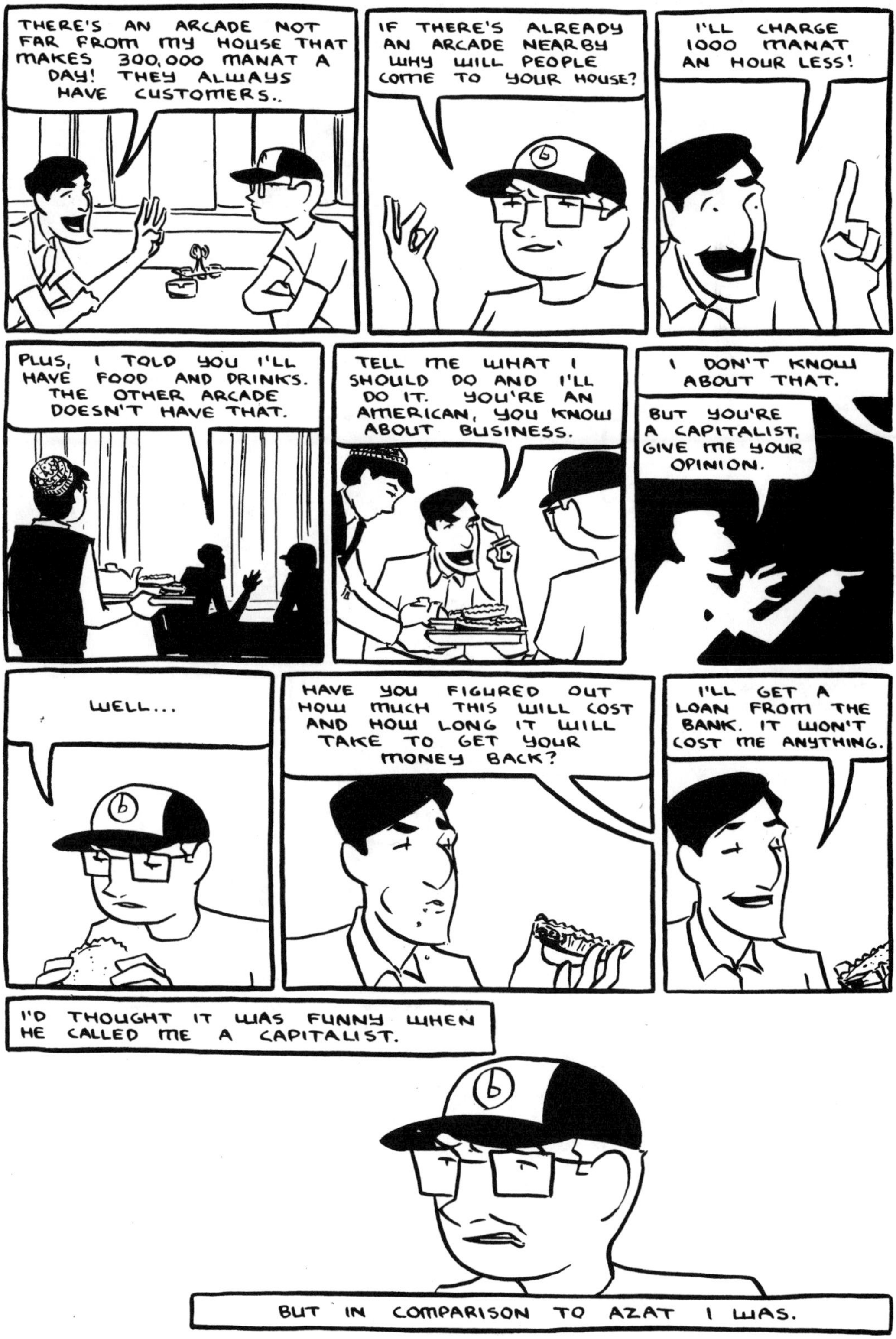
THERE'S AN ARCADE NOT FAR FROM MY HOUSE THAT MAKES 300,000 MANAT A DAY! THEY ALWAYS HAVE CUSTOMERS..
IF THERE'S ALREADY AN ARCADE NEARBY WHY WILL PEOPLE COME TO YOUR HOUSE?
I'LL CHARGE 1000 MANAT AN HOUR LESS!
PLUS, I TOLD YOU I'LL HAVE FOOD AND DRINKS. THE OTHER ARCADE DOESN'T HAVE THAT.
TELL ME WHAT I SHOULD DO AND I'LL DO IT. YOU'RE AN AMERICAN, YOU KNOW ABOUT BUSINESS.
I DON'T KNOW ABOUT THAT.
BUT YOU'RE A CAPITALIST, GIVE ME YOUR OPINION.
WELL...
HAVE YOU FIGURED OUT HOW MUCH THIS WILL COST AND HOW LONG IT WILL TAKE TO GET YOUR MONEY BACK?
I'LL GET A LOAN FROM THE BANK. IT WON'T COST ME ANYTHING.
I'D THOUGHT IT WAS FUNNY WHEN HE CALLED ME A CAPITALIST.
BUT IN COMPARISON TO AZAT I WAS.

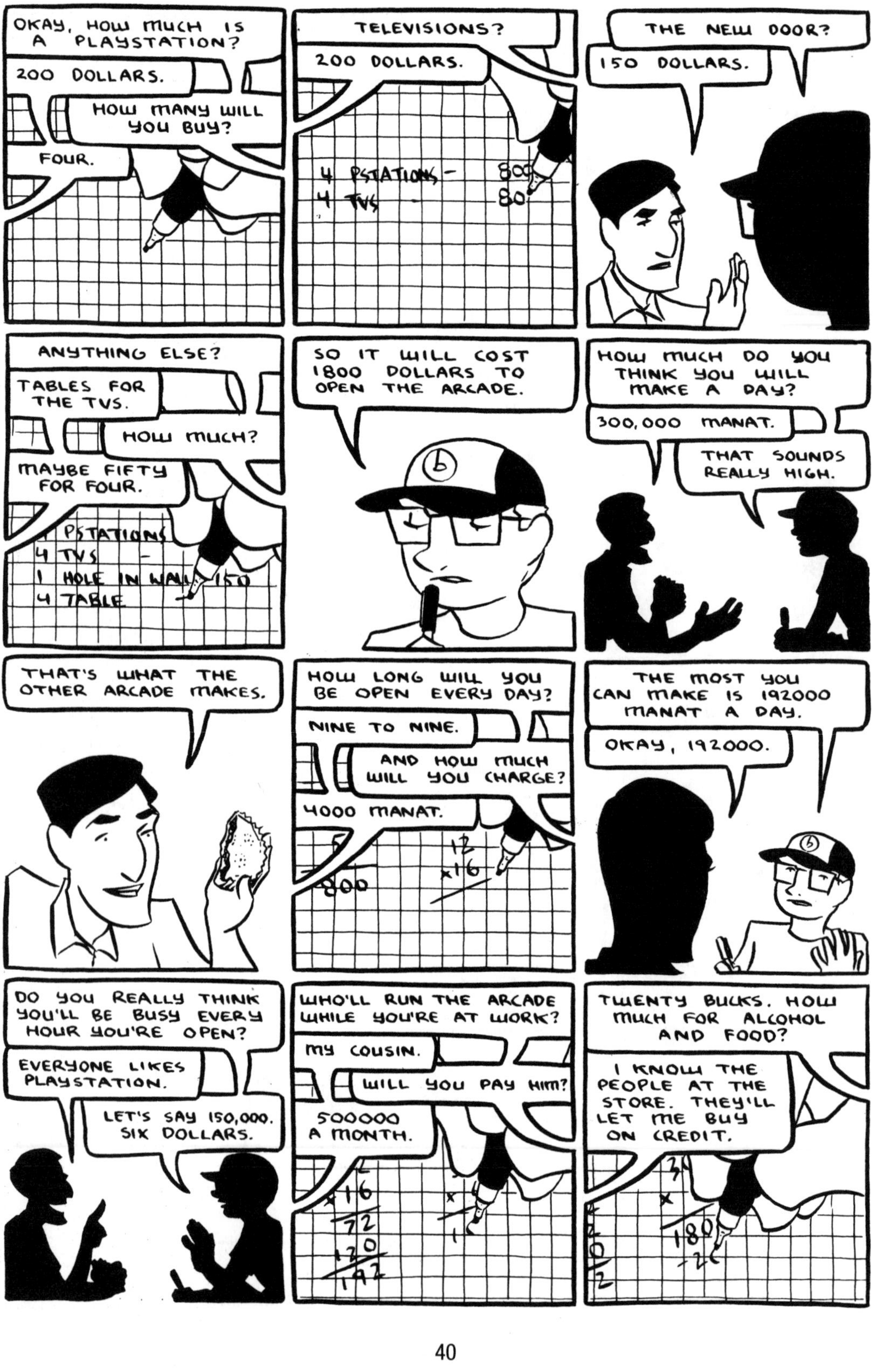
OKAY, HOW MUCH IS A PLAYSTATION?
200 DOLLARS.
HOW MANY WILL YOU BUY?
FOUR.
TELEVISIONS?
200 DOLLARS.
4 PSTATIONS - 800
4 TVS - 80
THE NEW DOOR?
150 DOLLARS.
ANYTHING ELSE?
TABLES FOR THE TVS.
HOW MUCH?
MAYBE FIFTY FOR FOUR.
4 PSTATIONS
4 TVS
1 HOLE IN WALL 150
4 TABLE
SO IT WILL COST 1800 DOLLARS TO OPEN THE ARCADE.
HOW MUCH DO YOU THINK YOU WILL MAKE A DAY?
300,000 MANAT.
THAT SOUNDS REALLY HIGH.
THAT'S WHAT THE OTHER ARCADE MAKES.
HOW LONG WILL YOU BE OPEN EVERY DAY?
NINE TO NINE.
AND HOW MUCH WILL YOU CHARGE?
4000 MANAT.
12
x16
THE MOST YOU CAN MAKE IS 192000 MANAT A DAY.
OKAY, 192000.
DO YOU REALLY THINK YOU'LL BE BUSY EVERY HOUR YOU'RE OPEN?
EVERYONE LIKES PLAYSTATION.
LET'S SAY 150,000. SIX DOLLARS.
WHO'LL RUN THE ARCADE WHILE YOU'RE AT WORK?
MY COUSIN.
WILL YOU PAY HIM?
500000 A MONTH.
x16
72
120
192
TWENTY BUCKS. HOW MUCH FOR ALCOHOL AND FOOD?
I KNOW THE PEOPLE AT THE STORE. THEY'LL LET ME BUY ON CREDIT.
180
-20

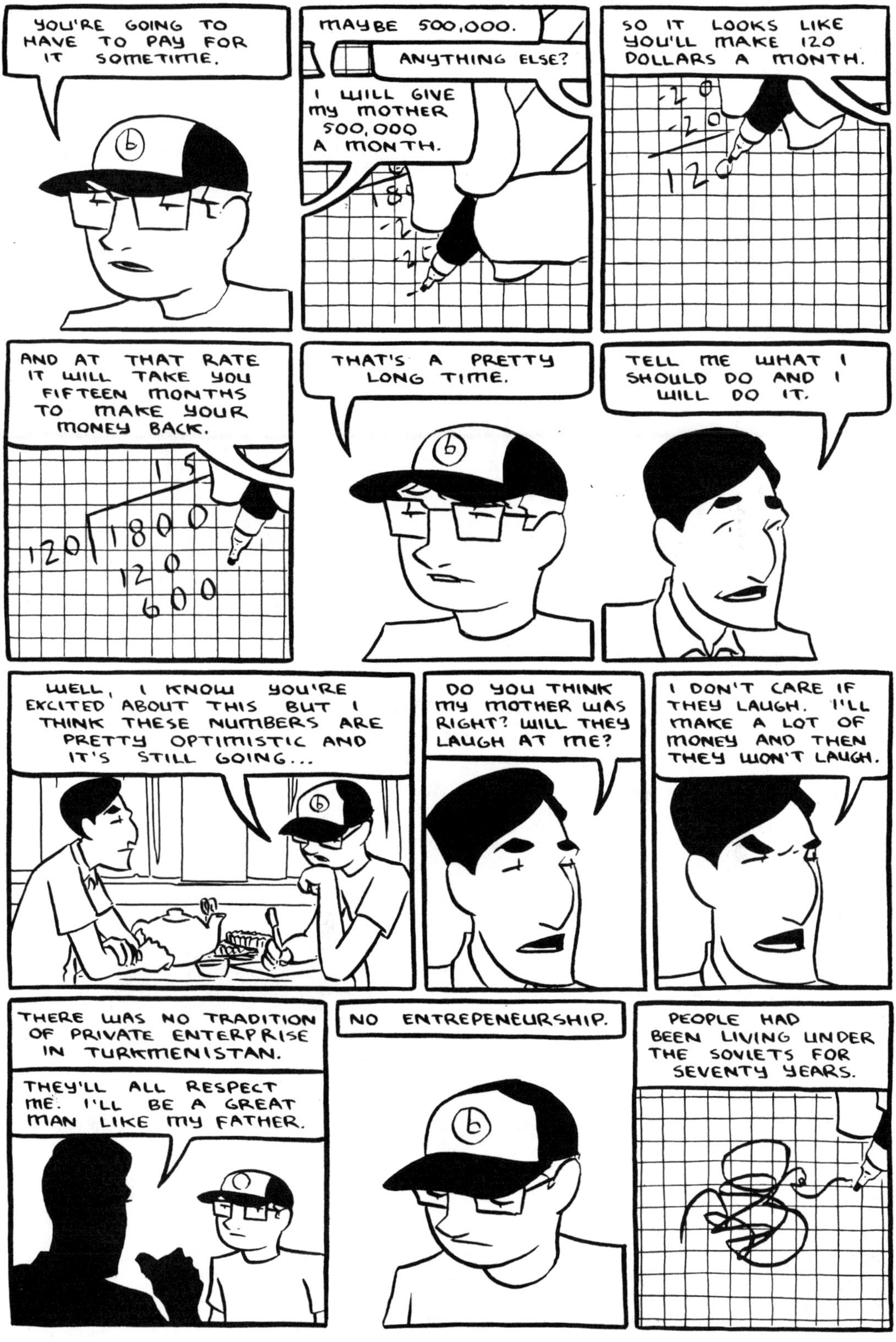

YOU'RE GOING TO HAVE TO PAY FOR IT SOMETIME.
MAYBE 500,000.
ANYTHING ELSE?
I WILL GIVE MY MOTHER 500,000 A MONTH.
SO IT LOOKS LIKE YOU'LL MAKE 120 DOLLARS A MONTH.
AND AT THAT RATE IT WILL TAKE YOU FIFTEEN MONTHS TO MAKE YOUR MONEY BACK.
THAT'S A PRETTY LONG TIME.
TELL ME WHAT I SHOULD DO AND I WILL DO IT.
WELL, I KNOW YOU'RE EXCITED ABOUT THIS BUT I THINK THESE NUMBERS ARE PRETTY OPTIMISTIC AND IT'S STILL GOING...
DO YOU THINK MY MOTHER WAS RIGHT? WILL THEY LAUGH AT ME?
I DON'T CARE IF THEY LAUGH. I'LL MAKE A LOT OF MONEY AND THEN THEY WON'T LAUGH.
THERE WAS NO TRADITION OF PRIVATE ENTERPRISE IN TURKMENISTAN.
THEY'LL ALL RESPECT ME. I'LL BE A GREAT MAN LIKE MY FATHER.
NO ENTREPENEURSHIP.
PEOPLE HAD BEEN LIVING UNDER THE SOVIETS FOR SEVENTY YEARS.

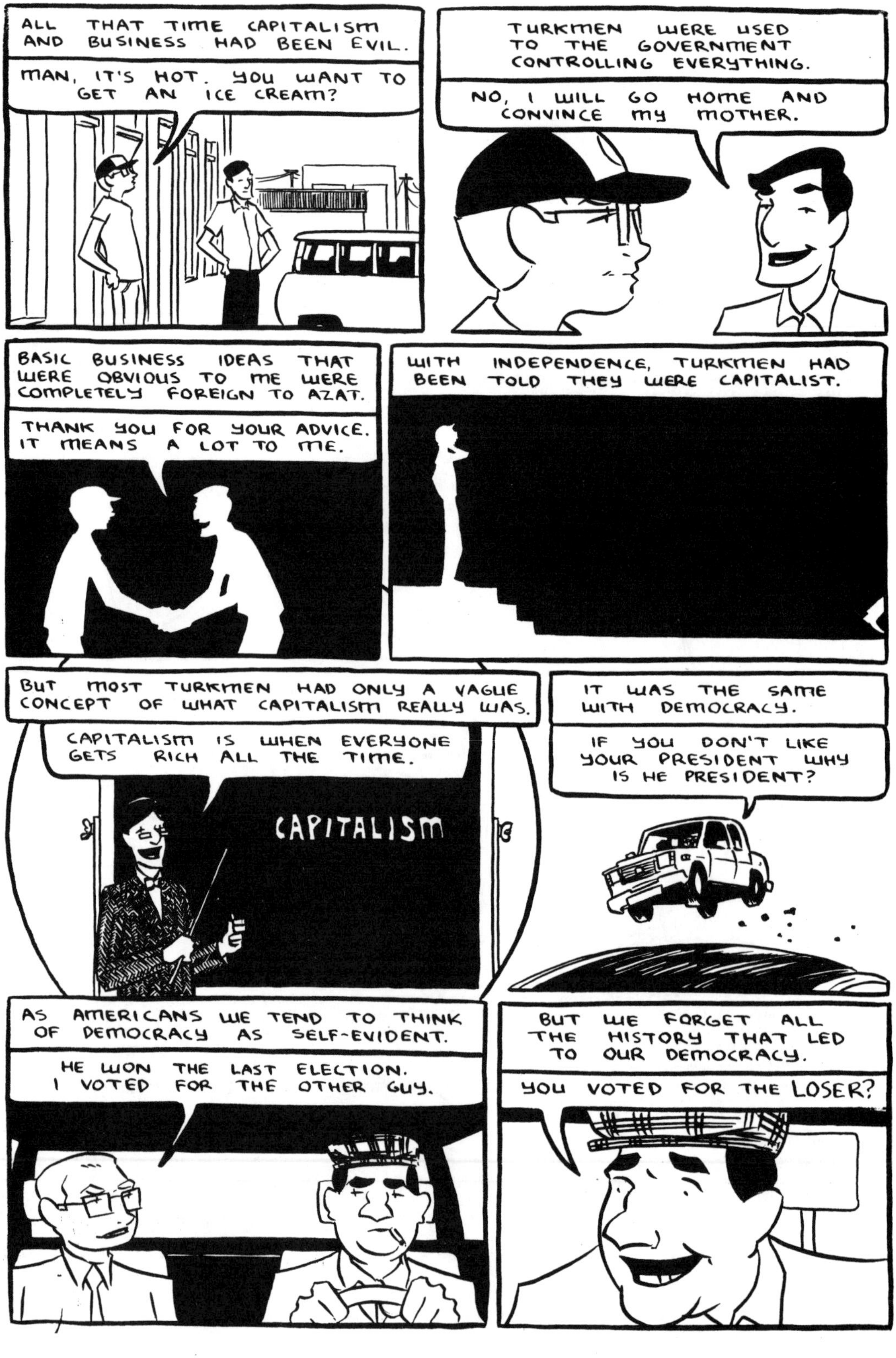
ALL THAT TIME CAPITALISM AND BUSINESS HAD BEEN EVIL.
MAN, IT'S HOT. YOU WANT TO GET AN ICE CREAM?
TURKMEN WERE USED TO THE GOVERNMENT CONTROLLING EVERYTHING.
NO, I WILL GO HOME AND CONVINCE MY MOTHER.
BASIC BUSINESS IDEAS THAT WERE OBVIOUS TO ME WERE COMPLETELY FOREIGN TO AZAT.
THANK YOU FOR YOUR ADVICE. IT MEANS A LOT TO ME.
WITH INDEPENDENCE, TURKMEN HAD BEEN TOLD THEY WERE CAPITALIST.
BUT MOST TURKMEN HAD ONLY A VAGUE CONCEPT OF WHAT CAPITALISM REALLY WAS.
CAPITALISM IS WHEN EVERYONE GETS RICH ALL THE TIME.
CAPITALISM
IT WAS THE SAME WITH DEMOCRACY.
IF YOU DON'T LIKE YOUR PRESIDENT WHY IS HE PRESIDENT?
AS AMERICANS WE TEND TO THINK OF DEMOCRACY AS SELF-EVIDENT.
HE WON THE LAST ELECTION. I VOTED FOR THE OTHER GUY.
BUT WE FORGET ALL THE HISTORY THAT LED TO OUR DEMOCRACY.
YOU VOTED FOR THE LOSER?

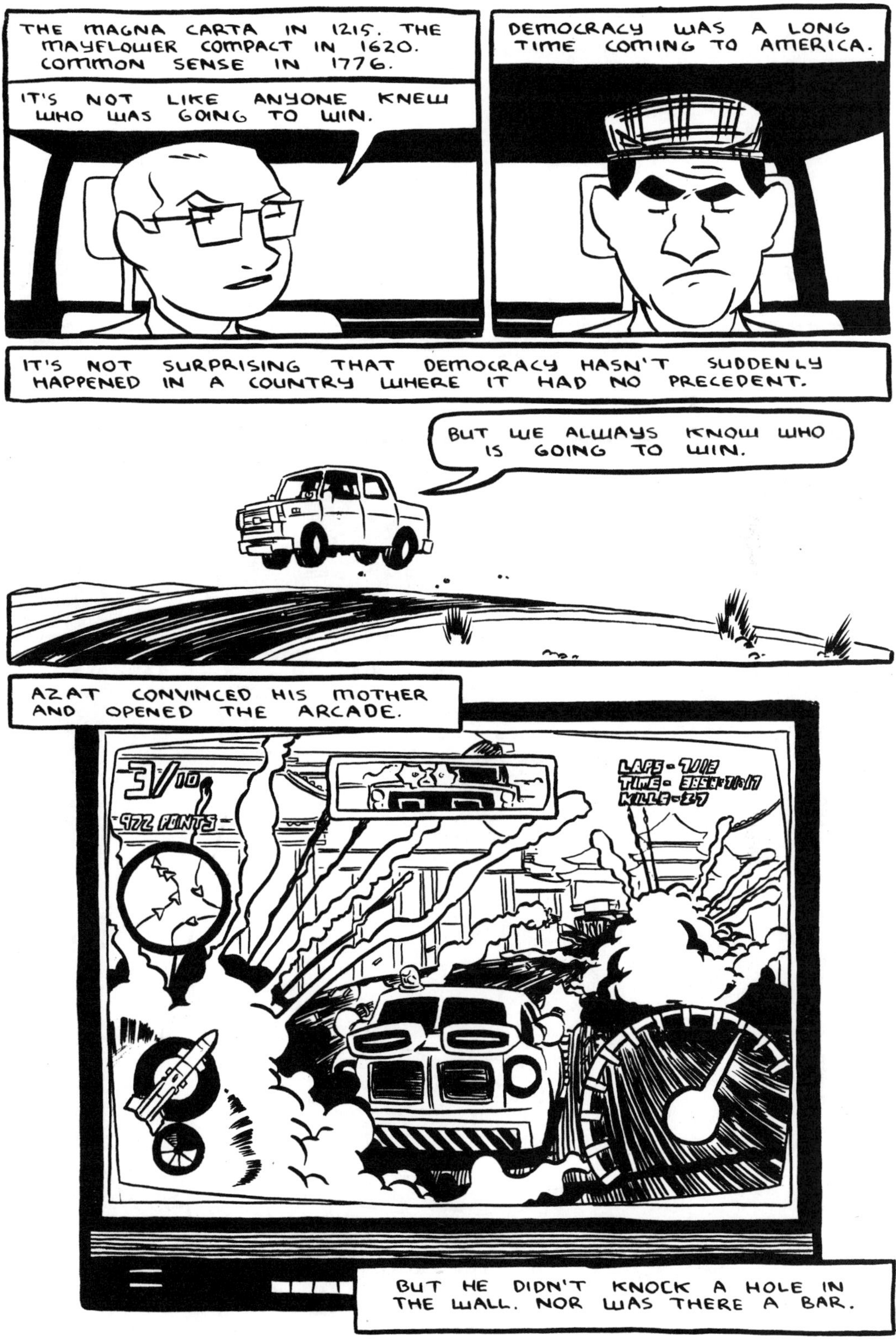
THE MAGNA CARTA IN 1215. THE MAYFLOWER COMPACT IN 1620. COMMON SENSE IN 1776.
IT'S NOT LIKE ANYONE KNEW WHO WAS GOING TO WIN.
DEMOCRACY WAS A LONG TIME COMING TO AMERICA.
IT'S NOT SURPRISING THAT DEMOCRACY HASN'T SUDDENLY HAPPENED IN A COUNTRY WHERE IT HAD NO PRECEDENT.
BUT WE ALWAYS KNOW WHO IS GOING TO WIN.
AZAT CONVINCED HIS MOTHER AND OPENED THE ARCADE.
972 POINTS
BUT HE DIDN'T KNOCK A HOLE IN THE WALL. NOR WAS THERE A BAR.

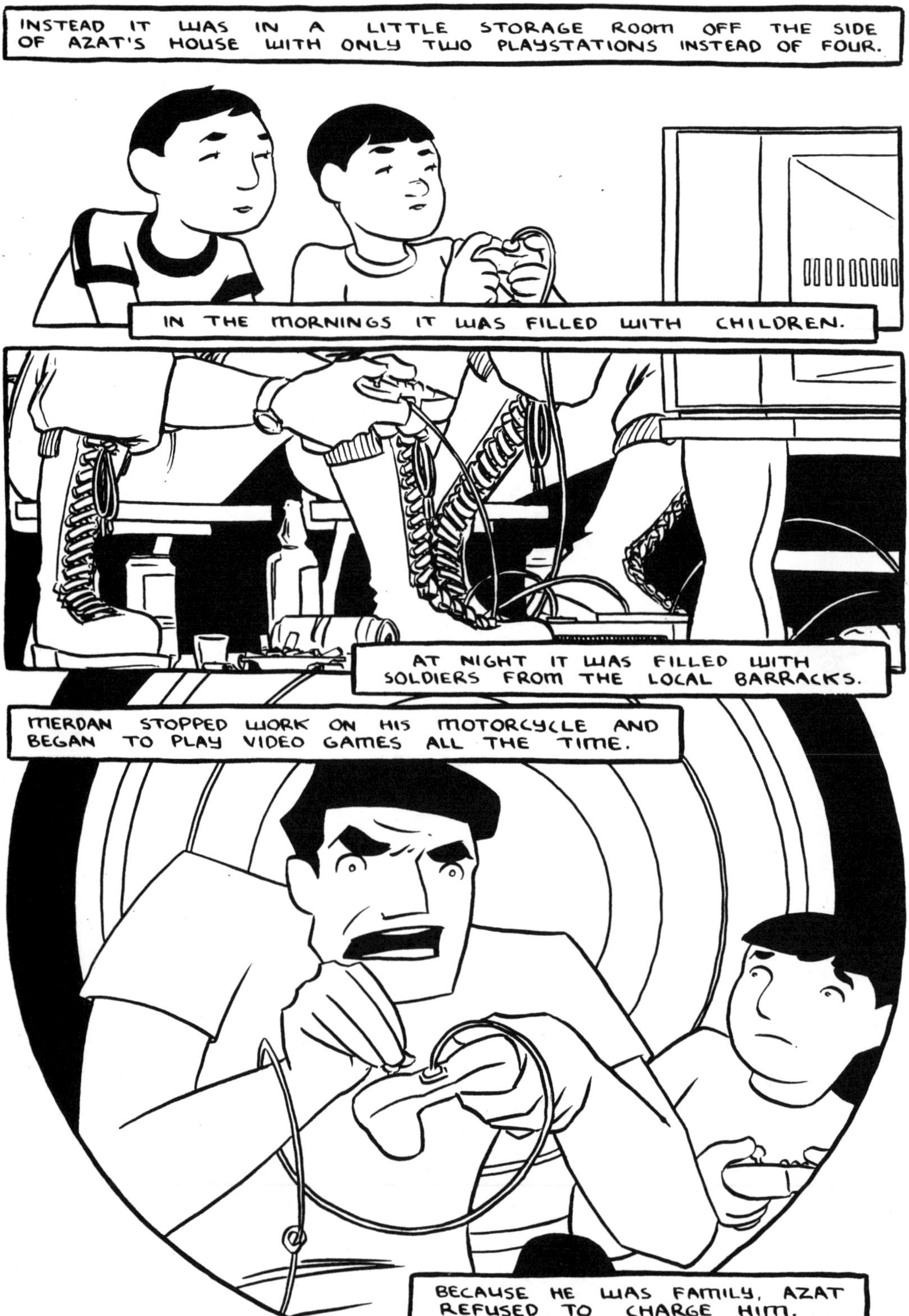
INSTEAD IT WAS IN A LITTLE STORAGE ROOM OFF THE SIDE OF AZAT'S HOUSE WITH ONLY TWO PLAYSTATIONS INSTEAD OF FOUR.
IN THE MORNINGS IT WAS FILLED WITH CHILDREN.
AT NIGHT IT WAS FILLED WITH SOLDIERS FROM THE LOCAL BARRACKS.
MERDAN STOPPED WORK ON HIS MOTORCYCLE AND BEGAN TO PLAY VIDEO GAMES ALL THE TIME.
BECAUSE HE WAS FAMILY, AZAT REFUSED TO CHARGE HIM.

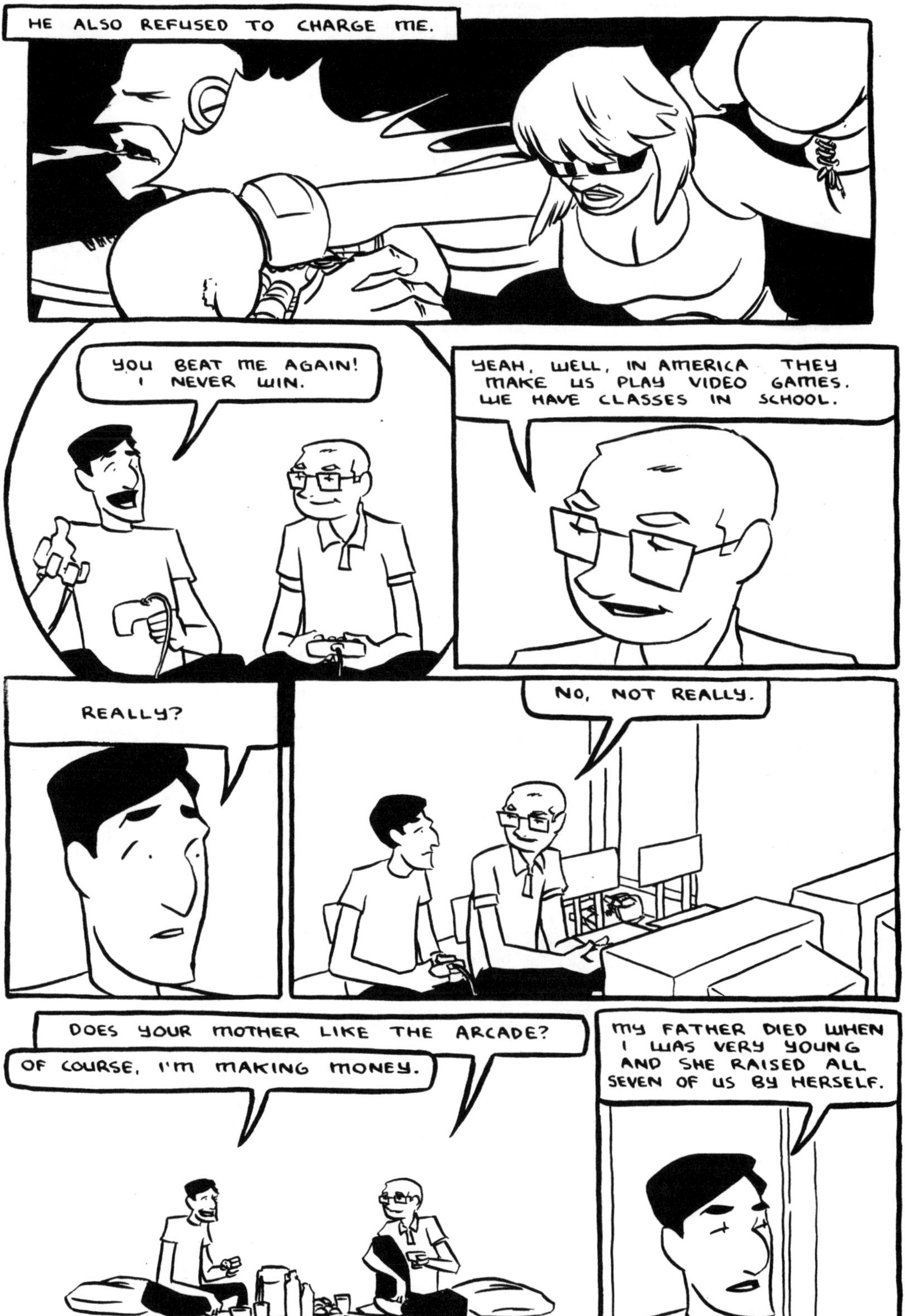
HE ALSO REFUSED TO CHARGE ME.
YOU BEAT ME AGAIN! I NEVER WIN.
YEAH, WELL, IN AMERICA THEY MAKE US PLAY VIDEO GAMES. WE HAVE CLASSES IN SCHOOL.
REALLY?
NO, NOT REALLY.
DOES YOUR MOTHER LIKE THE ARCADE?
OF COURSE, I'M MAKING MONEY.
MY FATHER DIED WHEN I WAS VERY YOUNG AND SHE RAISED ALL SEVEN OF US BY HERSELF.

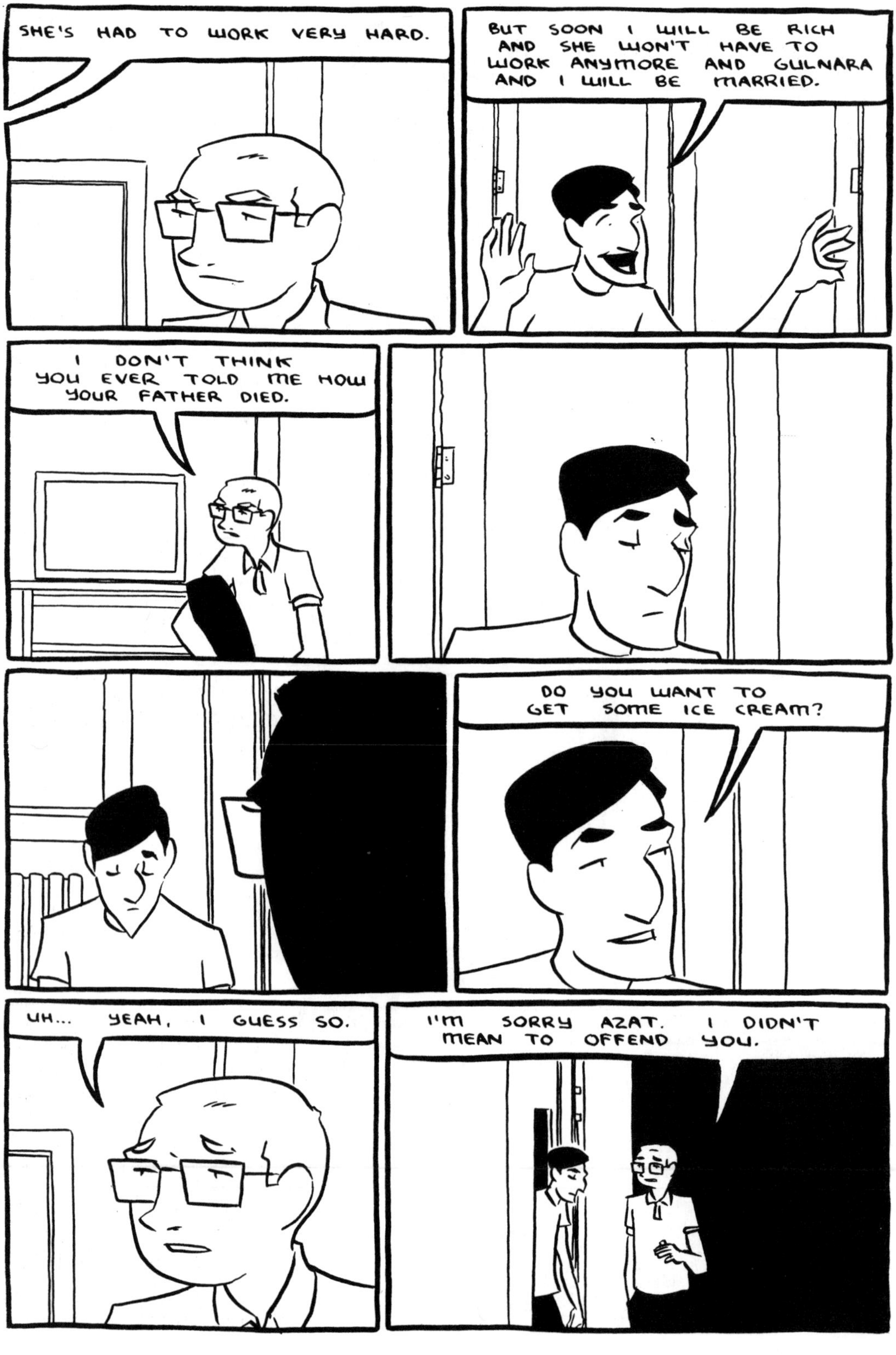
SHE'S HAD TO WORK VERY HARD.
BUT SOON I WILL BE RICH AND SHE WON'T HAVE TO WORK ANYMORE AND GULNARA AND I WILL BE MARRIED.
I DON'T THINK YOU EVER TOLD ME HOW YOUR FATHER DIED.
DO YOU WANT TO GET SOME ICE CREAM?
UH... YEAH, I GUESS SO.
I'M SORRY AZAT. I DIDN'T MEAN TO OFFEND YOU.

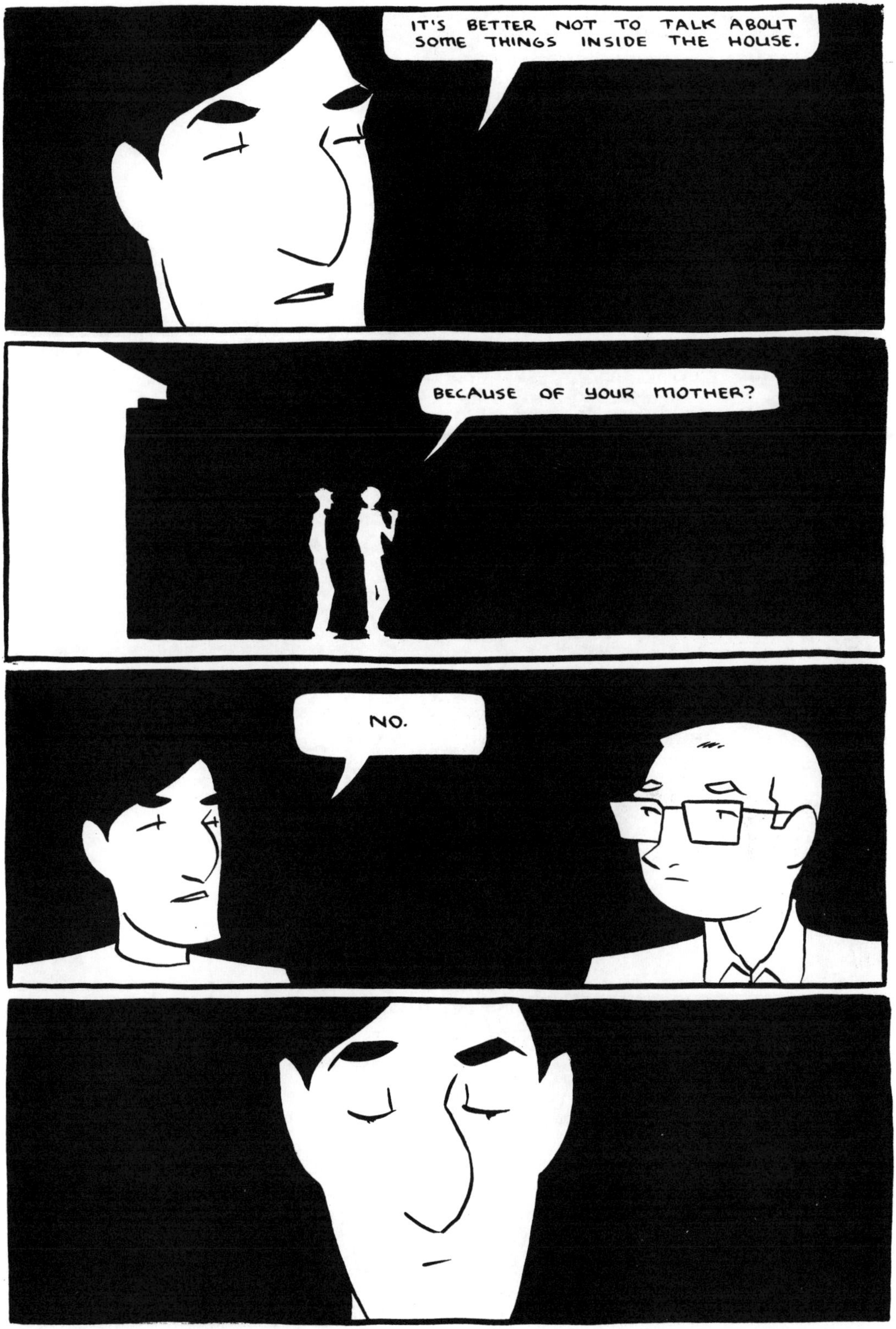
IT'S BETTER NOT TO TALK ABOUT SOME THINGS INSIDE THE HOUSE.
BECAUSE OF YOUR MOTHER?
NO.

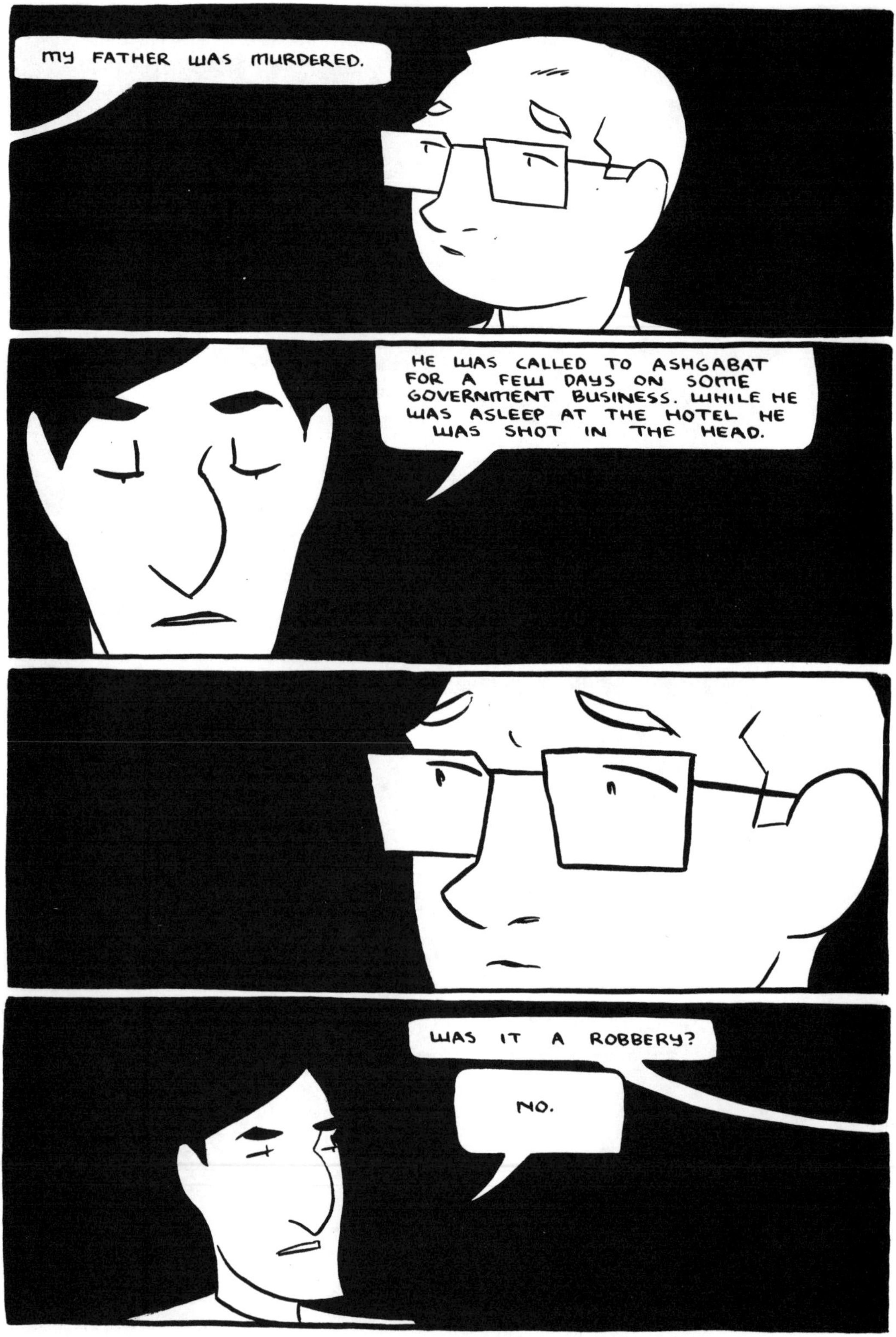
MY FATHER WAS MURDERED.
HE WAS CALLED TO ASHGABAT FOR A FEW DAYS ON SOME GOVERNMENT BUSINESS. WHILE HE WAS ASLEEP AT THE HOTEL HE WAS SHOT IN THE HEAD.
WAS IT A ROBBERY?
NO.

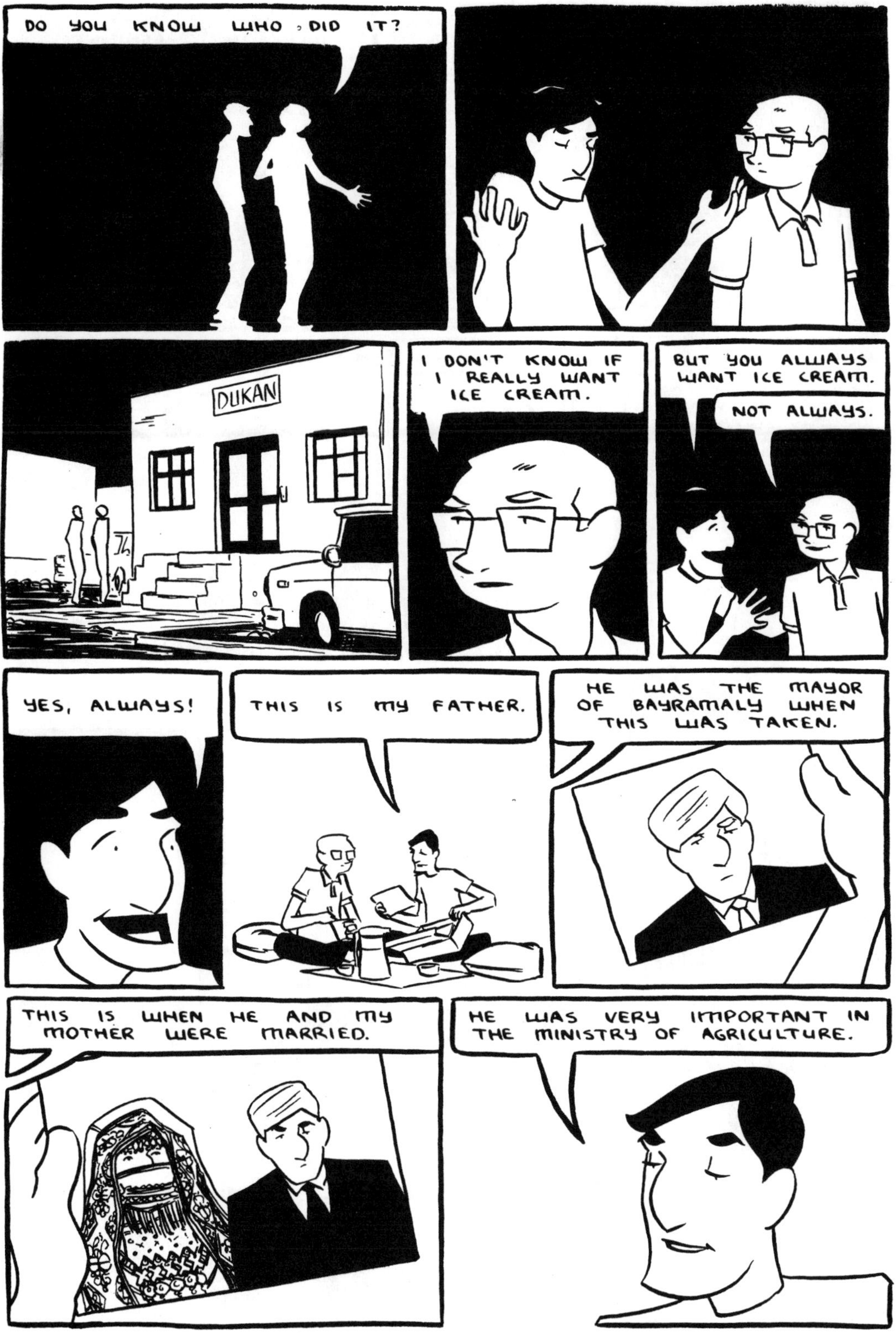

DO YOU KNOW WHO DID IT?
DUKAN
I DON'T KNOW IF I REALLY WANT ICE CREAM.
BUT YOU ALWAYS WANT ICE CREAM.
NOT ALWAYS.
YES, ALWAYS!
THIS IS MY FATHER.
HE WAS THE MAYOR OF BAYRAMALY WHEN THIS WAS TAKEN.
THIS IS WHEN HE AND MY MOTHER WERE MARRIED.
HE WAS VERY IMPORTANT IN THE MINISTRY OF AGRICULTURE.

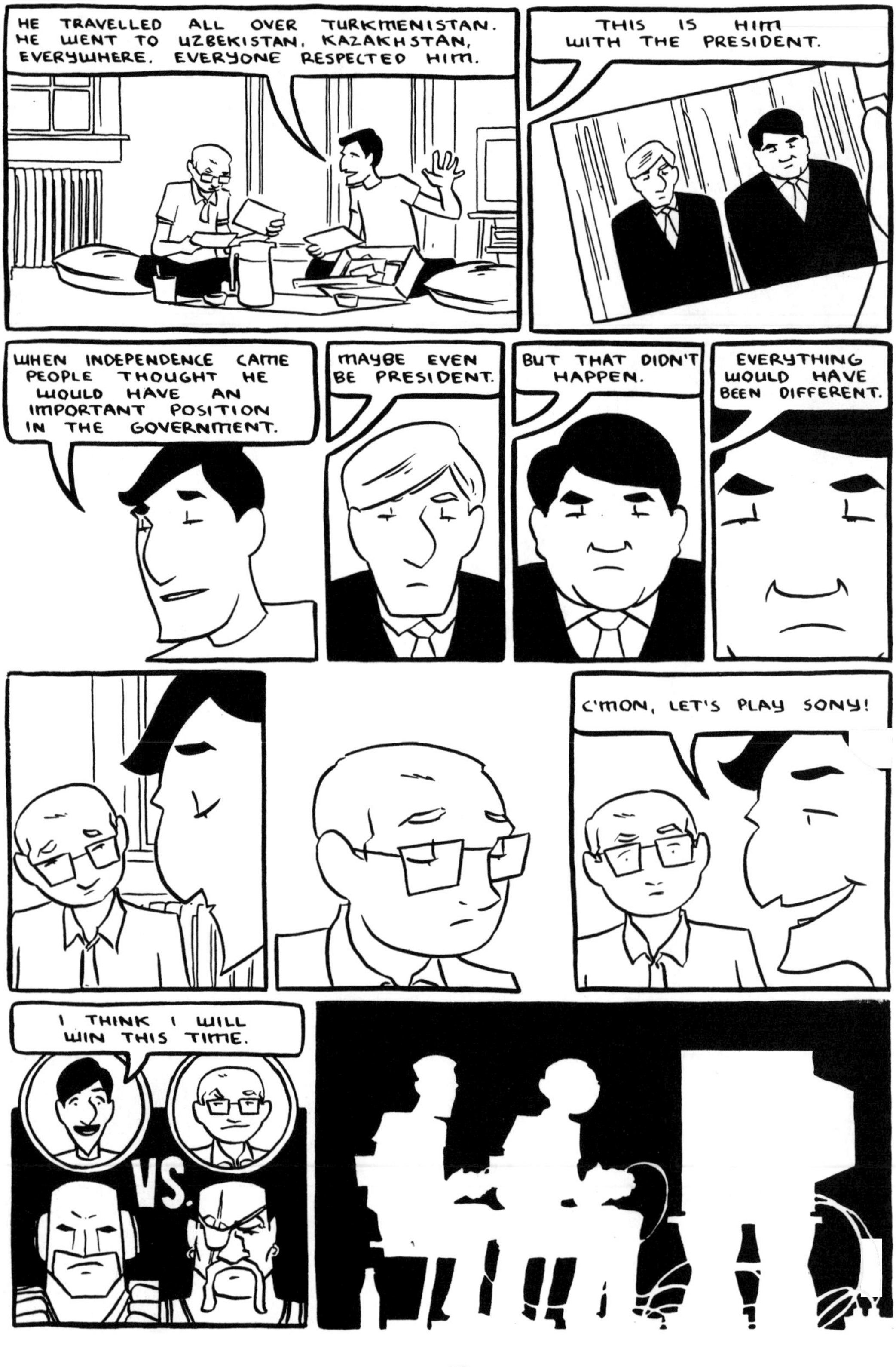
HE TRAVELLED ALL OVER TURKMENISTAN. HE WENT TO UZBEKISTAN, KAZAKHSTAN, EVERYWHERE. EVERYONE RESPECTED HIM.
THIS IS HIM WITH THE PRESIDENT.
WHEN INDEPENDENCE CAME PEOPLE THOUGHT HE WOULD HAVE AN IMPORTANT POSITION IN THE GOVERNMENT.
MAYBE EVEN BE PRESIDENT.
BUT THAT DIDN'T HAPPEN.
EVERYTHING WOULD HAVE BEEN DIFFERENT.
C'MON, LET'S PLAY SONY!
I THINK I WILL WIN THIS TIME.
VS.

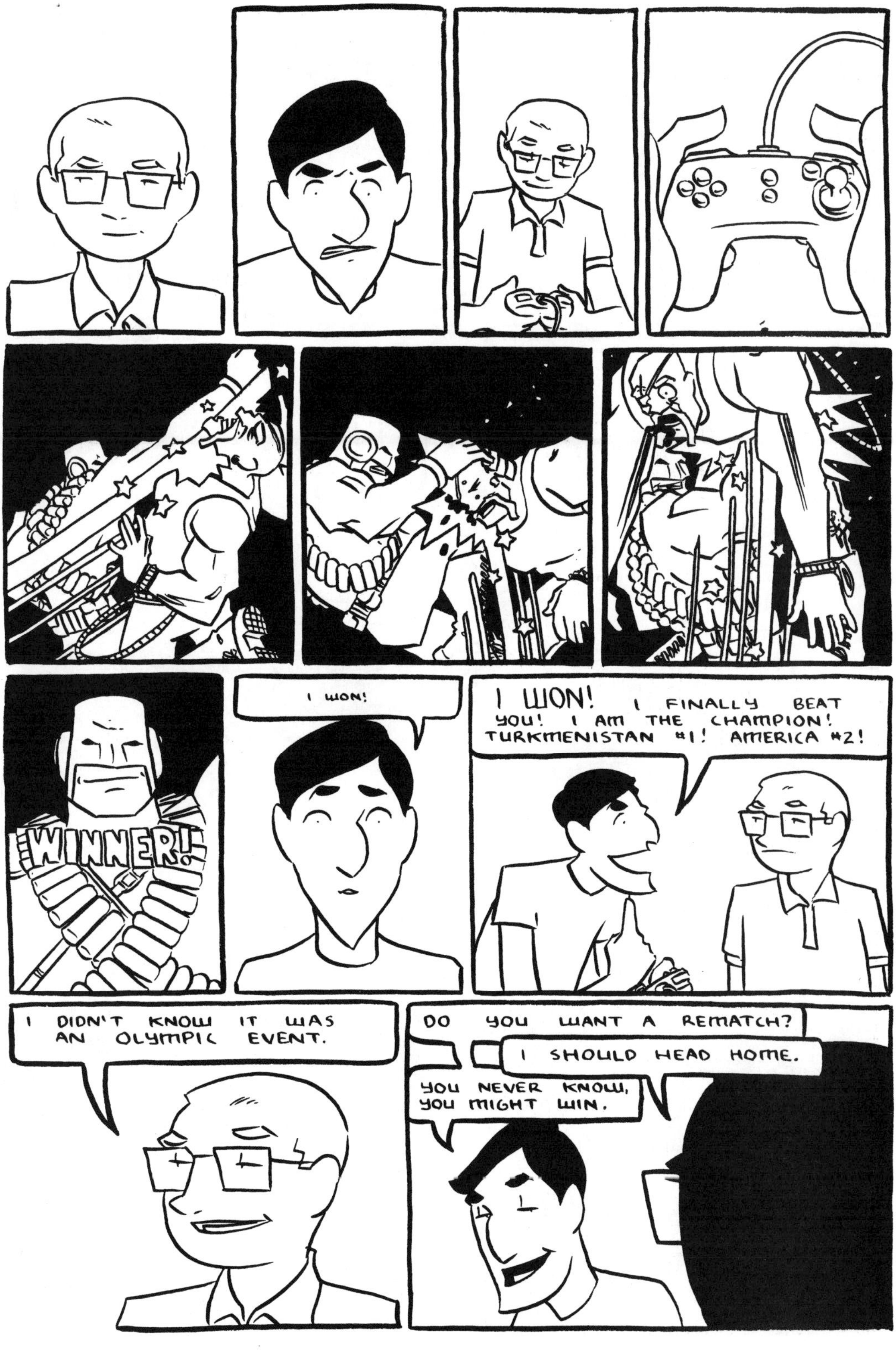
WINNER!
I WON!
I WON! I FINALLY BEAT YOU! I AM THE CHAMPION! TURKMENISTAN #1! AMERICA #2!
I DIDN'T KNOW IT WAS AN OLYMPIC EVENT.
DO YOU WANT A REMATCH?
I SHOULD HEAD HOME.
YOU NEVER KNOW, YOU MIGHT WIN.

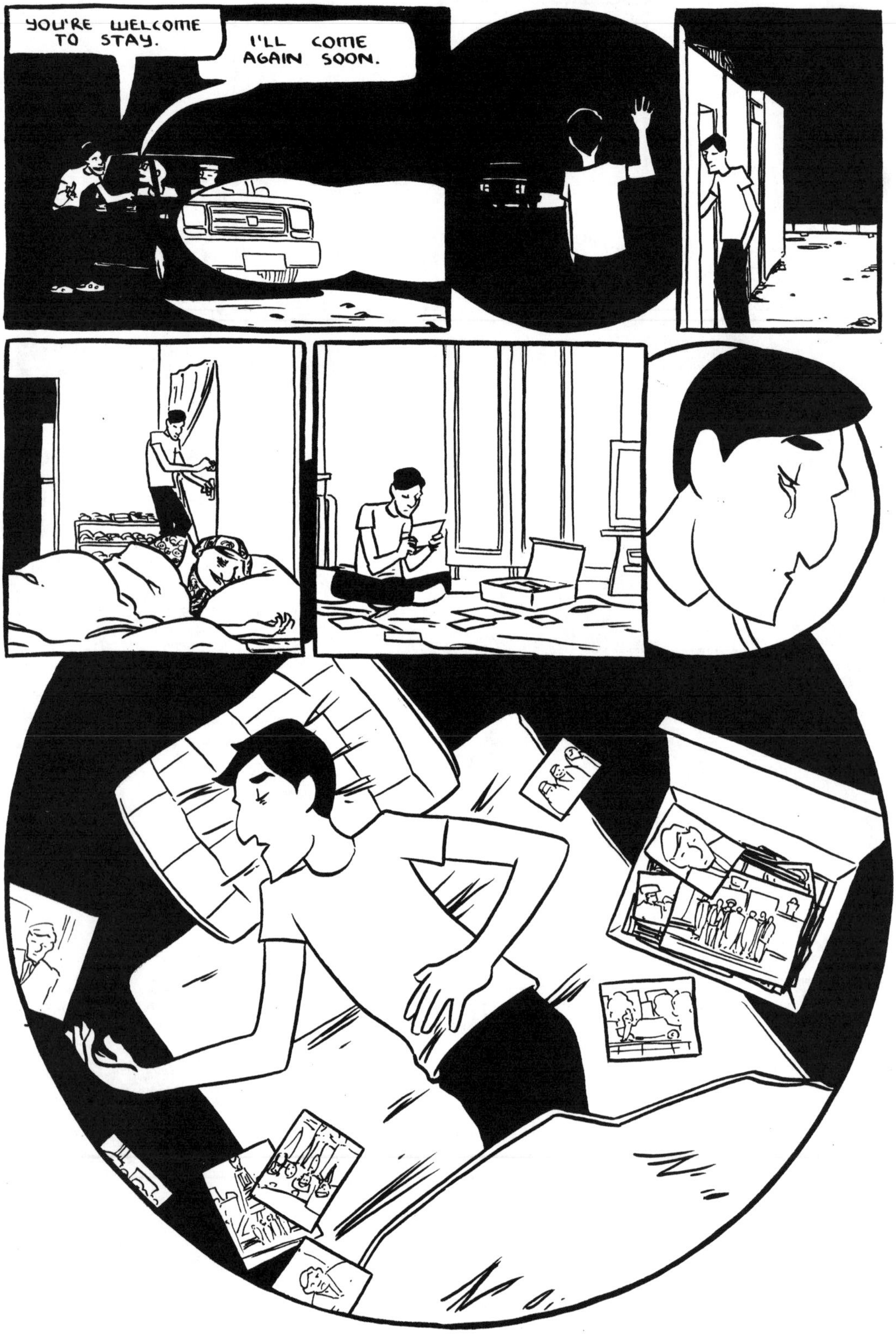
YOU'RE WELCOME TO STAY.
I'LL COME AGAIN SOON.

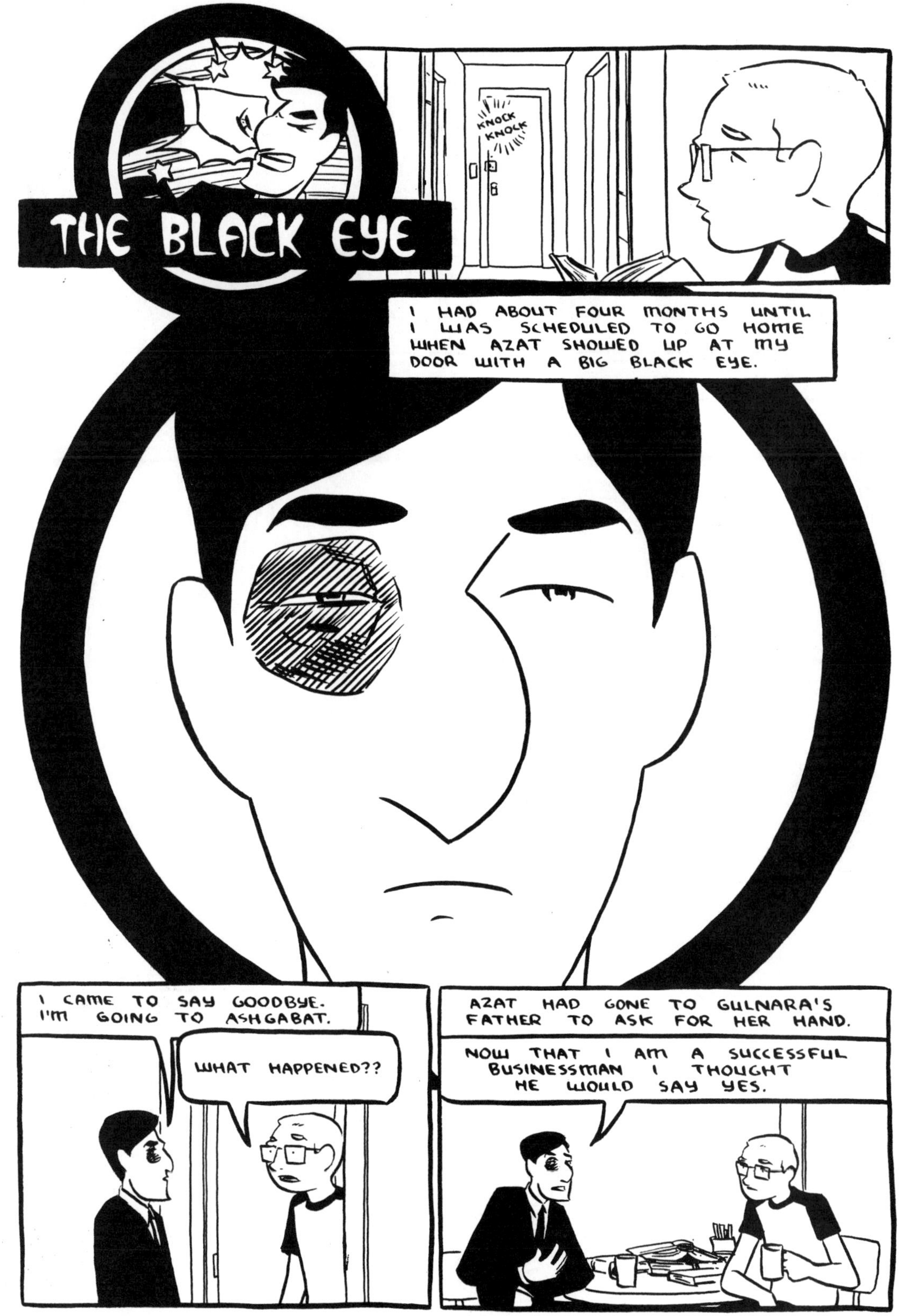
THE BLACK EYE
KNOCK KNOCK
I HAD ABOUT FOUR MONTHS UNTIL I WAS SCHEDULED TO GO HOME WHEN AZAT SHOWED UP AT MY DOOR WITH A BIG BLACK EYE.
I CAME TO SAY GOODBYE. I'M GOING TO ASHGABAT.
WHAT HAPPENED??
AZAT HAD GONE TO GULNARA'S FATHER TO ASK FOR HER HAND.
NOW THAT I AM A SUCCESSFUL BUSINESSMAN I THOUGHT HE WOULD SAY YES.

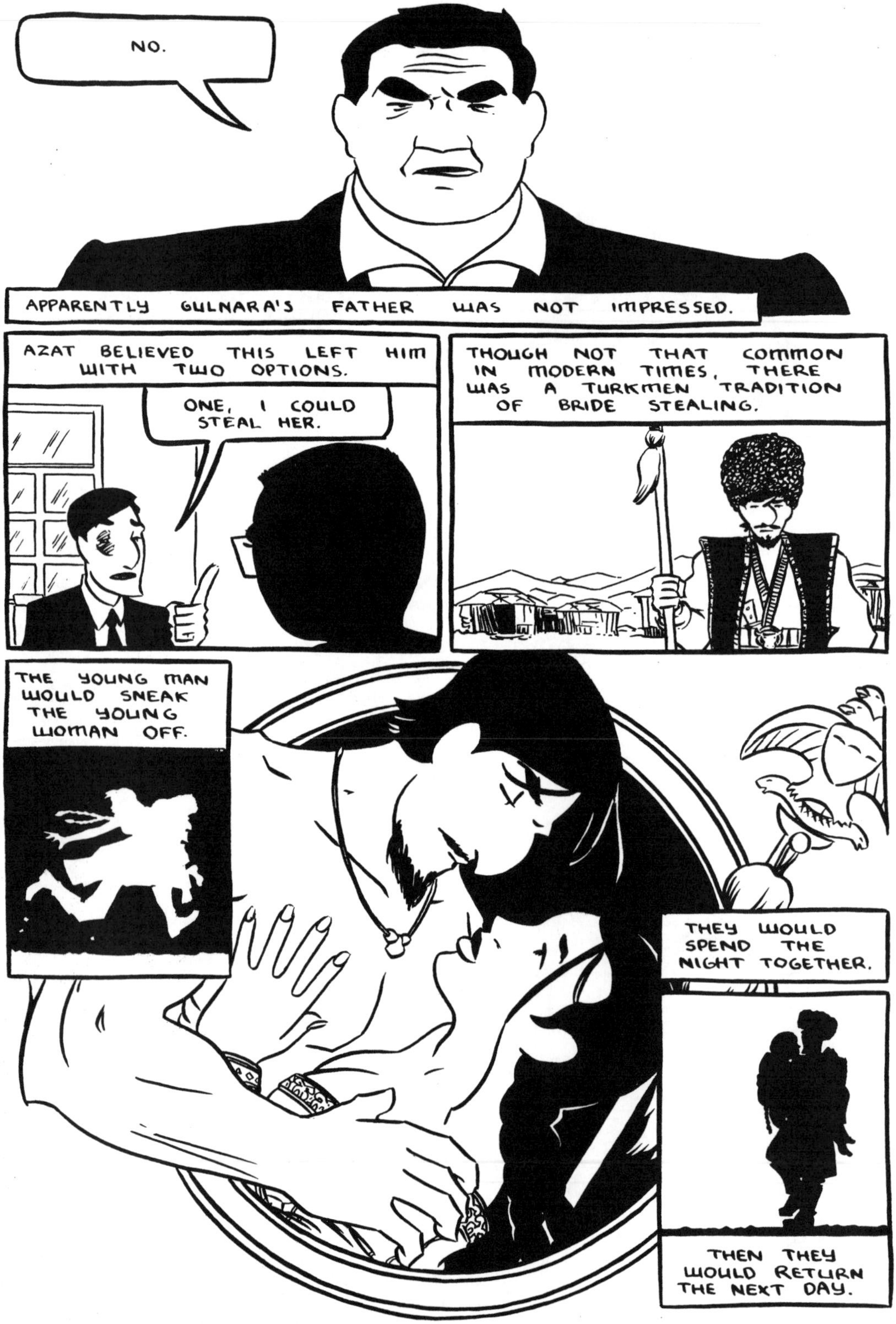
NO.
APPARENTLY GULNARA'S FATHER WAS NOT IMPRESSED.
AZAT BELIEVED THIS LEFT HIM WITH TWO OPTIONS.
ONE, I COULD STEAL HER.
THOUGH NOT THAT COMMON IN MODERN TIMES, THERE WAS A TURKMEN TRADITION OF BRIDE STEALING.
THE YOUNG MAN WOULD SNEAK THE YOUNG WOMAN OFF.
THEY WOULD SPEND THE NIGHT TOGETHER.
THEN THEY WOULD RETURN THE NEXT DAY.

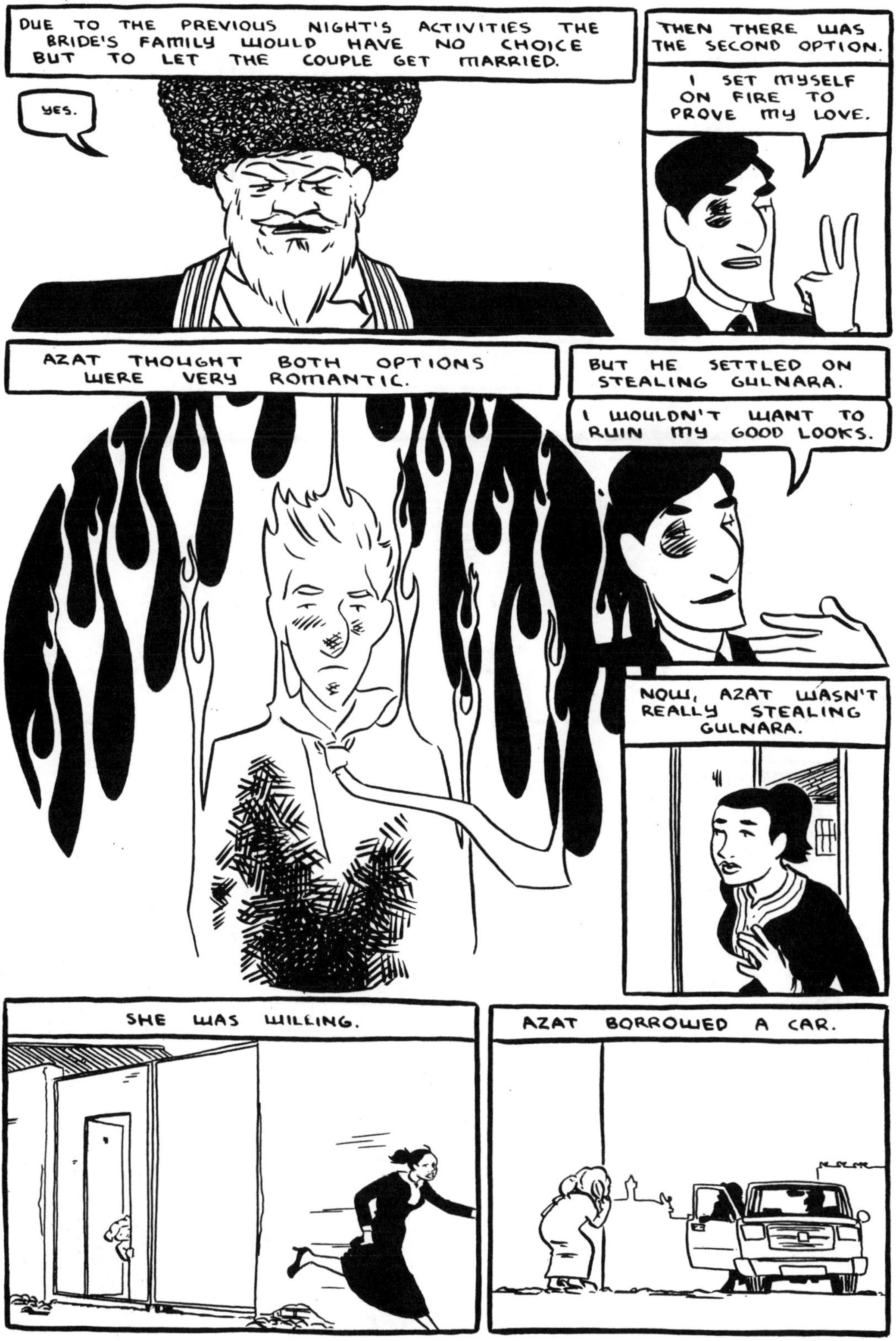
DUE TO THE PREVIOUS NIGHT'S ACTIVITIES THE BRIDE'S FAMILY WOULD HAVE NO CHOICE BUT TO LET THE COUPLE GET MARRIED.
YES.
THEN THERE WAS THE SECOND OPTION.
I SET MYSELF ON FIRE TO PROVE MY LOVE.
AZAT THOUGHT BOTH OPTIONS WERE VERY ROMANTIC.
BUT HE SETTLED ON STEALING GULNARA.
I WOULDN'T WANT TO RUIN MY GOOD LOOKS.
NOW, AZAT WASN'T REALLY STEALING GULNARA.
SHE WAS WILLING.
AZAT BORROWED A CAR.

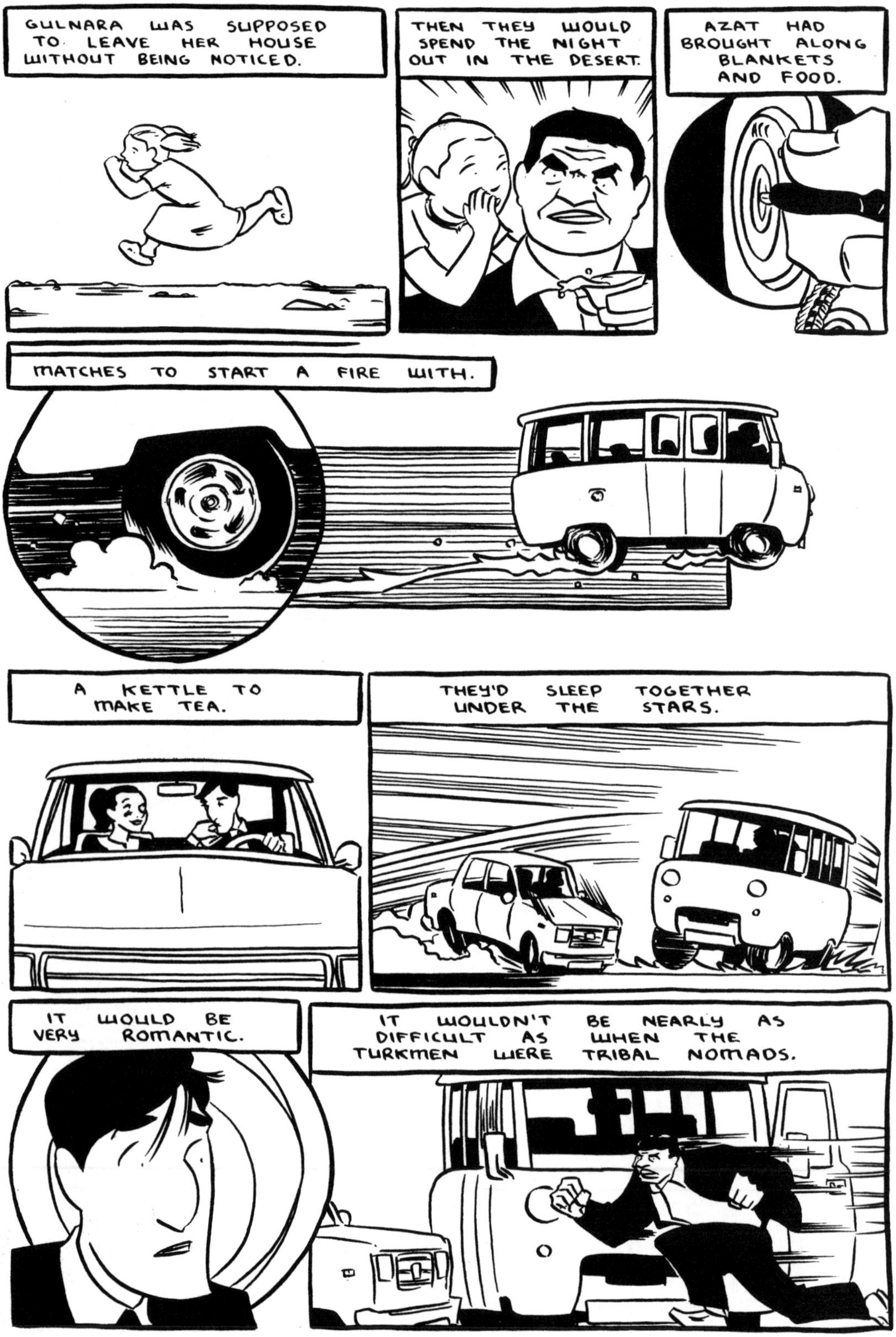
GULNARA WAS SUPPOSED TO LEAVE HER HOUSE WITHOUT BEING NOTICED.
THEN THEY WOULD SPEND THE NIGHT OUT IN THE DESERT.
AZAT HAD BROUGHT ALONG BLANKETS AND FOOD.
MATCHES TO START A FIRE WITH.
A KETTLE TO MAKE TEA.
THEY'D SLEEP TOGETHER UNDER THE STARS.
IT WOULD BE VERY ROMANTIC.
IT WOULDN'T BE NEARLY AS DIFFICULT AS WHEN THE TURKMEN WERE TRIBAL NOMADS.

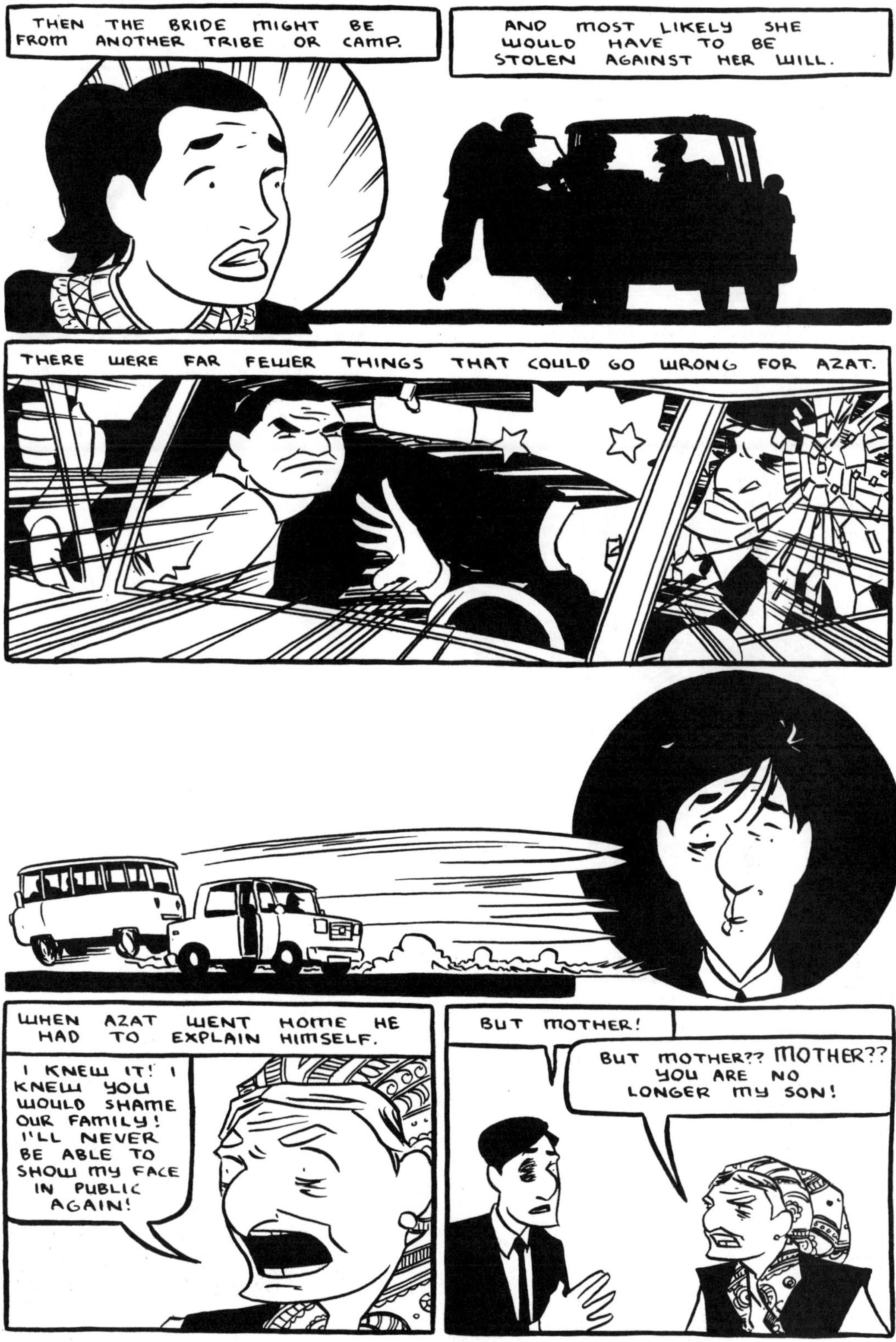
THEN THE BRIDE MIGHT BE FROM ANOTHER TRIBE OR CAMP.
AND MOST LIKELY SHE WOULD HAVE TO BE STOLEN AGAINST HER WILL.
THERE WERE FAR FEWER THINGS THAT COULD GO WRONG FOR AZAT.
WHEN AZAT WENT HOME HE HAD TO EXPLAIN HIMSELF.
I KNEW IT! I KNEW YOU WOULD SHAME OUR FAMILY! I'LL NEVER BE ABLE TO SHOW MY FACE IN PUBLIC AGAIN!
BUT MOTHER!
BUT MOTHER?? MOTHER?? YOU ARE NO LONGER MY SON!

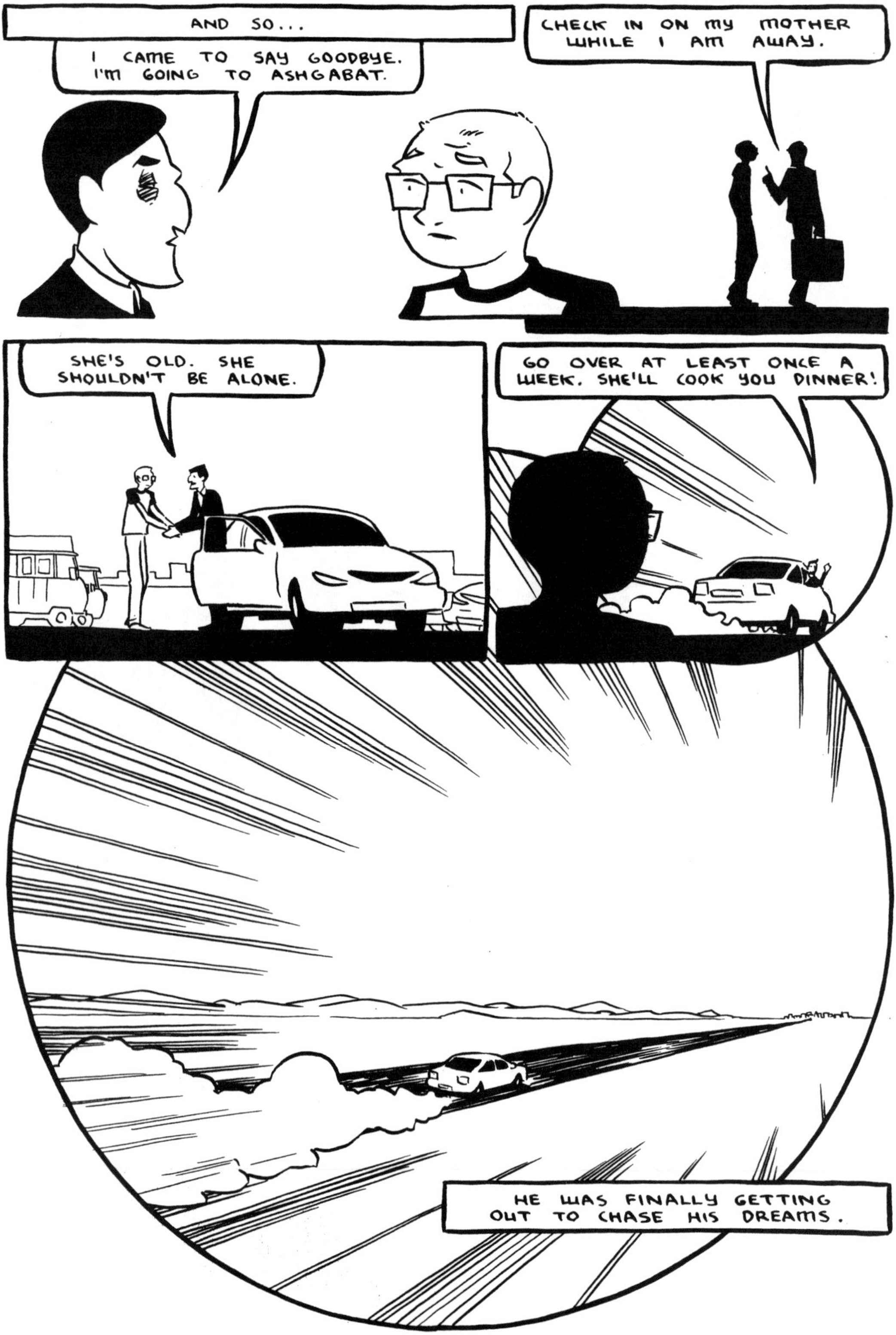
AND SO...
I CAME TO SAY GOODBYE. I'M GOING TO ASHGABAT.
CHECK IN ON MY MOTHER WHILE I AM AWAY.
SHE'S OLD. SHE SHOULDN'T BE ALONE.
GO OVER AT LEAST ONCE A WEEK. SHE'LL COOK YOU DINNER!
HE WAS FINALLY GETTING OUT TO CHASE HIS DREAMS.

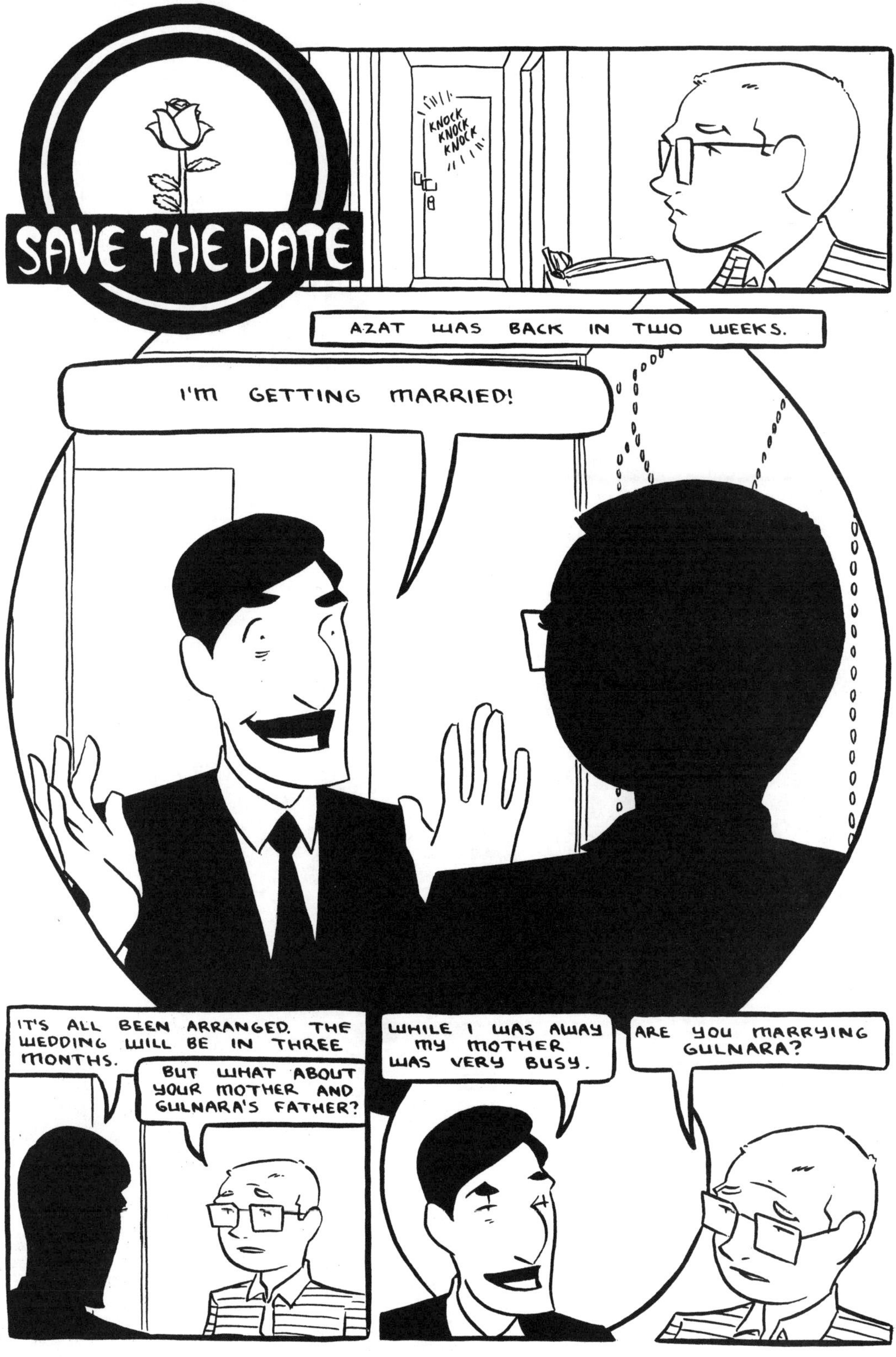
SAVE THE DATE
KNOCK KNOCK KNOCK
AZAT WAS BACK IN TWO WEEKS.
I'M GETTING MARRIED!
IT'S ALL BEEN ARRANGED. THE WEDDING WILL BE IN THREE MONTHS.
BUT WHAT ABOUT YOUR MOTHER AND GULNARA'S FATHER?
WHILE I WAS AWAY MY MOTHER WAS VERY BUSY.
ARE YOU MARRYING GULNARA?

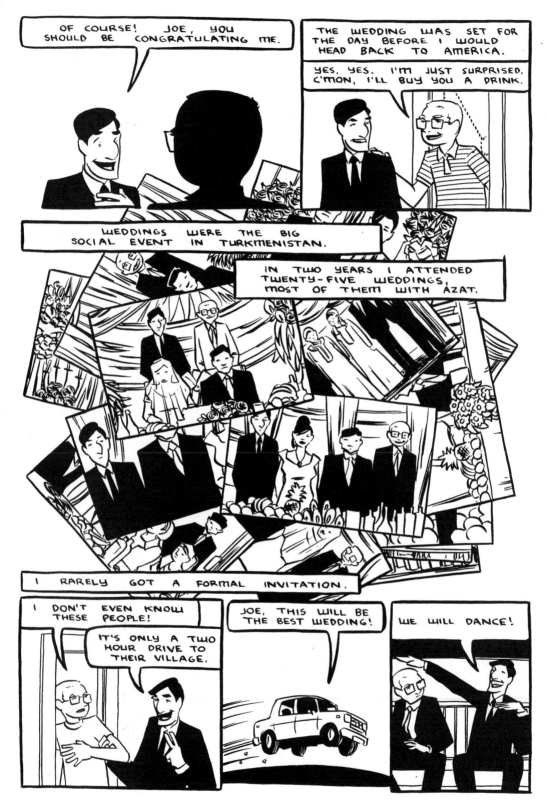

OF COURSE! JOE, YOU SHOULD BE CONGRATULATING ME.

THE WEDDING WAS SET FOR THE DAY BEFORE I WOULD HEAD BACK TO AMERICA.

YES, YES. I'M JUST SURPRISED. C'MON, I'LL BUY YOU A DRINK.

WEDDINGS WERE THE BIG SOCIAL EVENT IN TURKMENISTAN.

IN TWO YEARS I ATTENDED TWENTY-FIVE WEDDINGS, MOST OF THEM WITH AZAT.

I RARELY GOT A FORMAL INVITATION.

I DON'T EVEN KNOW THESE PEOPLE!

IT'S ONLY A TWO HOUR DRIVE TO THEIR VILLAGE.

JOE, THIS WILL BE THE BEST WEDDING!

WE WILL DANCE!

60

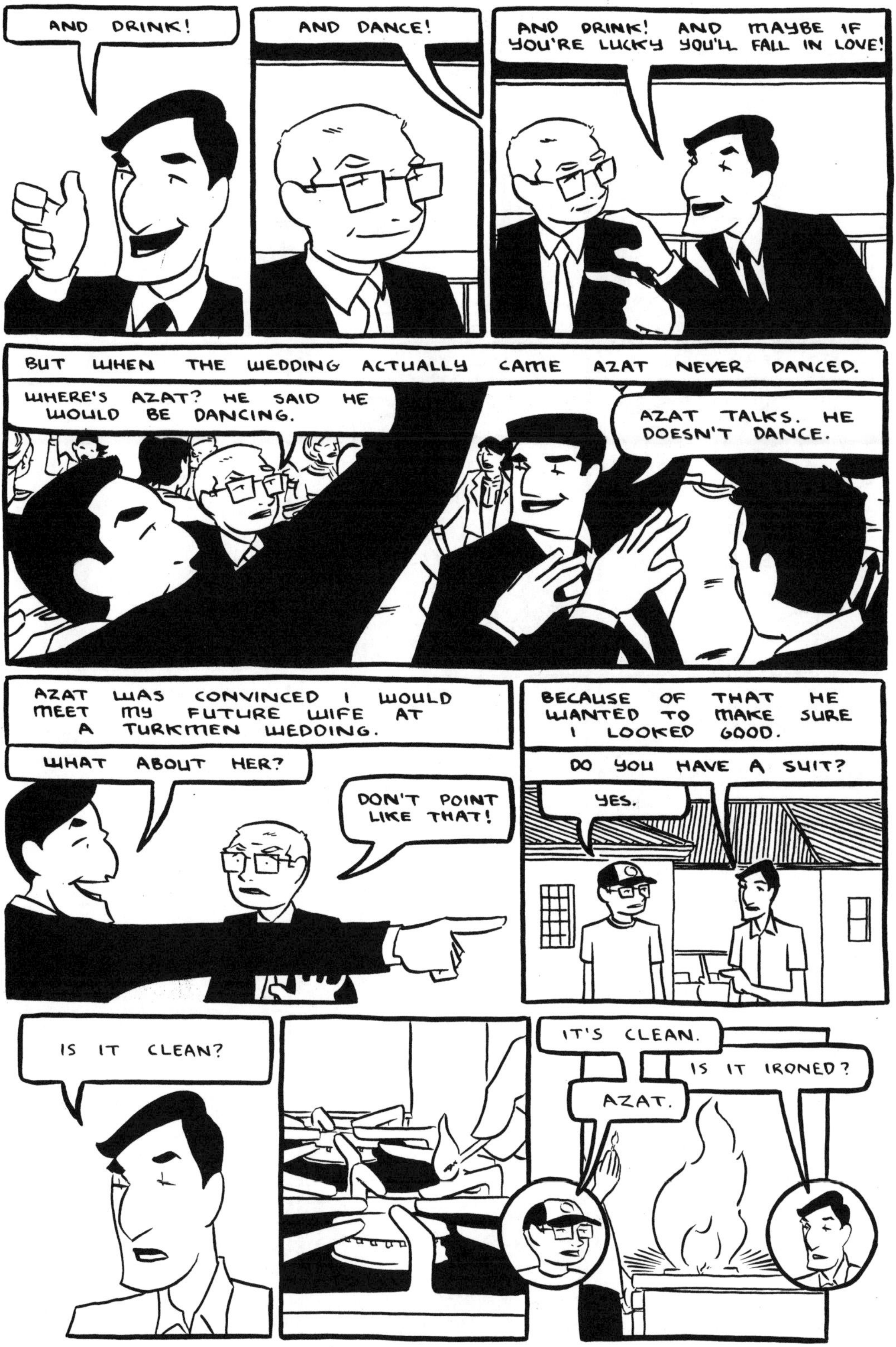
AND DRINK!
AND DANCE!
AND DRINK! AND MAYBE IF YOU'RE LUCKY YOU'LL FALL IN LOVE!
BUT WHEN THE WEDDING ACTUALLY CAME AZAT NEVER DANCED.
WHERE'S AZAT? HE SAID HE WOULD BE DANCING.
AZAT TALKS. HE DOESN'T DANCE.
AZAT WAS CONVINCED I WOULD MEET MY FUTURE WIFE AT A TURKMEN WEDDING.
WHAT ABOUT HER?
DON'T POINT LIKE THAT!
BECAUSE OF THAT HE WANTED TO MAKE SURE I LOOKED GOOD.
DO YOU HAVE A SUIT?
YES.
IS IT CLEAN?
IT'S CLEAN.
IS IT IRONED?
AZAT.

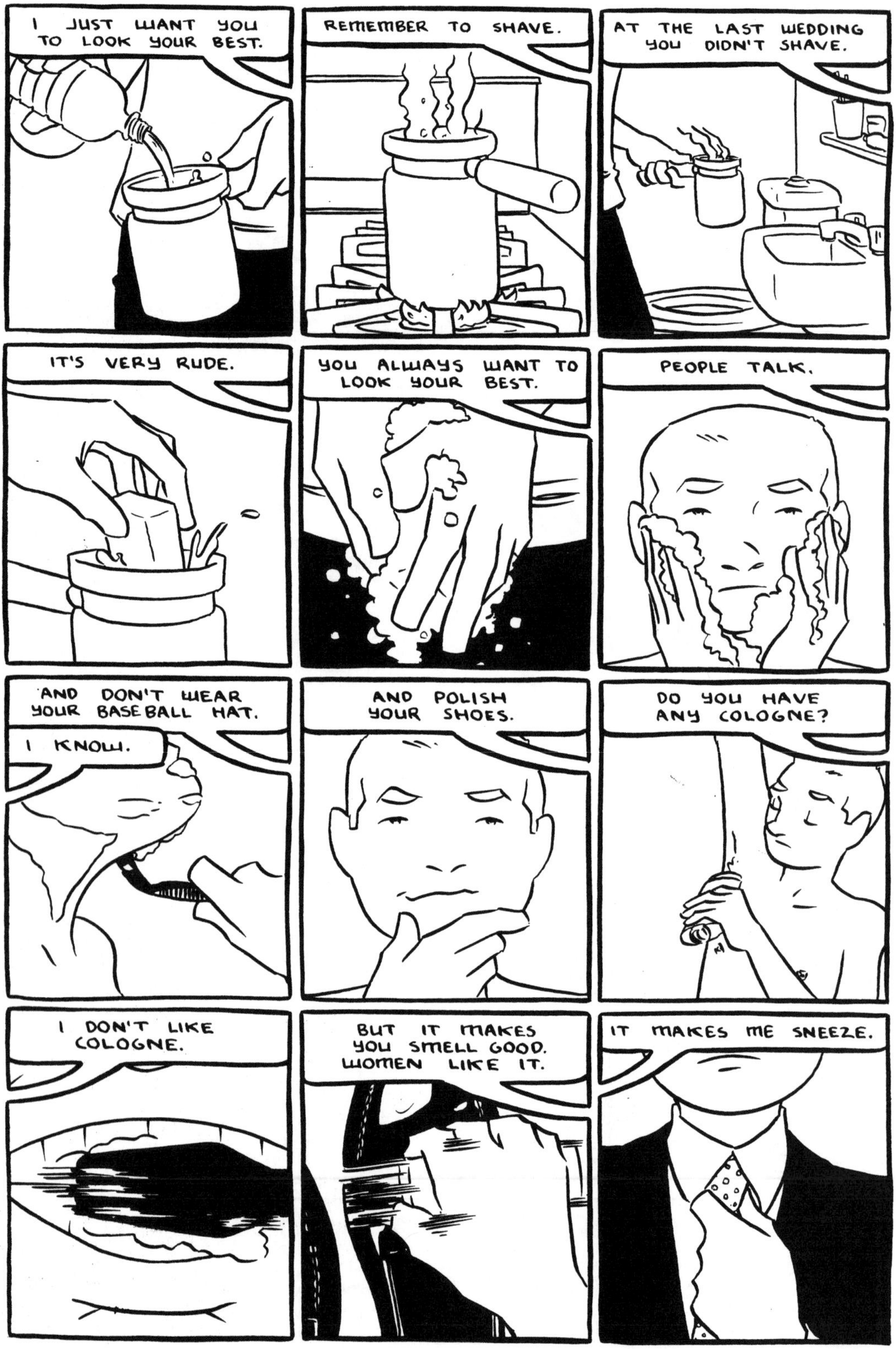
I JUST WANT YOU TO LOOK YOUR BEST.
REMEMBER TO SHAVE.
AT THE LAST WEDDING YOU DIDN'T SHAVE.
IT'S VERY RUDE.
YOU ALWAYS WANT TO LOOK YOUR BEST.
PEOPLE TALK.
AND DON'T WEAR YOUR BASEBALL HAT.
I KNOW.
AND POLISH YOUR SHOES.
DO YOU HAVE ANY COLOGNE?
I DON'T LIKE COLOGNE.
BUT IT MAKES YOU SMELL GOOD. WOMEN LIKE IT.
IT MAKES ME SNEEZE.

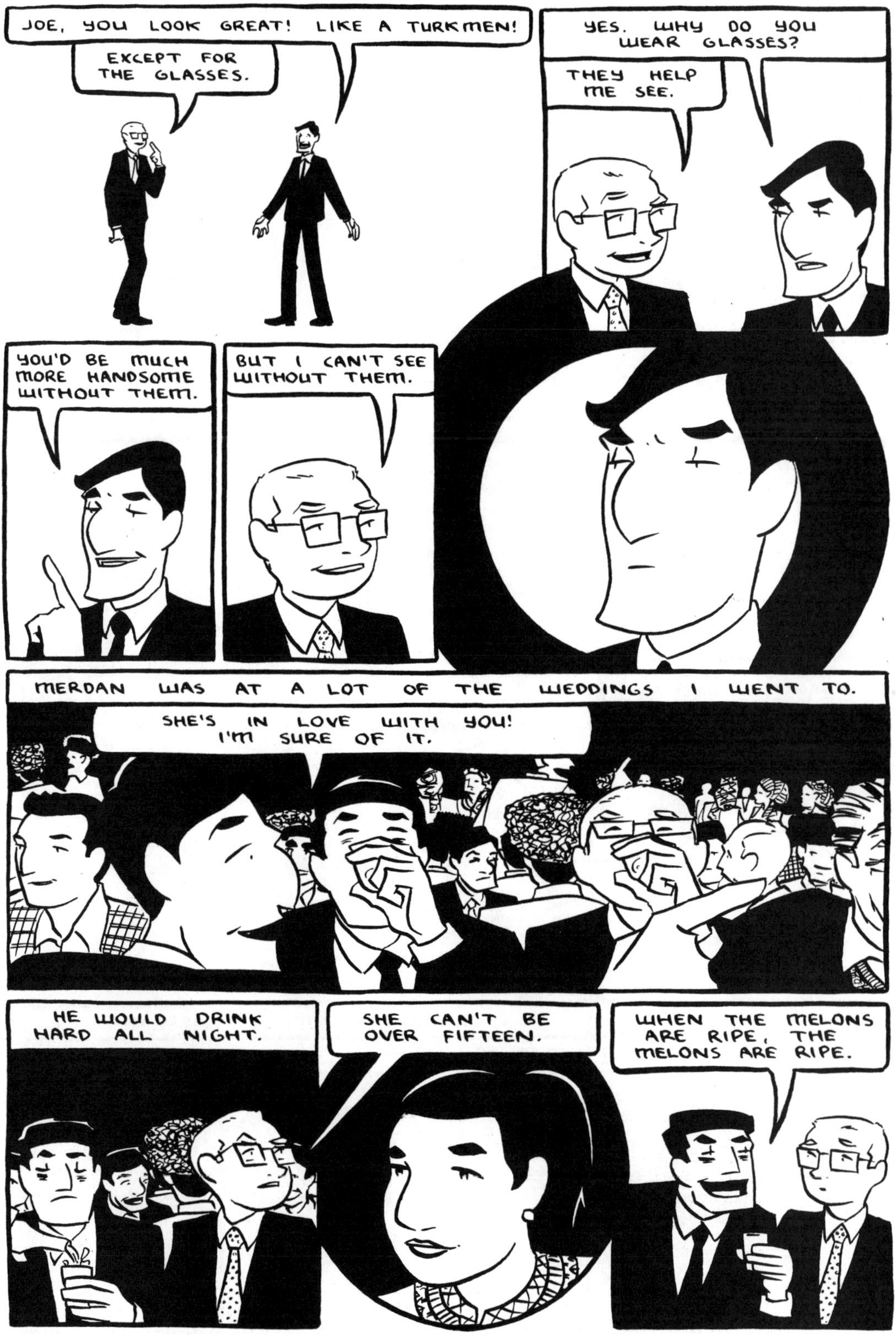

JOE, YOU LOOK GREAT! LIKE A TURKMEN!
EXCEPT FOR THE GLASSES.
YES. WHY DO YOU WEAR GLASSES?
THEY HELP ME SEE.
YOU'D BE MUCH MORE HANDSOME WITHOUT THEM.
BUT I CAN'T SEE WITHOUT THEM.
MERDAN WAS AT A LOT OF THE WEDDINGS I WENT TO.
SHE'S IN LOVE WITH YOU! I'M SURE OF IT.
HE WOULD DRINK HARD ALL NIGHT.
SHE CAN'T BE OVER FIFTEEN.
WHEN THE MELONS ARE RIPE, THE MELONS ARE RIPE.

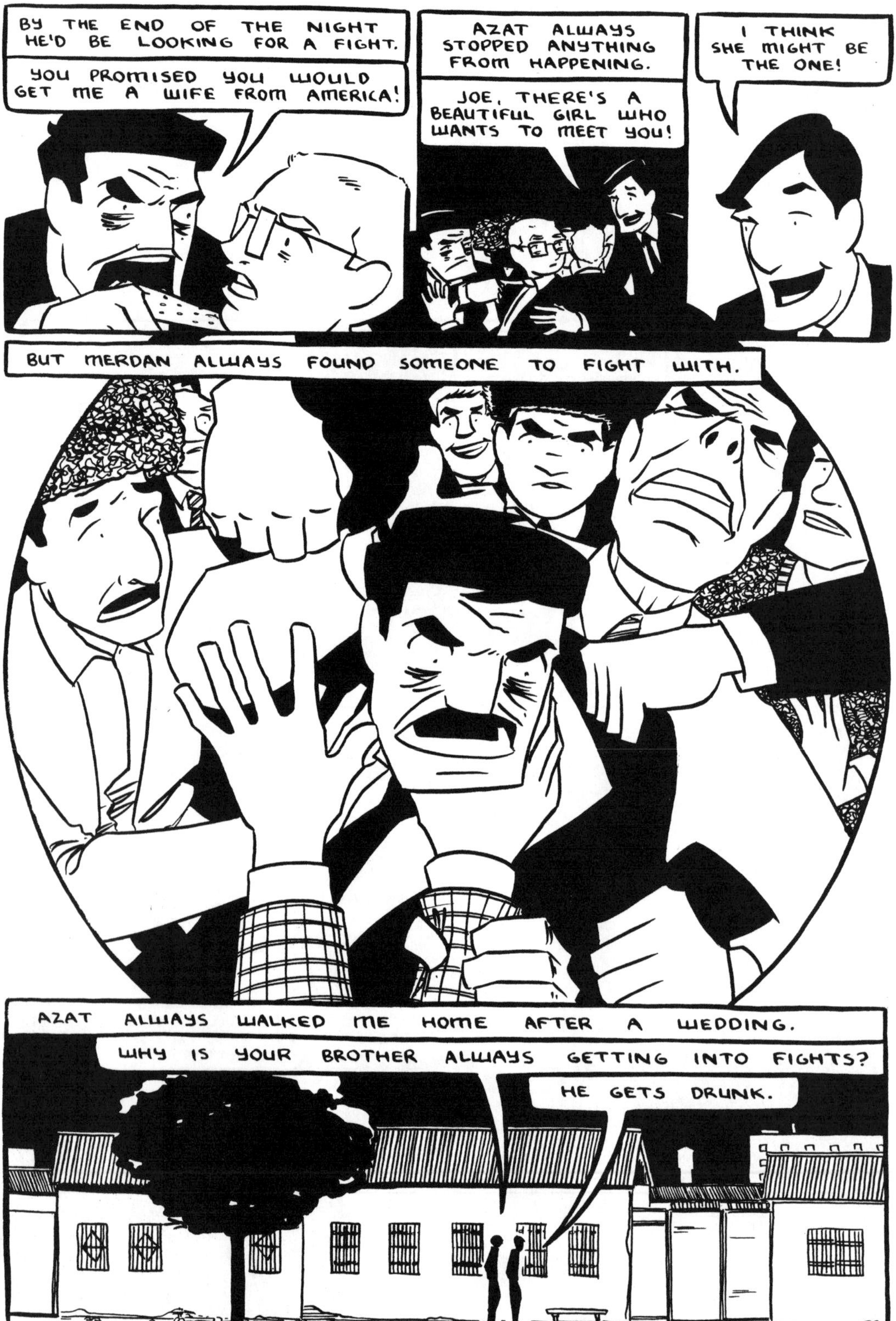

BY THE END OF THE NIGHT HE'D BE LOOKING FOR A FIGHT.
YOU PROMISED YOU WOULD GET ME A WIFE FROM AMERICA!
AZAT ALWAYS STOPPED ANYTHING FROM HAPPENING.
JOE, THERE'S A BEAUTIFUL GIRL WHO WANTS TO MEET YOU!
I THINK SHE MIGHT BE THE ONE!
BUT MERDAN ALWAYS FOUND SOMEONE TO FIGHT WITH.
AZAT ALWAYS WALKED ME HOME AFTER A WEDDING.
WHY IS YOUR BROTHER ALWAYS GETTING INTO FIGHTS?
HE GETS DRUNK.

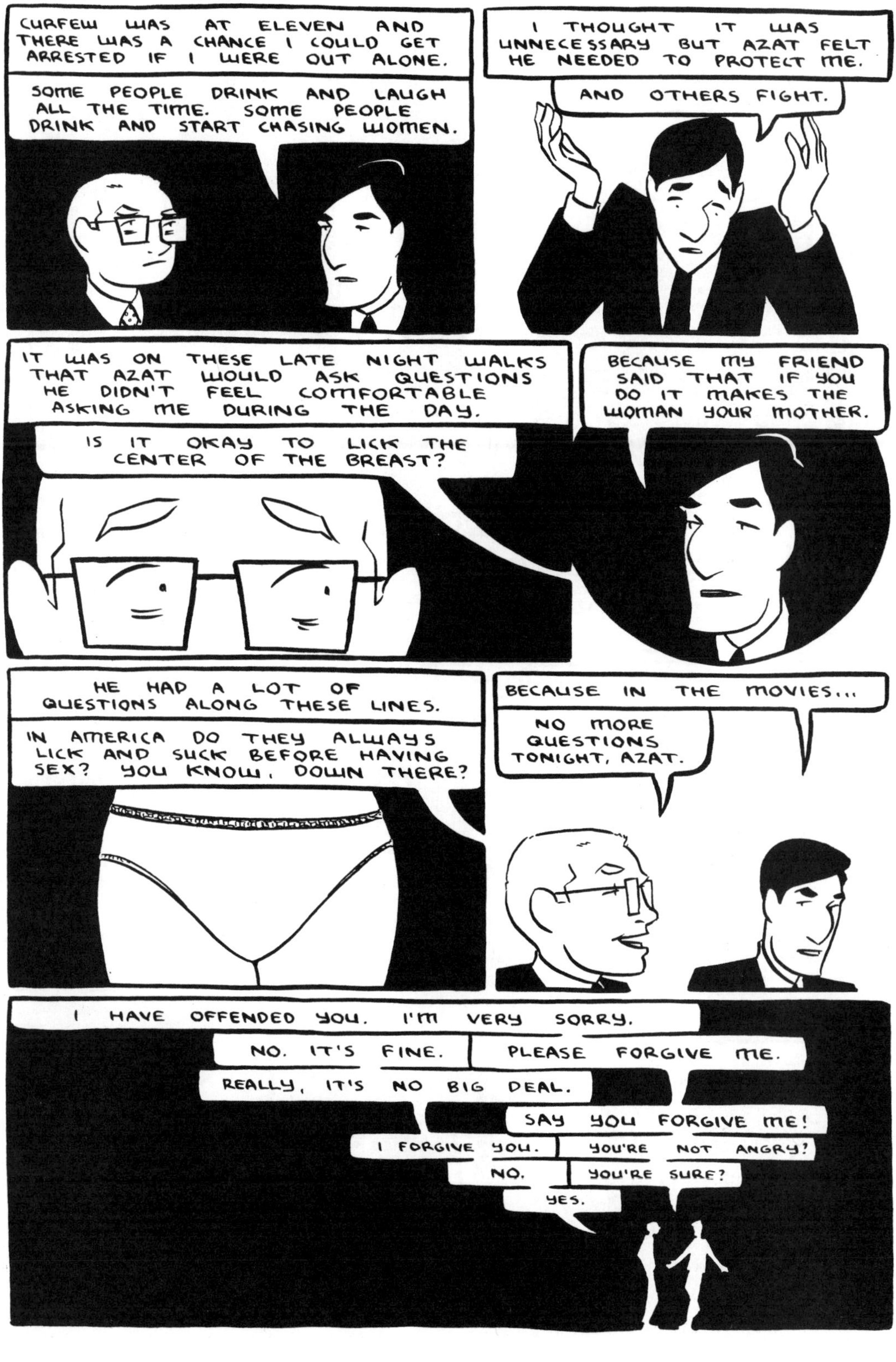

CURFEW WAS AT ELEVEN AND THERE WAS A CHANCE I COULD GET ARRESTED IF I WERE OUT ALONE.
SOME PEOPLE DRINK AND LAUGH ALL THE TIME. SOME PEOPLE DRINK AND START CHASING WOMEN.
I THOUGHT IT WAS UNNECESSARY BUT AZAT FELT HE NEEDED TO PROTECT ME.
AND OTHERS FIGHT.
IT WAS ON THESE LATE NIGHT WALKS THAT AZAT WOULD ASK QUESTIONS HE DIDN'T FEEL COMFORTABLE ASKING ME DURING THE DAY.
IS IT OKAY TO LICK THE CENTER OF THE BREAST?
BECAUSE MY FRIEND SAID THAT IF YOU DO IT MAKES THE WOMAN YOUR MOTHER.
HE HAD A LOT OF QUESTIONS ALONG THESE LINES.
IN AMERICA DO THEY ALWAYS LICK AND SUCK BEFORE HAVING SEX? YOU KNOW. DOWN THERE?
BECAUSE IN THE MOVIES...
NO MORE QUESTIONS TONIGHT, AZAT.
I HAVE OFFENDED YOU. I'M VERY SORRY.
NO. IT'S FINE.
PLEASE FORGIVE ME.
REALLY, IT'S NO BIG DEAL.
SAY YOU FORGIVE ME!
I FORGIVE YOU.
YOU'RE NOT ANGRY?
NO.
YOU'RE SURE?
YES.

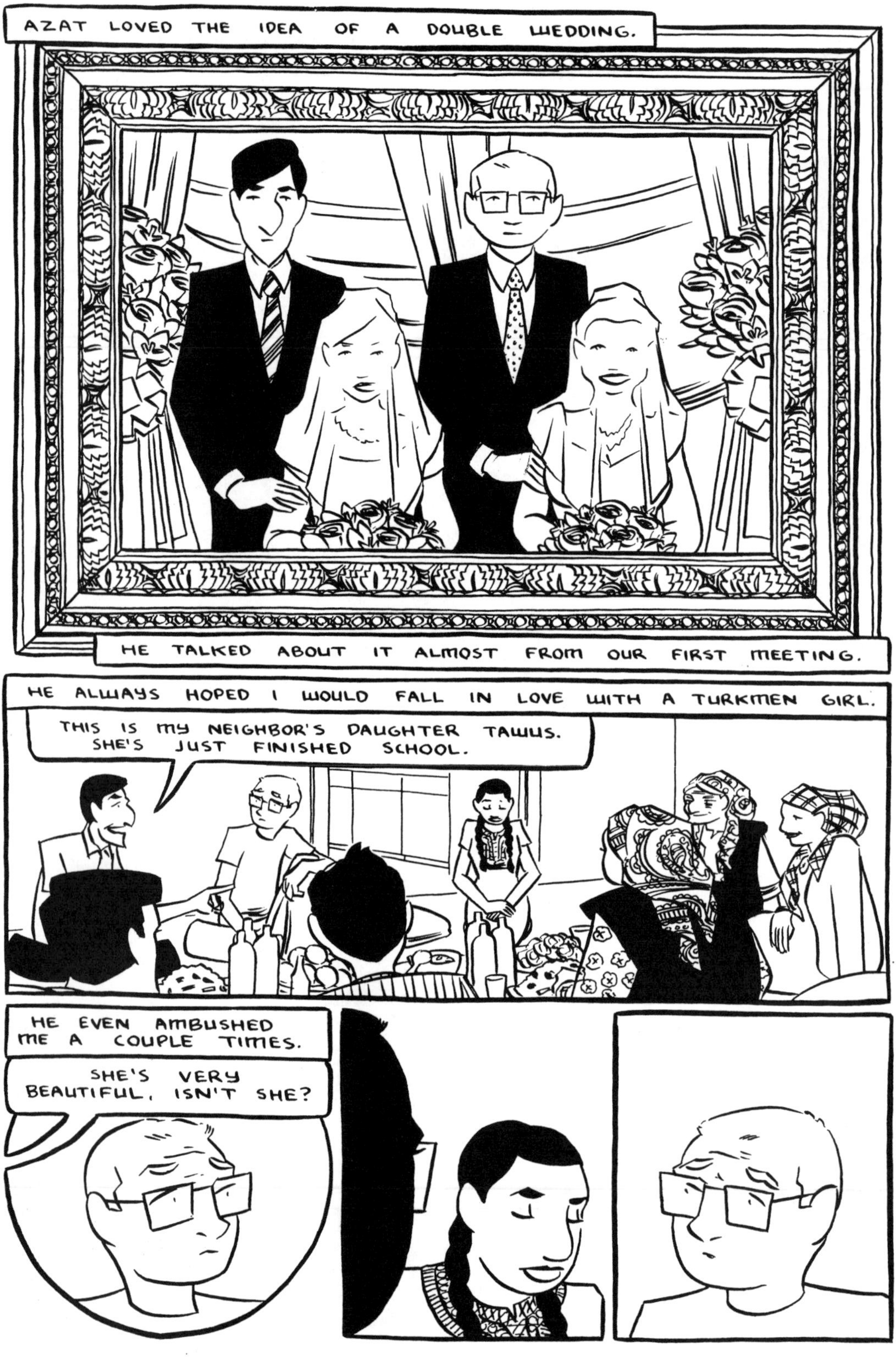
AZAT LOVED THE IDEA OF A DOUBLE WEDDING.
HE TALKED ABOUT IT ALMOST FROM OUR FIRST MEETING.
HE ALWAYS HOPED I WOULD FALL IN LOVE WITH A TURKMEN GIRL.
THIS IS MY NEIGHBOR'S DAUGHTER TAWUS. SHE'S JUST FINISHED SCHOOL.
HE EVEN AMBUSHED ME A COUPLE TIMES.
SHE'S VERY BEAUTIFUL, ISN'T SHE?

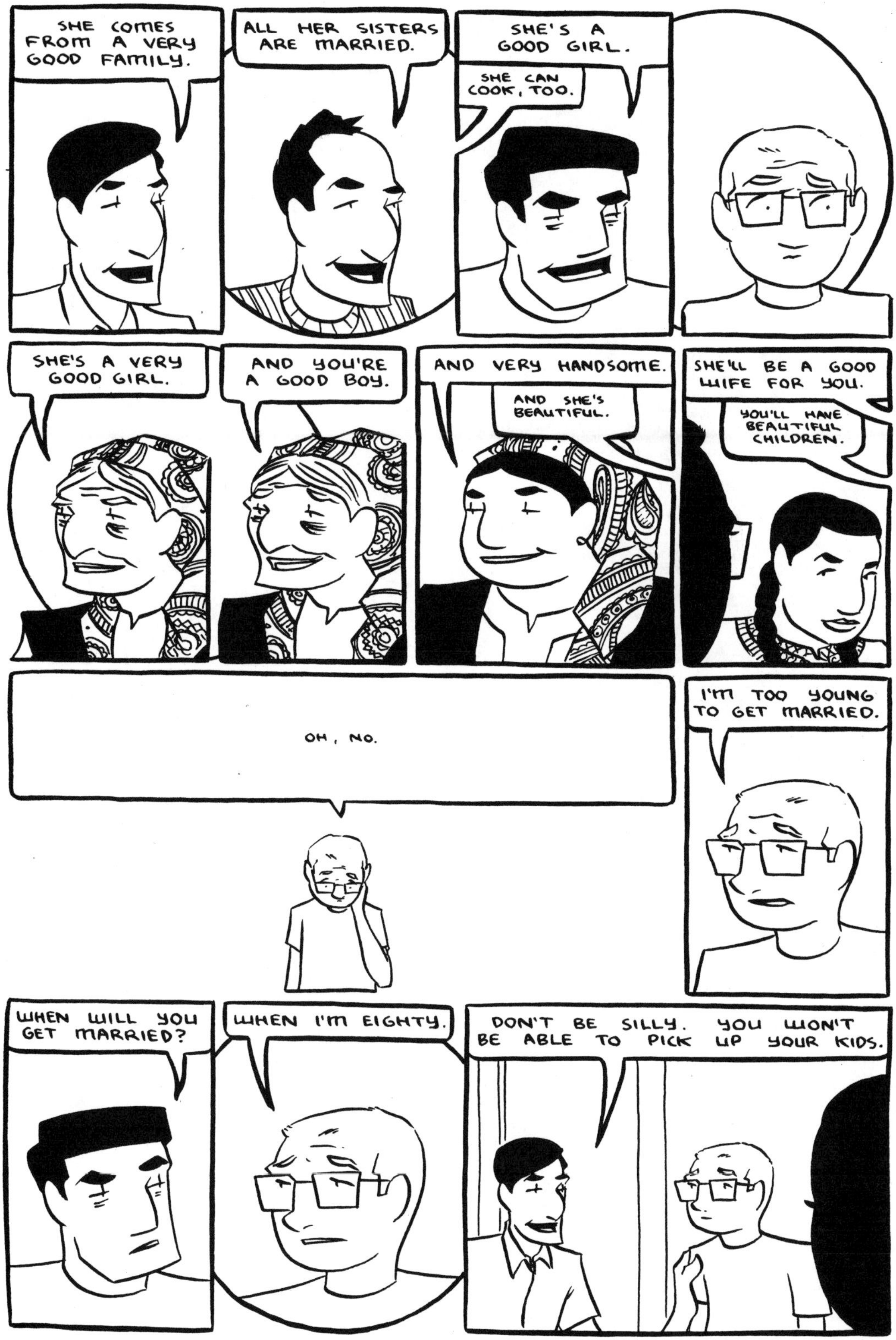
SHE COMES FROM A VERY GOOD FAMILY.
ALL HER SISTERS ARE MARRIED.
SHE'S A GOOD GIRL.
SHE CAN COOK, TOO.
SHE'S A VERY GOOD GIRL.
AND YOU'RE A GOOD BOY.
AND VERY HANDSOME.
AND SHE'S BEAUTIFUL.
SHE'LL BE A GOOD WIFE FOR YOU.
YOU'LL HAVE BEAUTIFUL CHILDREN.
OH, NO.
I'M TOO YOUNG TO GET MARRIED.
WHEN WILL YOU GET MARRIED?
WHEN I'M EIGHTY.
DON'T BE SILLY. YOU WON'T BE ABLE TO PICK UP YOUR KIDS.

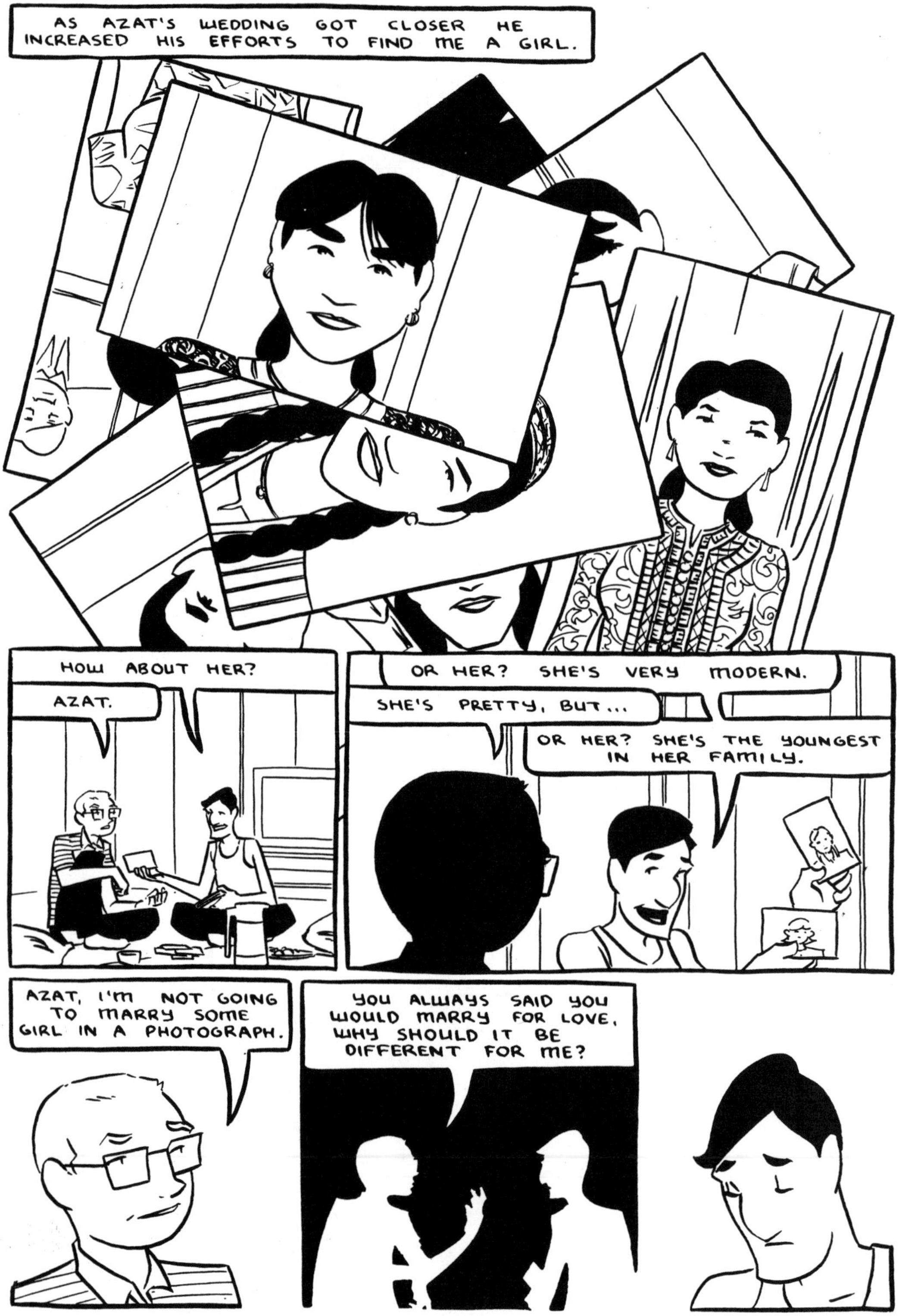
AS AZAT'S WEDDING GOT CLOSER HE INCREASED HIS EFFORTS TO FIND ME A GIRL.
HOW ABOUT HER?
AZAT.
OR HER? SHE'S VERY MODERN.
SHE'S PRETTY, BUT...
OR HER? SHE'S THE YOUNGEST IN HER FAMILY.
AZAT, I'M NOT GOING TO MARRY SOME GIRL IN A PHOTOGRAPH.
YOU ALWAYS SAID YOU WOULD MARRY FOR LOVE. WHY SHOULD IT BE DIFFERENT FOR ME?

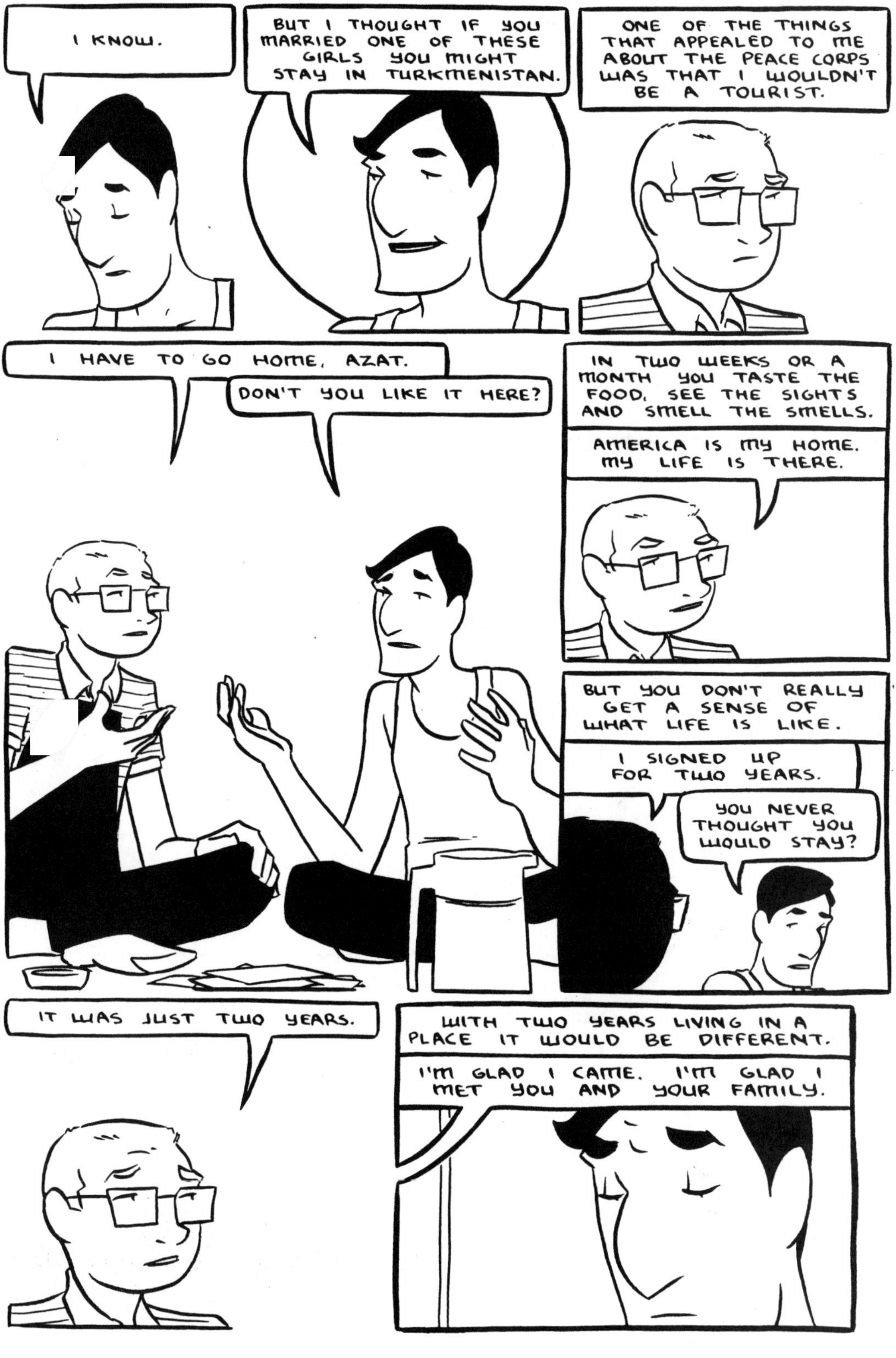
I KNOW.
BUT I THOUGHT IF YOU MARRIED ONE OF THESE GIRLS YOU MIGHT STAY IN TURKMENISTAN.
ONE OF THE THINGS THAT APPEALED TO ME ABOUT THE PEACE CORPS WAS THAT I WOULDN'T BE A TOURIST.
I HAVE TO GO HOME, AZAT.
DON'T YOU LIKE IT HERE?
IN TWO WEEKS OR A MONTH YOU TASTE THE FOOD, SEE THE SIGHTS AND SMELL THE SMELLS.
AMERICA IS MY HOME. MY LIFE IS THERE.
BUT YOU DON'T REALLY GET A SENSE OF WHAT LIFE IS LIKE.
I SIGNED UP FOR TWO YEARS.
YOU NEVER THOUGHT YOU WOULD STAY?
IT WAS JUST TWO YEARS.
WITH TWO YEARS LIVING IN A PLACE IT WOULD BE DIFFERENT.
I'M GLAD I CAME. I'M GLAD I MET YOU AND YOUR FAMILY.

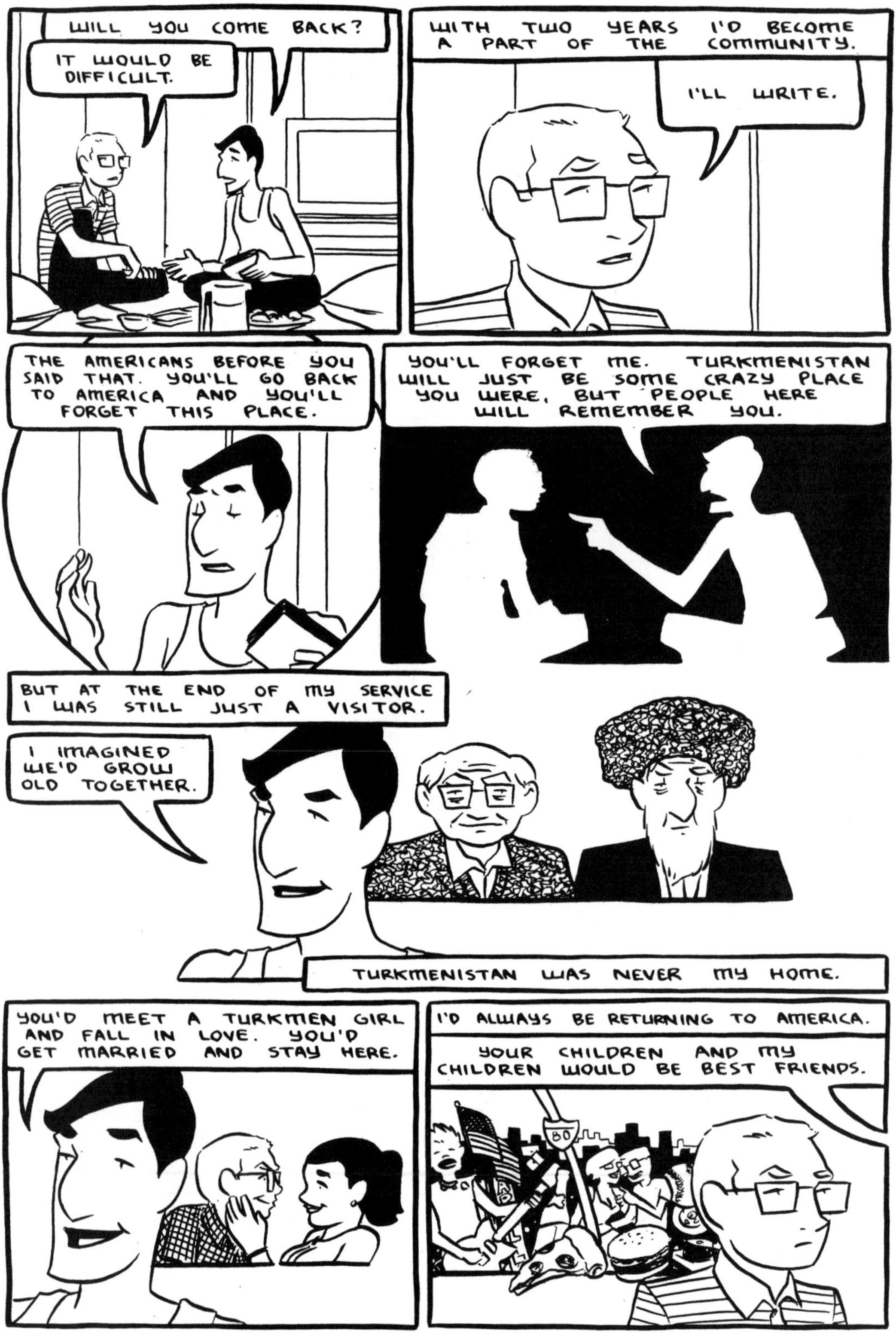
WILL YOU COME BACK?
IT WOULD BE DIFFICULT.
WITH TWO YEARS I'D BECOME A PART OF THE COMMUNITY.
I'LL WRITE.
THE AMERICANS BEFORE YOU SAID THAT. YOU'LL GO BACK TO AMERICA AND YOU'LL FORGET THIS PLACE.
YOU'LL FORGET ME. TURKMENISTAN WILL JUST BE SOME CRAZY PLACE YOU WERE, BUT PEOPLE HERE WILL REMEMBER YOU.
BUT AT THE END OF MY SERVICE I WAS STILL JUST A VISITOR.
I IMAGINED WE'D GROW OLD TOGETHER.
TURKMENISTAN WAS NEVER MY HOME.
YOU'D MEET A TURKMEN GIRL AND FALL IN LOVE. YOU'D GET MARRIED AND STAY HERE.
I'D ALWAYS BE RETURNING TO AMERICA.
YOUR CHILDREN AND MY CHILDREN WOULD BE BEST FRIENDS.
80

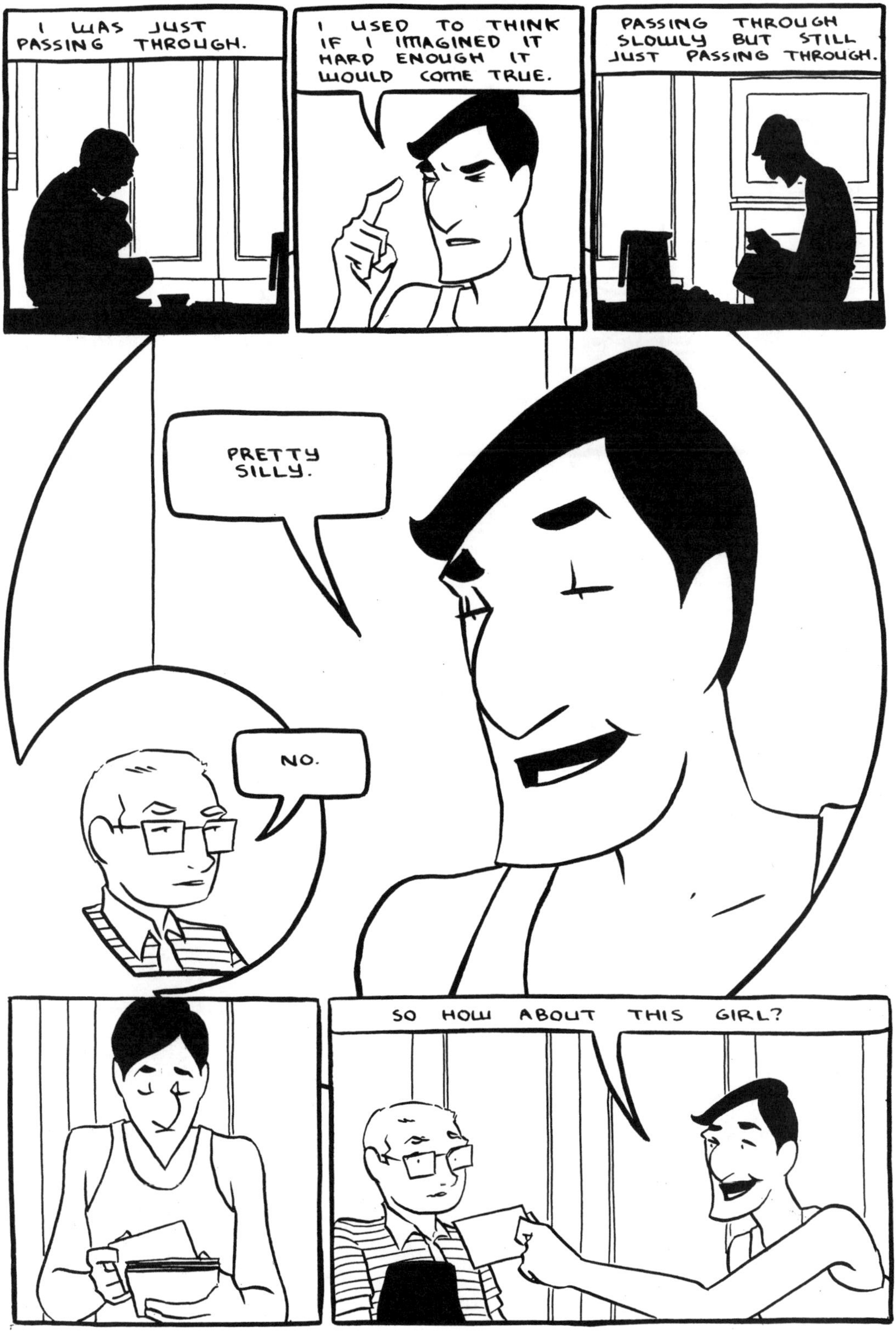
I WAS JUST PASSING THROUGH.
I USED TO THINK IF I IMAGINED IT HARD ENOUGH IT WOULD COME TRUE.
PASSING THROUGH SLOWLY BUT STILL JUST PASSING THROUGH.
PRETTY SILLY.
NO.
SO HOW ABOUT THIS GIRL?

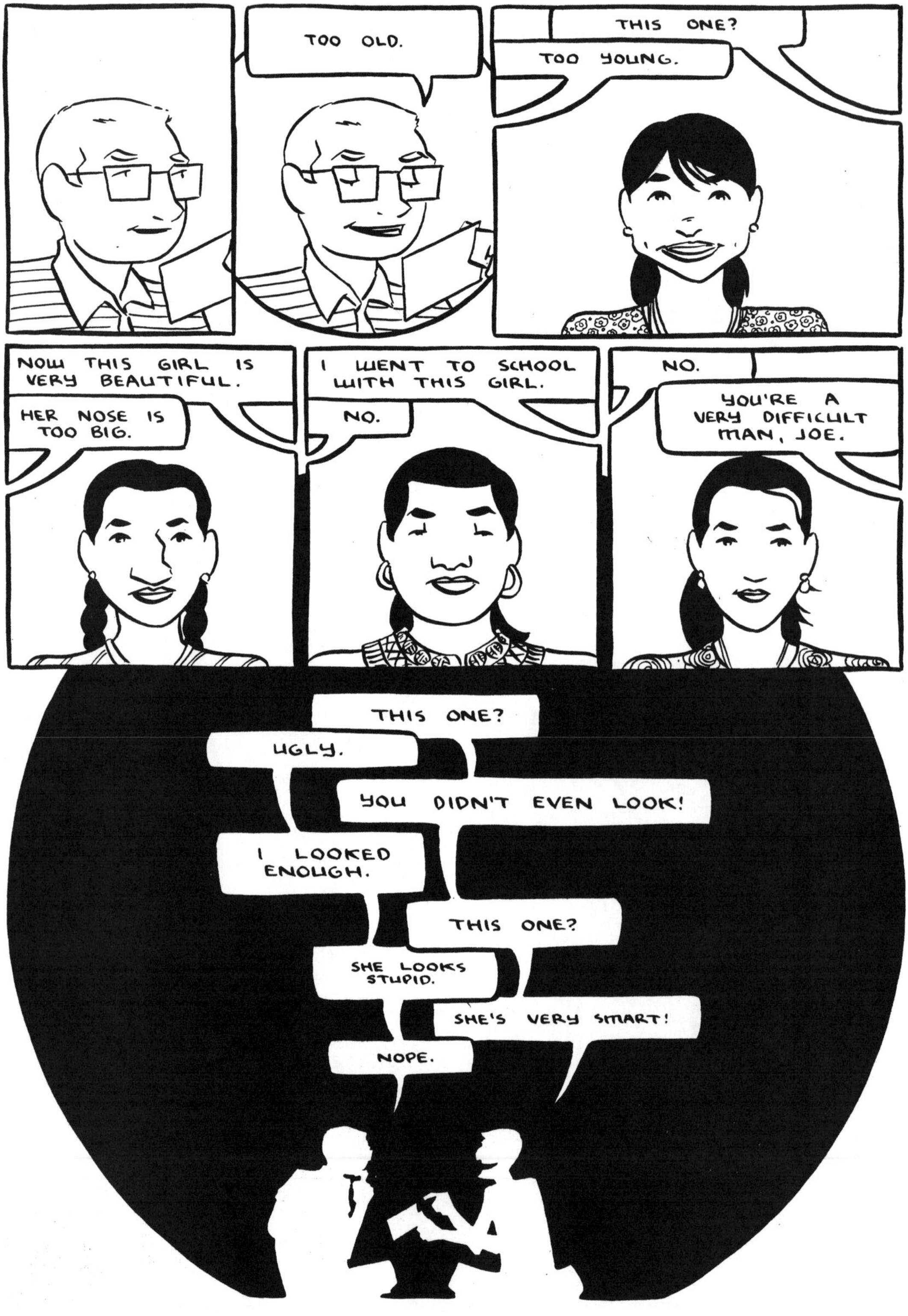

TOO OLD.
THIS ONE?
TOO YOUNG.
NOW THIS GIRL IS VERY BEAUTIFUL.
HER NOSE IS TOO BIG.
I WENT TO SCHOOL WITH THIS GIRL.
NO.
NO.
YOU'RE A VERY DIFFICULT MAN, JOE.
THIS ONE?
UGLY.
YOU DIDN'T EVEN LOOK!
I LOOKED ENOUGH.
THIS ONE?
SHE LOOKS STUPID.
SHE'S VERY SMART!
NOPE.

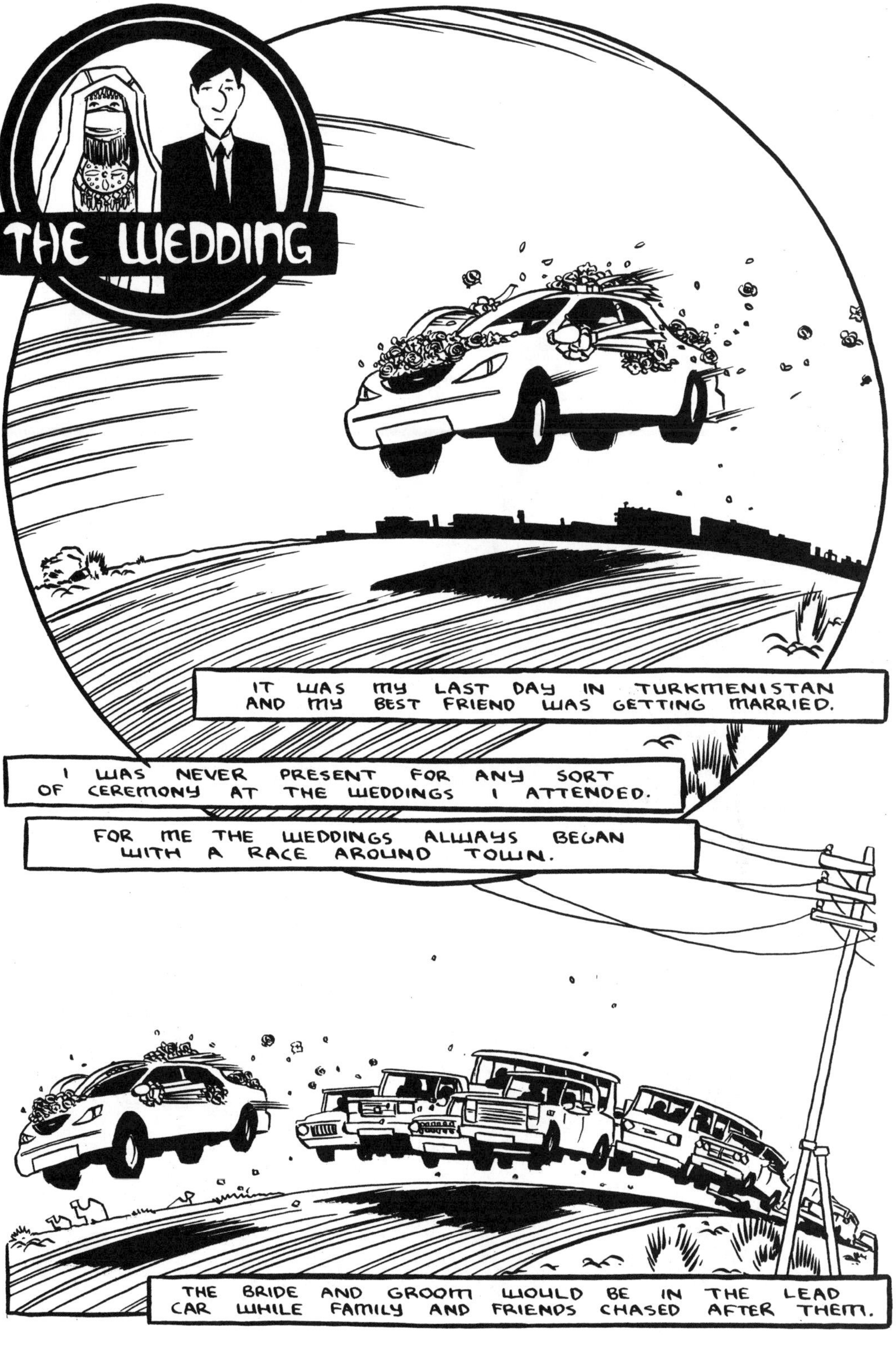
THE WEDDING
IT WAS MY LAST DAY IN TURKMENISTAN AND MY BEST FRIEND WAS GETTING MARRIED.
I WAS NEVER PRESENT FOR ANY SORT OF CEREMONY AT THE WEDDINGS I ATTENDED.
FOR ME THE WEDDINGS ALWAYS BEGAN WITH A RACE AROUND TOWN.
THE BRIDE AND GROOM WOULD BE IN THE LEAD CAR WHILE FAMILY AND FRIENDS CHASED AFTER THEM.

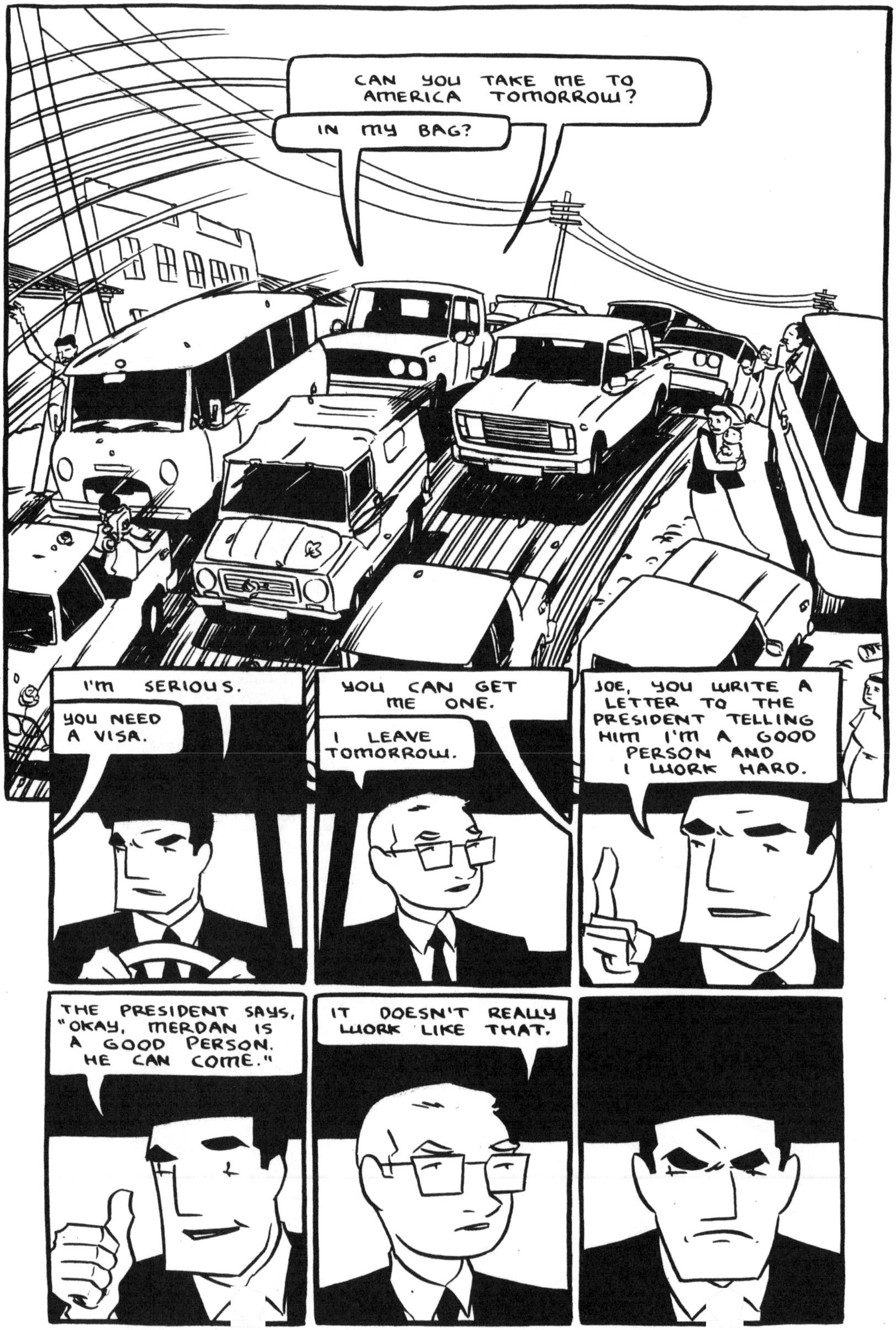
CAN YOU TAKE ME TO AMERICA TOMORROW?
IN MY BAG?
I'M SERIOUS.
YOU NEED A VISA.
YOU CAN GET ME ONE.
I LEAVE TOMORROW.
JOE, YOU WRITE A LETTER TO THE PRESIDENT TELLING HIM I'M A GOOD PERSON AND I WORK HARD.
THE PRESIDENT SAYS, "OKAY, MERDAN IS A GOOD PERSON. HE CAN COME."
IT DOESN'T REALLY WORK LIKE THAT.

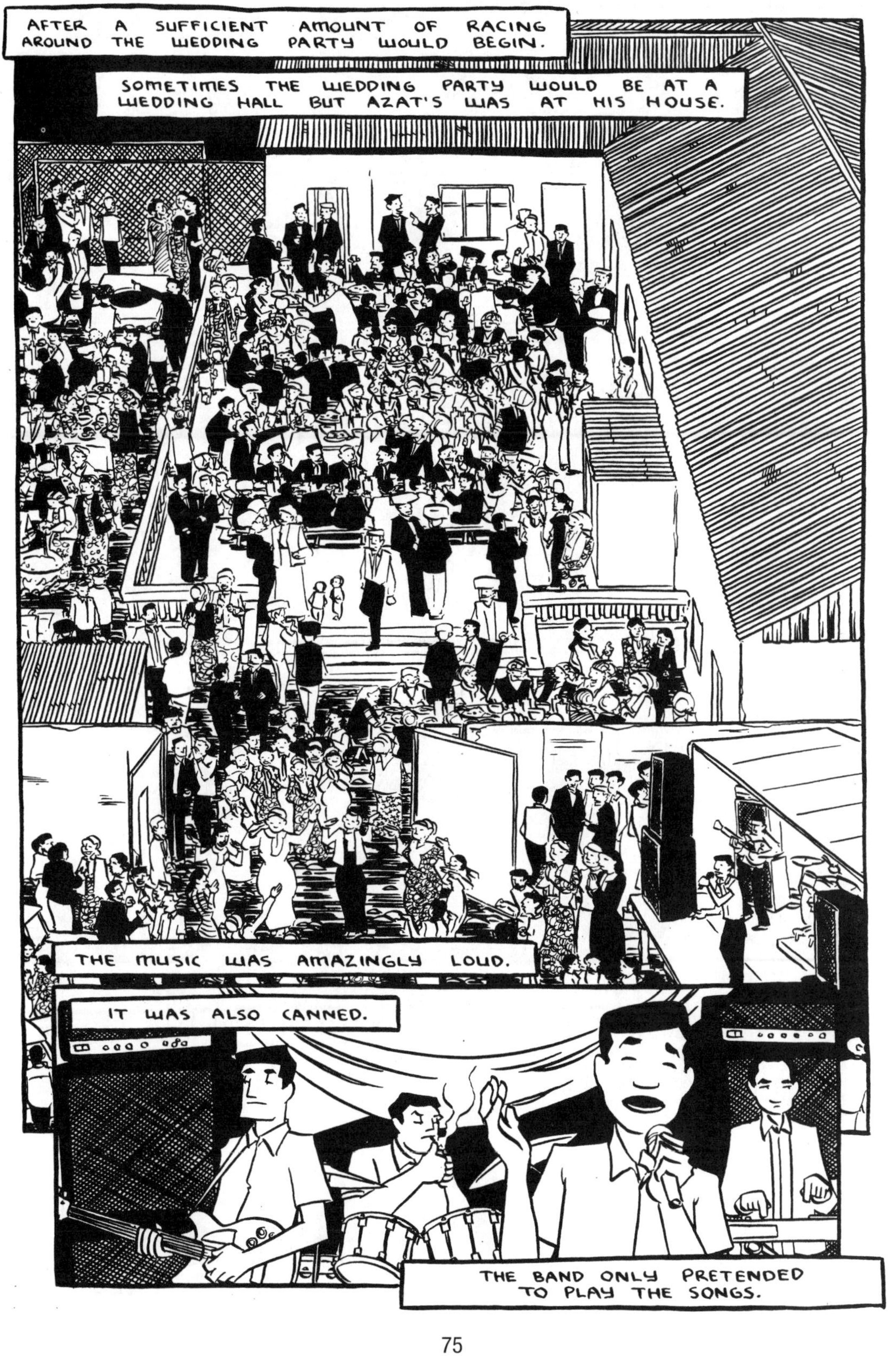
AFTER A SUFFICIENT AMOUNT OF RACING AROUND THE WEDDING PARTY WOULD BEGIN.
SOMETIMES THE WEDDING PARTY WOULD BE AT A WEDDING HALL BUT AZAT'S WAS AT HIS HOUSE.
THE MUSIC WAS AMAZINGLY LOUD.
IT WAS ALSO CANNED.
THE BAND ONLY PRETENDED TO PLAY THE SONGS.

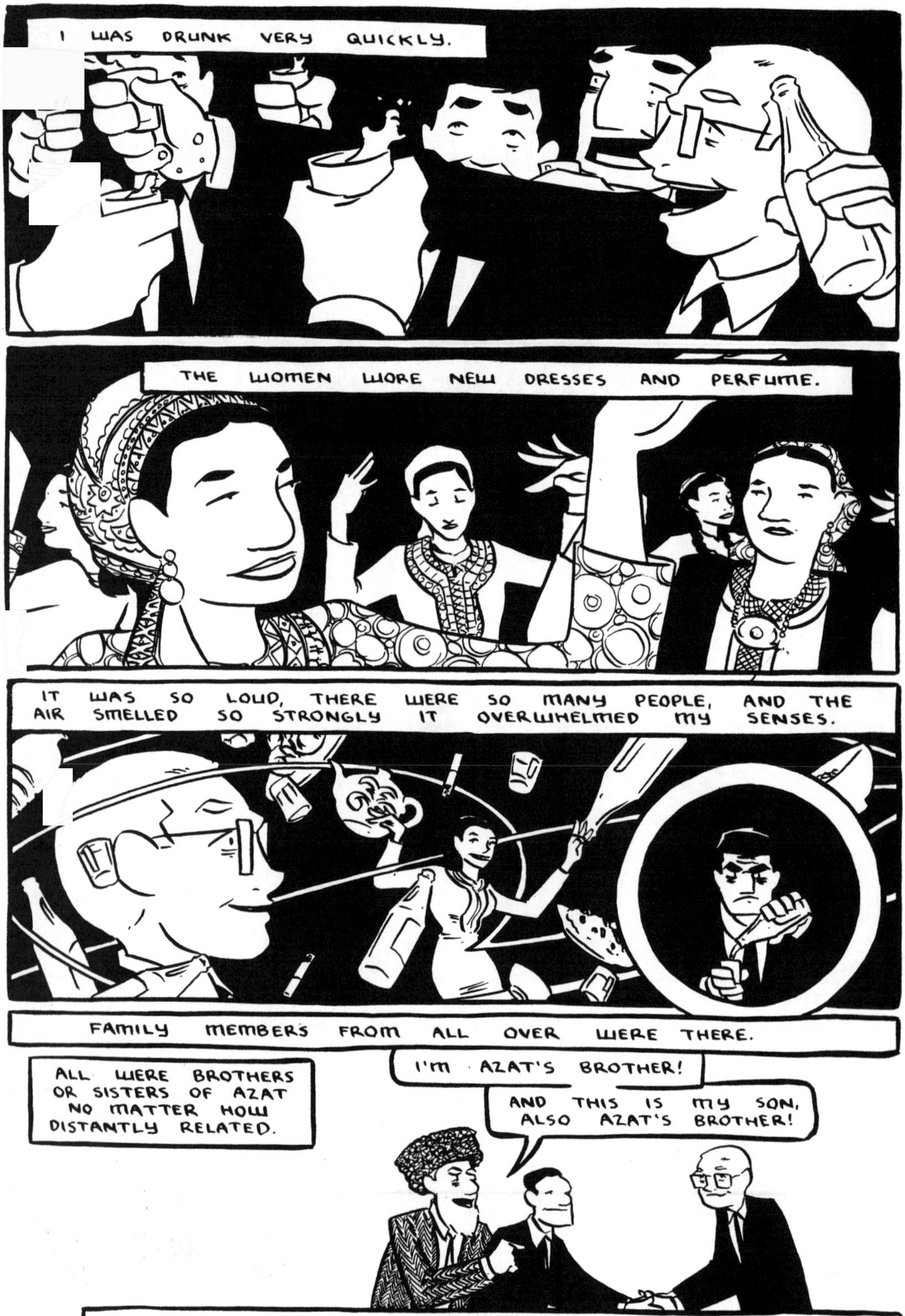
I WAS DRUNK VERY QUICKLY.
THE WOMEN WORE NEW DRESSES AND PERFUME.
IT WAS SO LOUD, THERE WERE SO MANY PEOPLE, AND THE AIR SMELLED SO STRONGLY IT OVERWHELMED MY SENSES.
FAMILY MEMBERS FROM ALL OVER WERE THERE.
ALL WERE BROTHERS OR SISTERS OF AZAT NO MATTER HOW DISTANTLY RELATED.
I'M AZAT'S BROTHER!
AND THIS IS MY SON, ALSO AZAT'S BROTHER!
THEIR NAMES WERE FORGOTTEN ALMOST IMMEDIATELY.

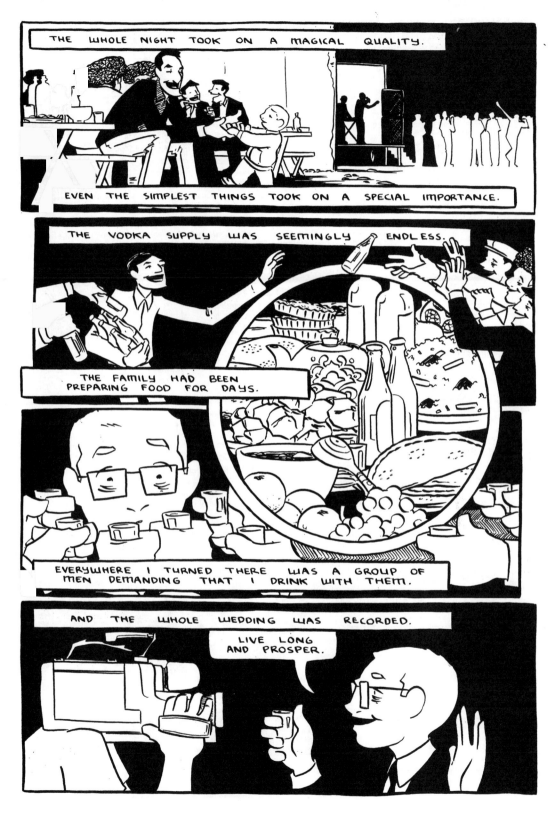

THE WHOLE NIGHT TOOK ON A MAGICAL QUALITY.

EVEN THE SIMPLEST THINGS TOOK ON A SPECIAL IMPORTANCE.

THE VODKA SUPPLY WAS SEEMINGLY ENDLESS.

THE FAMILY HAD BEEN PREPARING FOOD FOR DAYS.

EVERYWHERE I TURNED THERE WAS A GROUP OF MEN DEMANDING THAT I DRINK WITH THEM.

AND THE WHOLE WEDDING WAS RECORDED.

LIVE LONG AND PROSPER.

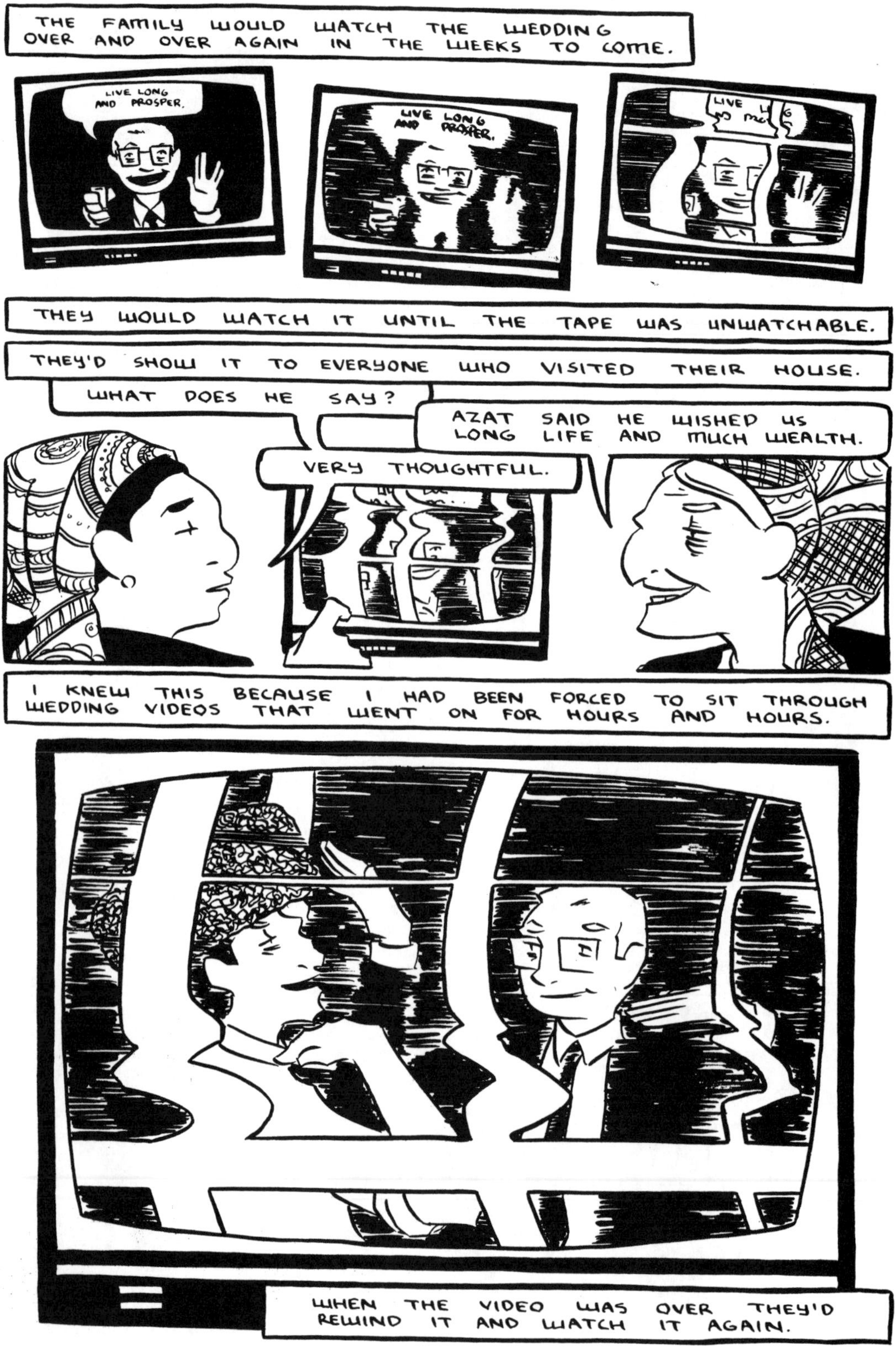
THE FAMILY WOULD WATCH THE WEDDING OVER AND OVER AGAIN IN THE WEEKS TO COME.
LIVE LONG AND PROSPER.
LIVE LONG AND PROSPER.
THEY WOULD WATCH IT UNTIL THE TAPE WAS UNWATCHABLE.
THEY'D SHOW IT TO EVERYONE WHO VISITED THEIR HOUSE.
WHAT DOES HE SAY?
AZAT SAID HE WISHED US LONG LIFE AND MUCH WEALTH.
VERY THOUGHTFUL.
I KNEW THIS BECAUSE I HAD BEEN FORCED TO SIT THROUGH WEDDING VIDEOS THAT WENT ON FOR HOURS AND HOURS.
WHEN THE VIDEO WAS OVER THEY'D REWIND IT AND WATCH IT AGAIN.

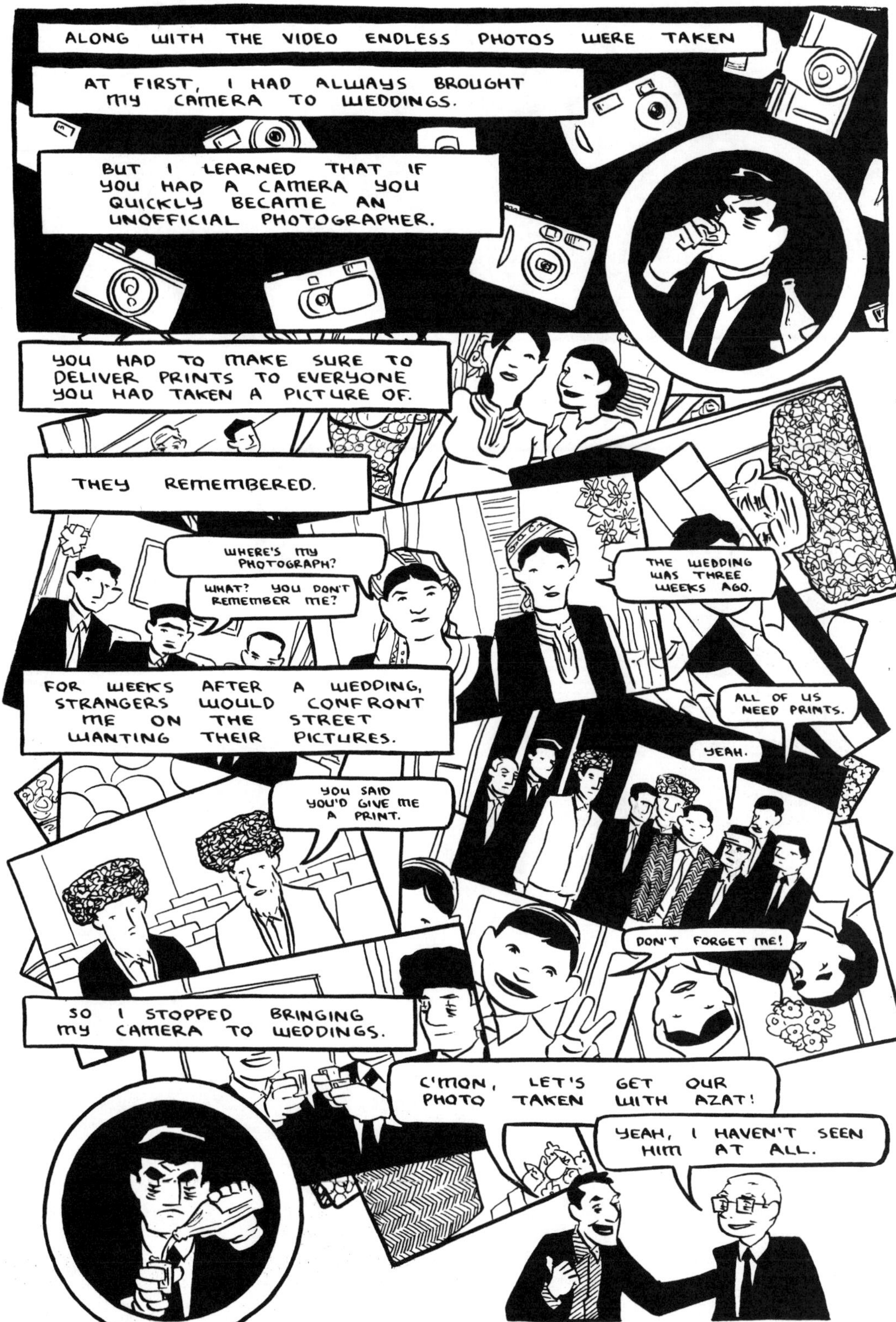

ALONG WITH THE VIDEO ENDLESS PHOTOS WERE TAKEN
AT FIRST, I HAD ALWAYS BROUGHT MY CAMERA TO WEDDINGS.
BUT I LEARNED THAT IF YOU HAD A CAMERA YOU QUICKLY BECAME AN UNOFFICIAL PHOTOGRAPHER.
YOU HAD TO MAKE SURE TO DELIVER PRINTS TO EVERYONE YOU HAD TAKEN A PICTURE OF.
THEY REMEMBERED.
WHERE'S MY PHOTOGRAPH?
WHAT? YOU DON'T REMEMBER ME?
THE WEDDING WAS THREE WEEKS AGO.
FOR WEEKS AFTER A WEDDING, STRANGERS WOULD CONFRONT ME ON THE STREET WANTING THEIR PICTURES.
ALL OF US NEED PRINTS.
YEAH.
YOU SAID YOU'D GIVE ME A PRINT.
DON'T FORGET ME!
SO I STOPPED BRINGING MY CAMERA TO WEDDINGS.
C'MON, LET'S GET OUR PHOTO TAKEN WITH AZAT!
YEAH, I HAVEN'T SEEN HIM AT ALL.

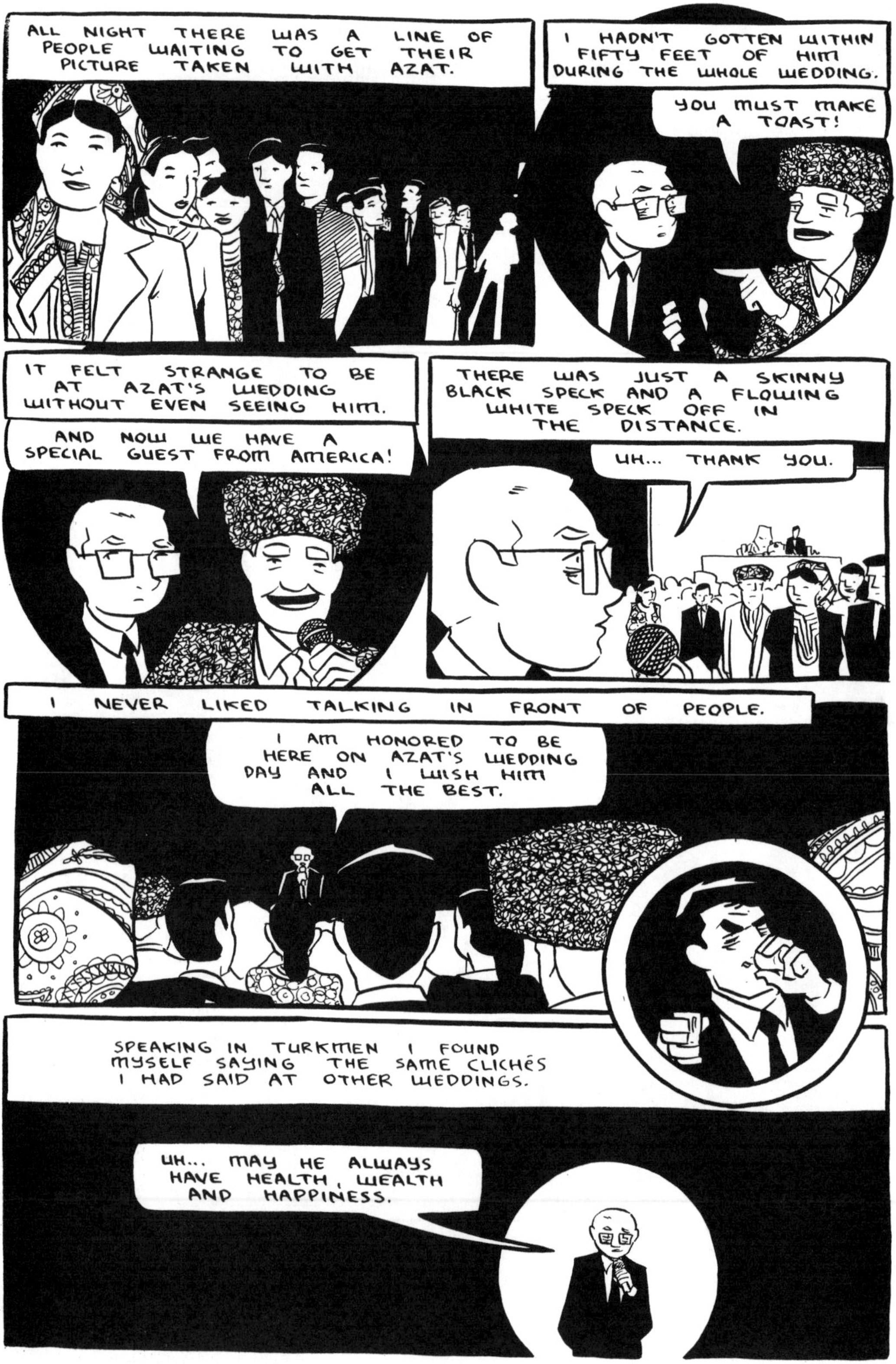
ALL NIGHT THERE WAS A LINE OF PEOPLE WAITING TO GET THEIR PICTURE TAKEN WITH AZAT.
I HADN'T GOTTEN WITHIN FIFTY FEET OF HIM DURING THE WHOLE WEDDING.
YOU MUST MAKE A TOAST!
IT FELT STRANGE TO BE AT AZAT'S WEDDING WITHOUT EVEN SEEING HIM.
AND NOW WE HAVE A SPECIAL GUEST FROM AMERICA!
THERE WAS JUST A SKINNY BLACK SPECK AND A FLOWING WHITE SPECK OFF IN THE DISTANCE.
UH... THANK YOU.
I NEVER LIKED TALKING IN FRONT OF PEOPLE.
I AM HONORED TO BE HERE ON AZAT'S WEDDING DAY AND I WISH HIM ALL THE BEST.
SPEAKING IN TURKMEN I FOUND MYSELF SAYING THE SAME CLICHÉS I HAD SAID AT OTHER WEDDINGS.
UH... MAY HE ALWAYS HAVE HEALTH, WEALTH AND HAPPINESS.

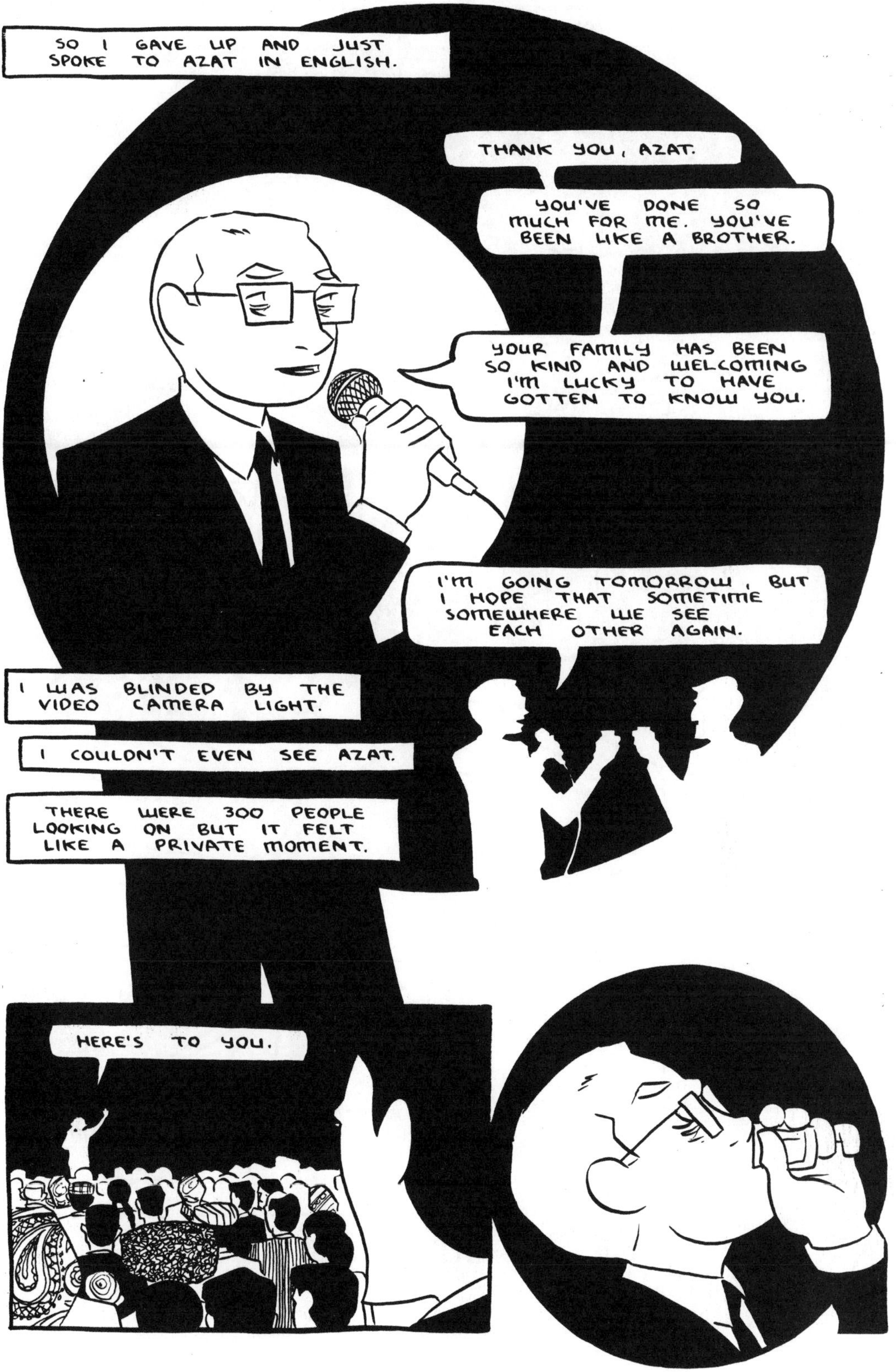
SO I GAVE UP AND JUST SPOKE TO AZAT IN ENGLISH.
THANK YOU, AZAT.
YOU'VE DONE SO MUCH FOR ME. YOU'VE BEEN LIKE A BROTHER.
YOUR FAMILY HAS BEEN SO KIND AND WELCOMING I'M LUCKY TO HAVE GOTTEN TO KNOW YOU.
I'M GOING TOMORROW, BUT I HOPE THAT SOMETIME SOMEWHERE WE SEE EACH OTHER AGAIN.
I WAS BLINDED BY THE VIDEO CAMERA LIGHT.
I COULDN'T EVEN SEE AZAT.
THERE WERE 300 PEOPLE LOOKING ON BUT IT FELT LIKE A PRIVATE MOMENT.
HERE'S TO YOU.

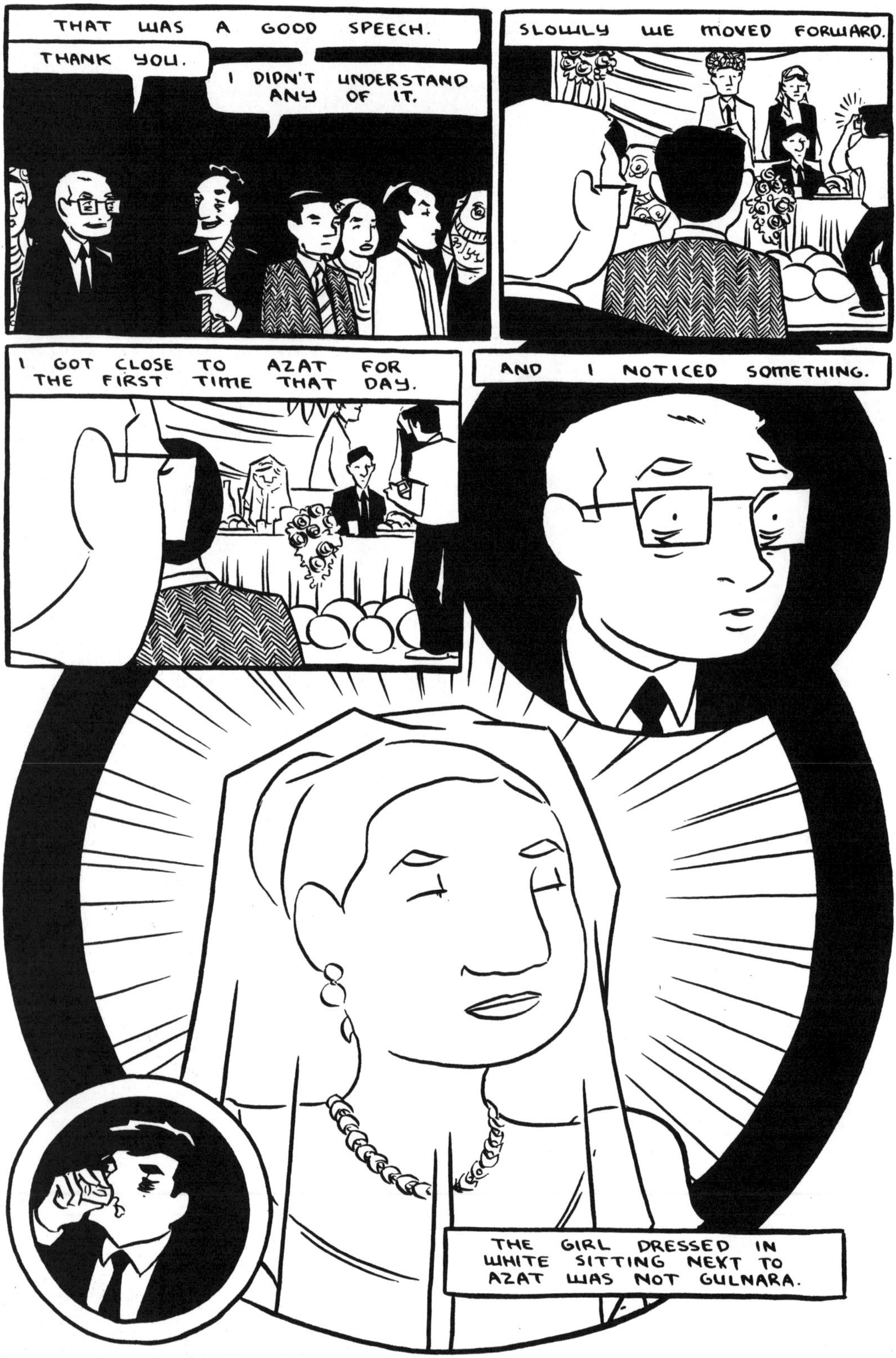
THAT WAS A GOOD SPEECH.
THANK YOU.
I DIDN'T UNDERSTAND ANY OF IT.
SLOWLY WE MOVED FORWARD.
I GOT CLOSE TO AZAT FOR THE FIRST TIME THAT DAY.
AND I NOTICED SOMETHING.
THE GIRL DRESSED IN WHITE SITTING NEXT TO AZAT WAS NOT GULNARA.

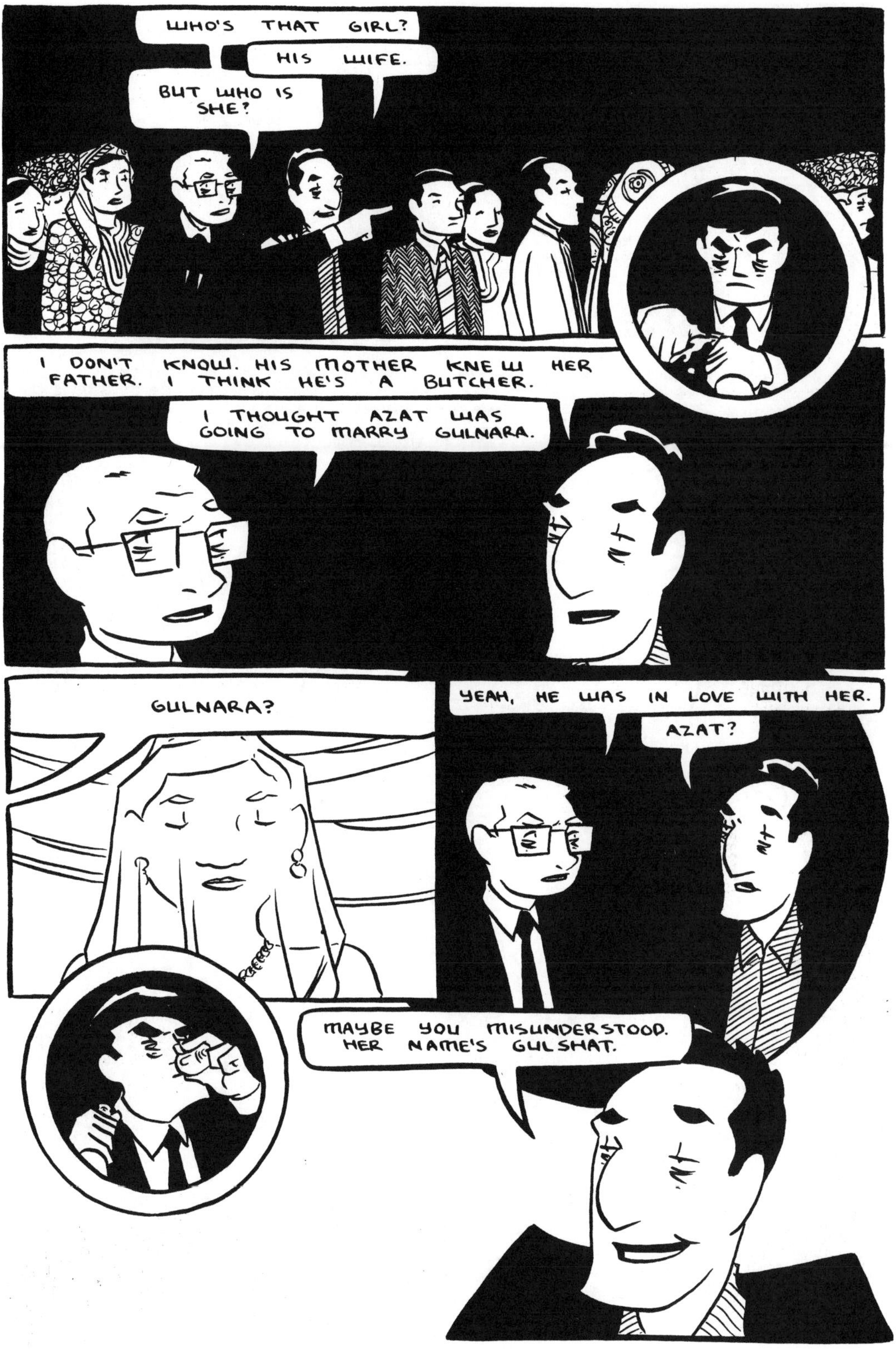
WHO'S THAT GIRL?
HIS WIFE.
BUT WHO IS SHE?
I DON'T KNOW. HIS MOTHER KNEW HER FATHER. I THINK HE'S A BUTCHER.
I THOUGHT AZAT WAS GOING TO MARRY GULNARA.
GULNARA?
YEAH, HE WAS IN LOVE WITH HER.
AZAT?
MAYBE YOU MISUNDERSTOOD. HER NAME'S GULSHAT.

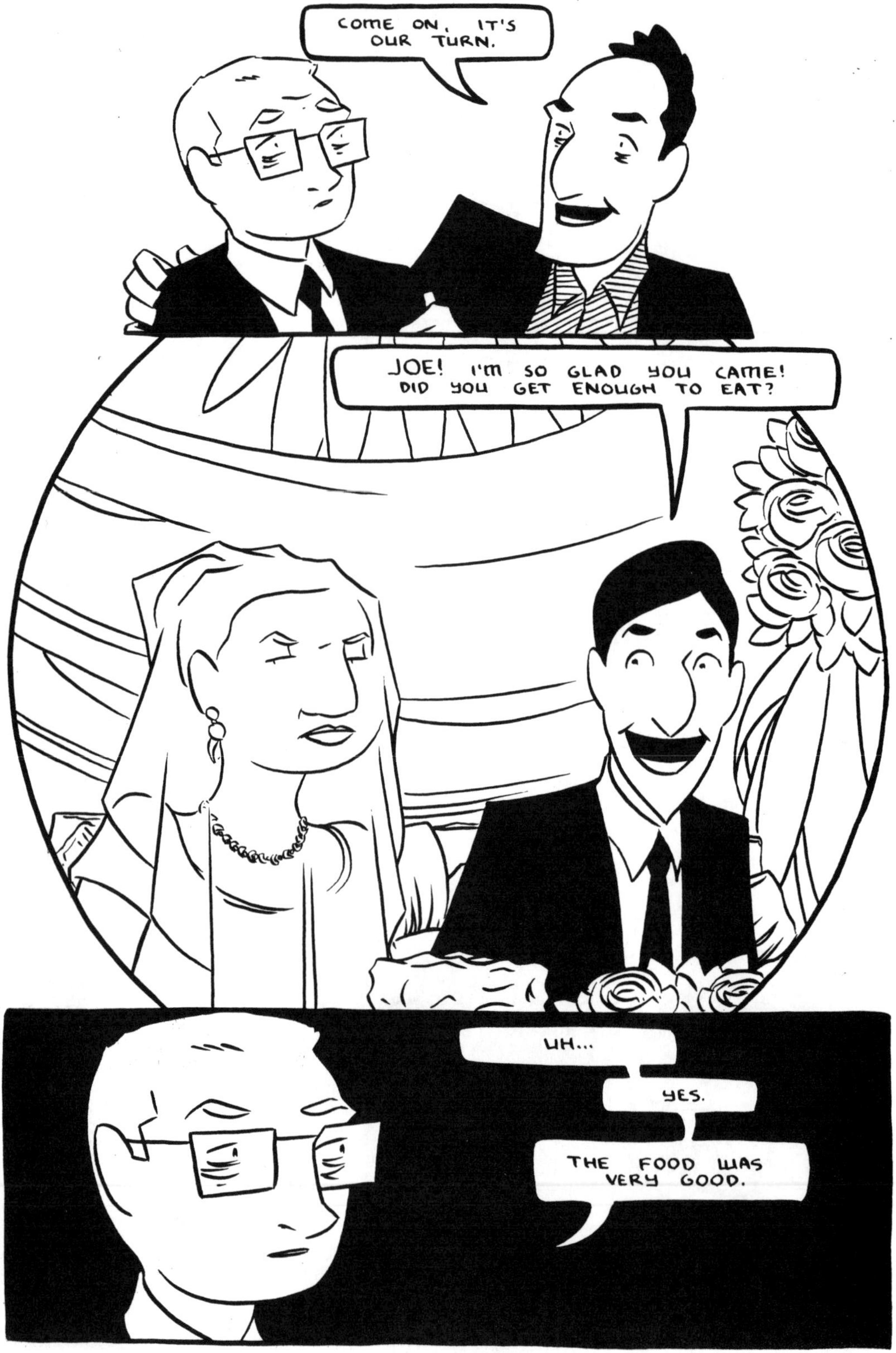
COME ON, IT'S OUR TURN.
JOE! I'M SO GLAD YOU CAME! DID YOU GET ENOUGH TO EAT?
UH...
YES.
THE FOOD WAS VERY GOOD.

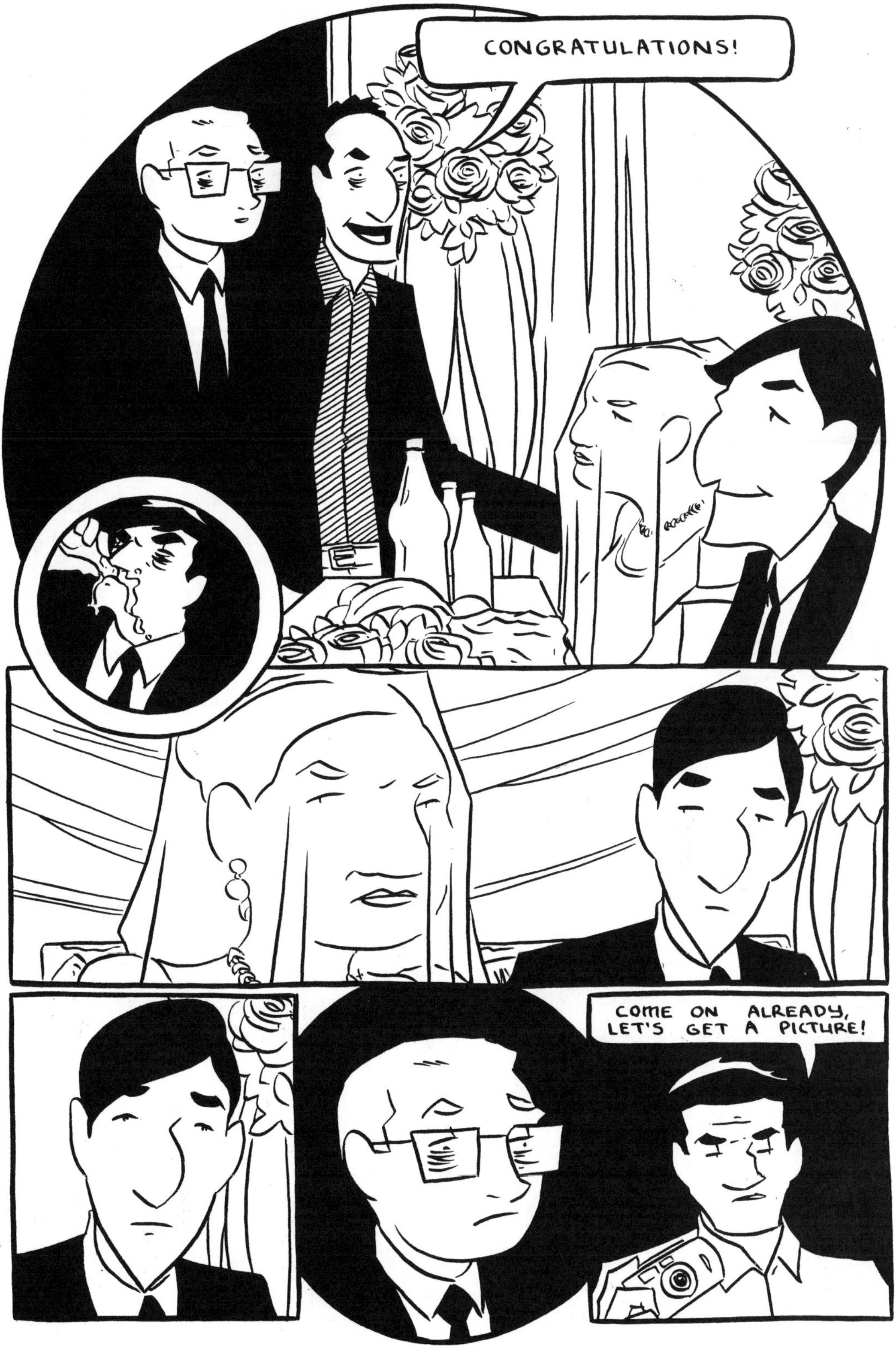
CONGRATULATIONS!
COME ON ALREADY, LET'S GET A PICTURE!

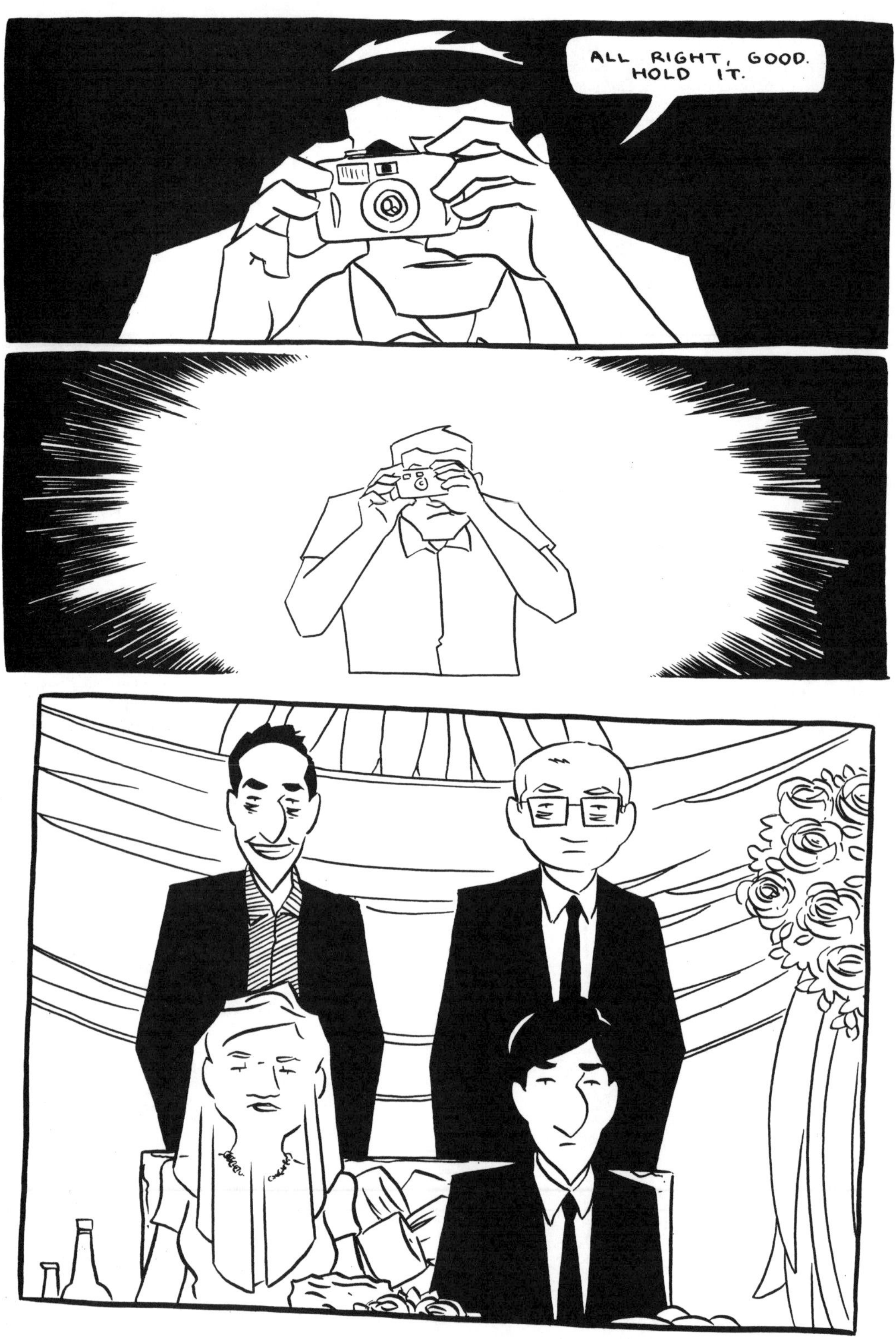
ALL RIGHT, GOOD.
HOLD IT.

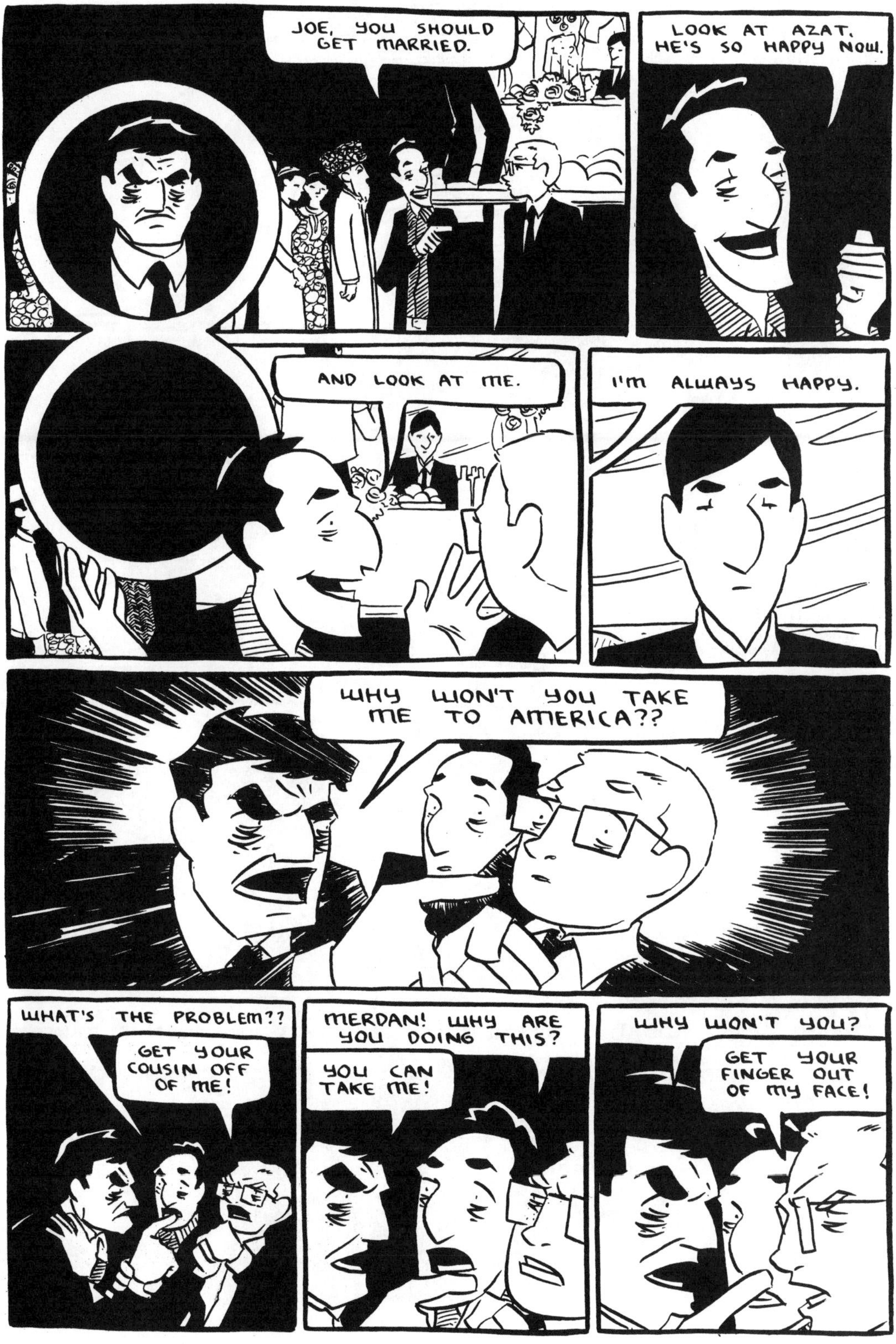
JOE, YOU SHOULD GET MARRIED.
LOOK AT AZAT. HE'S SO HAPPY NOW.
AND LOOK AT ME.
I'M ALWAYS HAPPY.
WHY WON'T YOU TAKE ME TO AMERICA??
WHAT'S THE PROBLEM??
GET YOUR COUSIN OFF OF ME!
MERDAN! WHY ARE YOU DOING THIS?
YOU CAN TAKE ME!
WHY WON'T YOU?
GET YOUR FINGER OUT OF MY FACE!

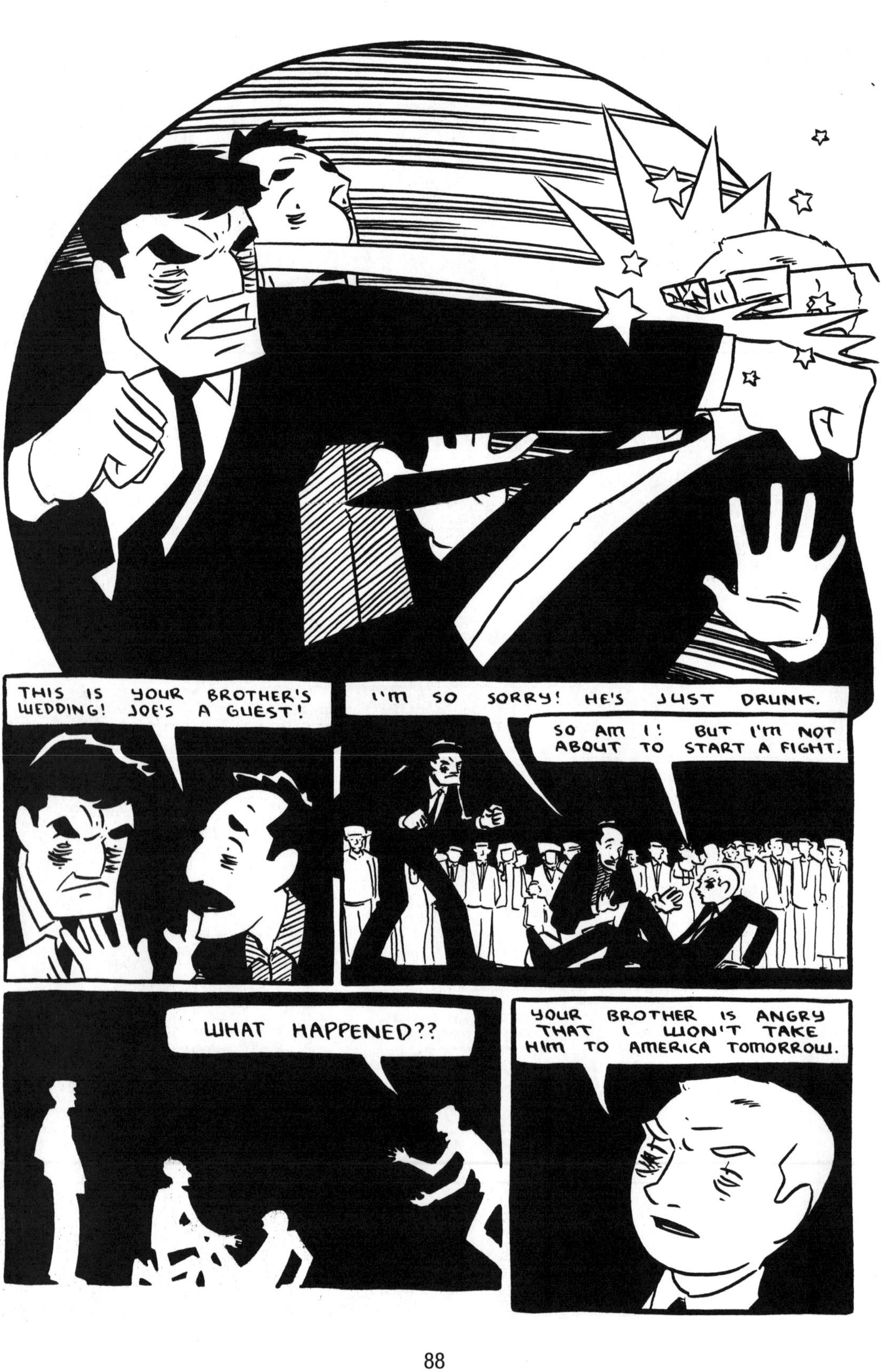
THIS IS YOUR BROTHER'S WEDDING! JOE'S A GUEST!
I'M SO SORRY! HE'S JUST DRUNK.
SO AM I! BUT I'M NOT ABOUT TO START A FIGHT.
WHAT HAPPENED??
YOUR BROTHER IS ANGRY THAT I WON'T TAKE HIM TO AMERICA TOMORROW.

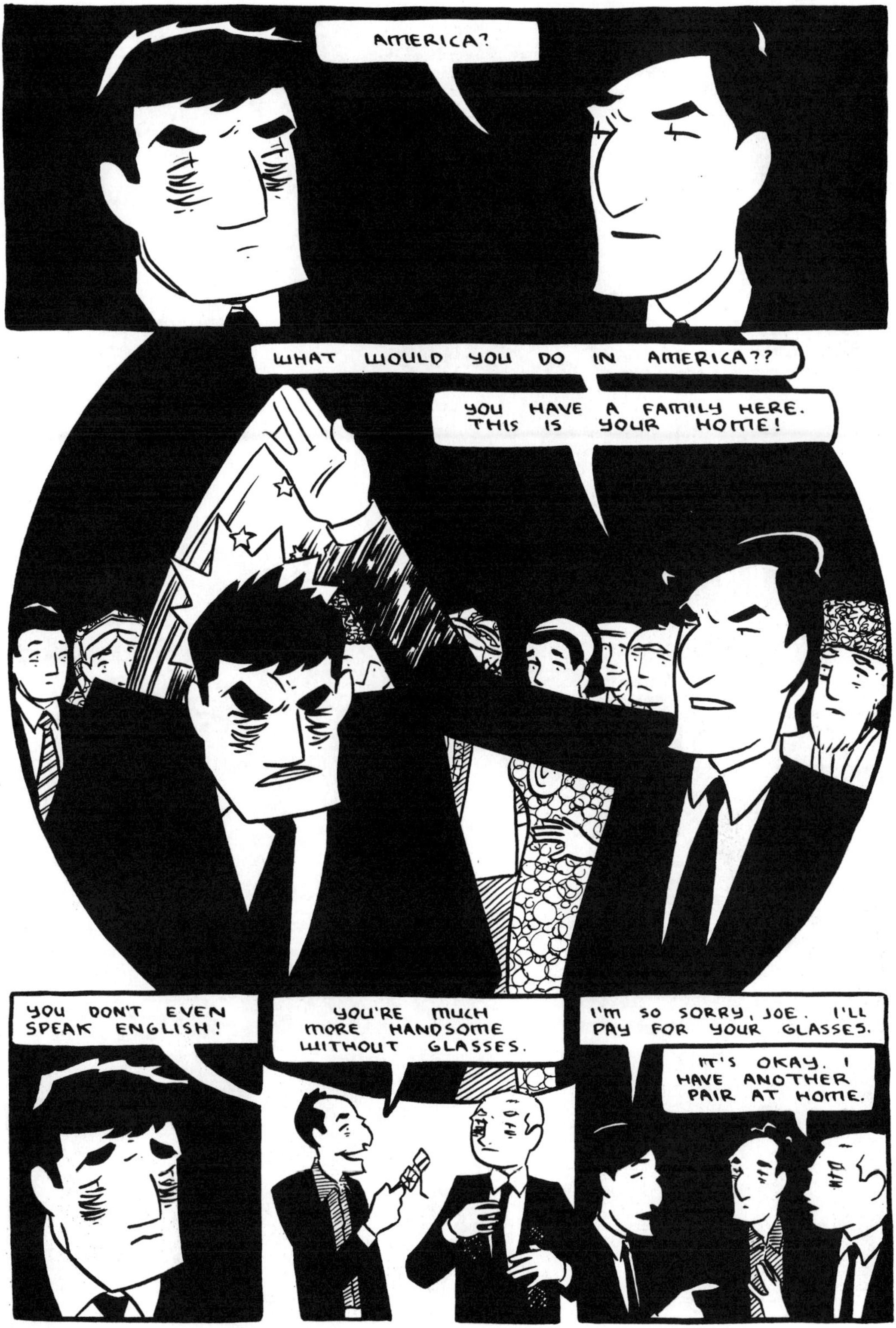
AMERICA?
WHAT WOULD YOU DO IN AMERICA??
YOU HAVE A FAMILY HERE. THIS IS YOUR HOME!
YOU DON'T EVEN SPEAK ENGLISH!
YOU'RE MUCH MORE HANDSOME WITHOUT GLASSES.
I'M SO SORRY, JOE. I'LL PAY FOR YOUR GLASSES.
IT'S OKAY. I HAVE ANOTHER PAIR AT HOME.

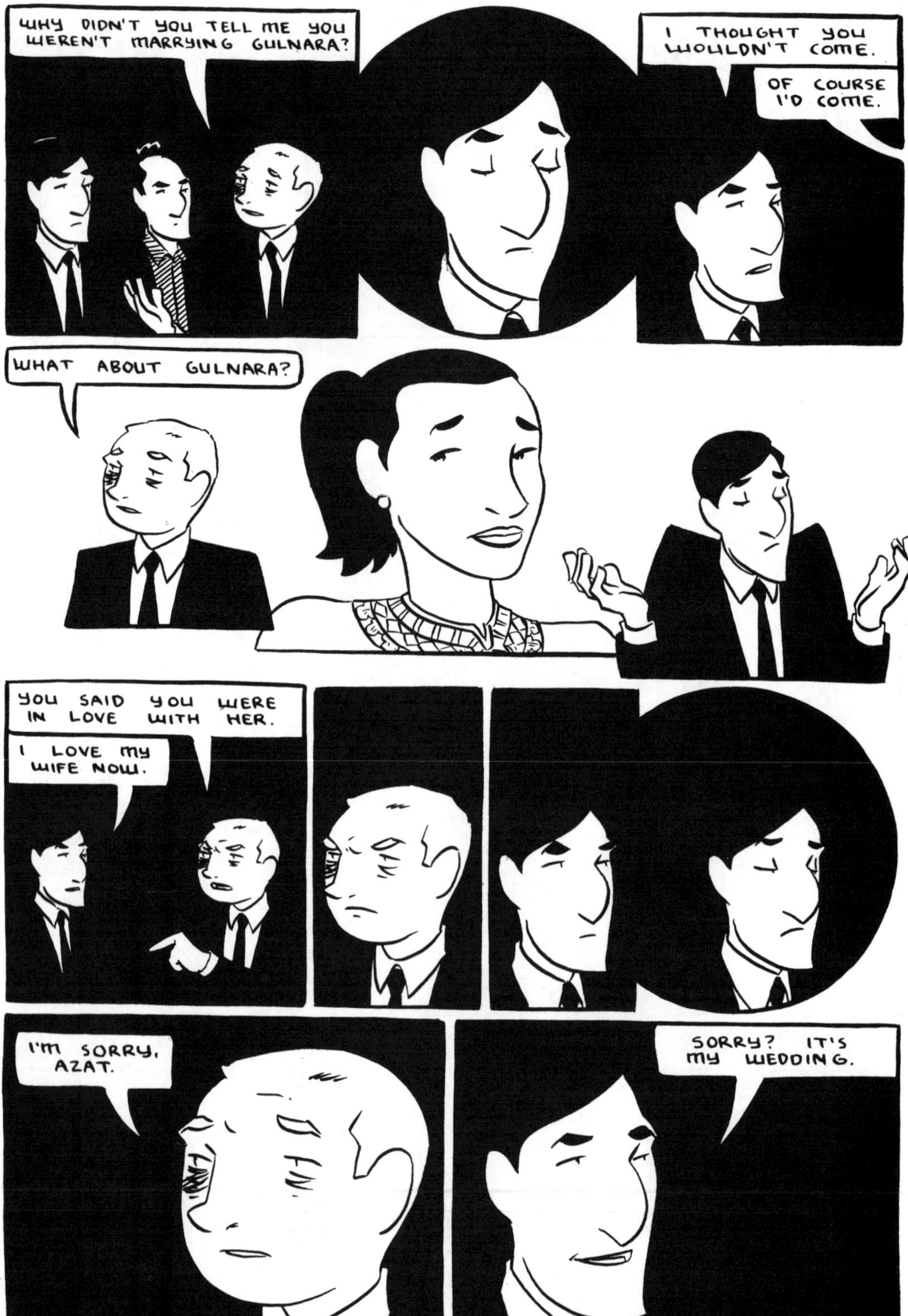
WHY DIDN'T YOU TELL ME YOU WEREN'T MARRYING GULNARA?
I THOUGHT YOU WOULDN'T COME.
OF COURSE I'D COME.
WHAT ABOUT GULNARA?
YOU SAID YOU WERE IN LOVE WITH HER.
I LOVE MY WIFE NOW.
I'M SORRY, AZAT.
SORRY? IT'S MY WEDDING.

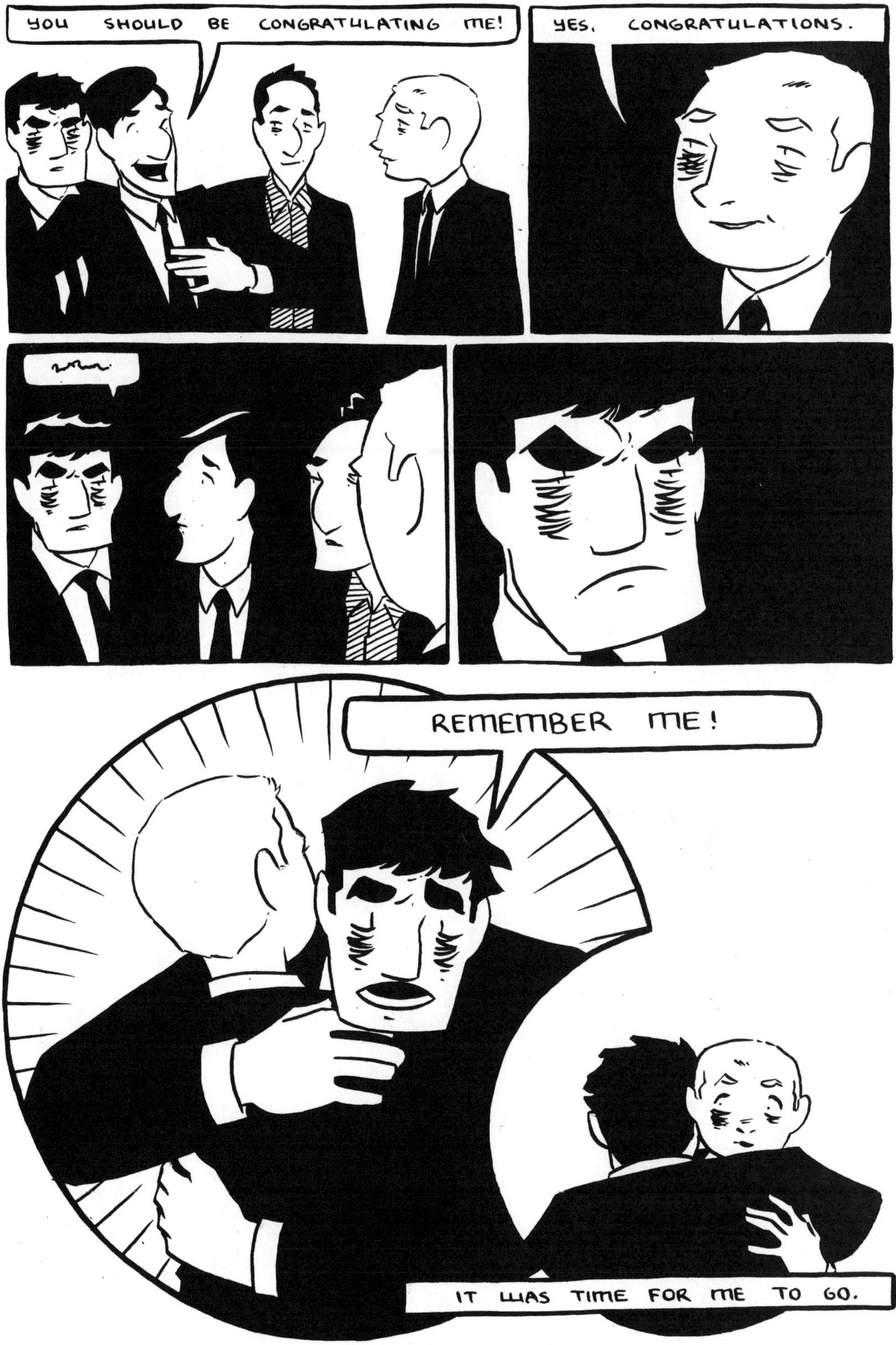
YOU SHOULD BE CONGRATULATING ME!
YES, CONGRATULATIONS.
REMEMBER ME!
IT WAS TIME FOR ME TO GO.

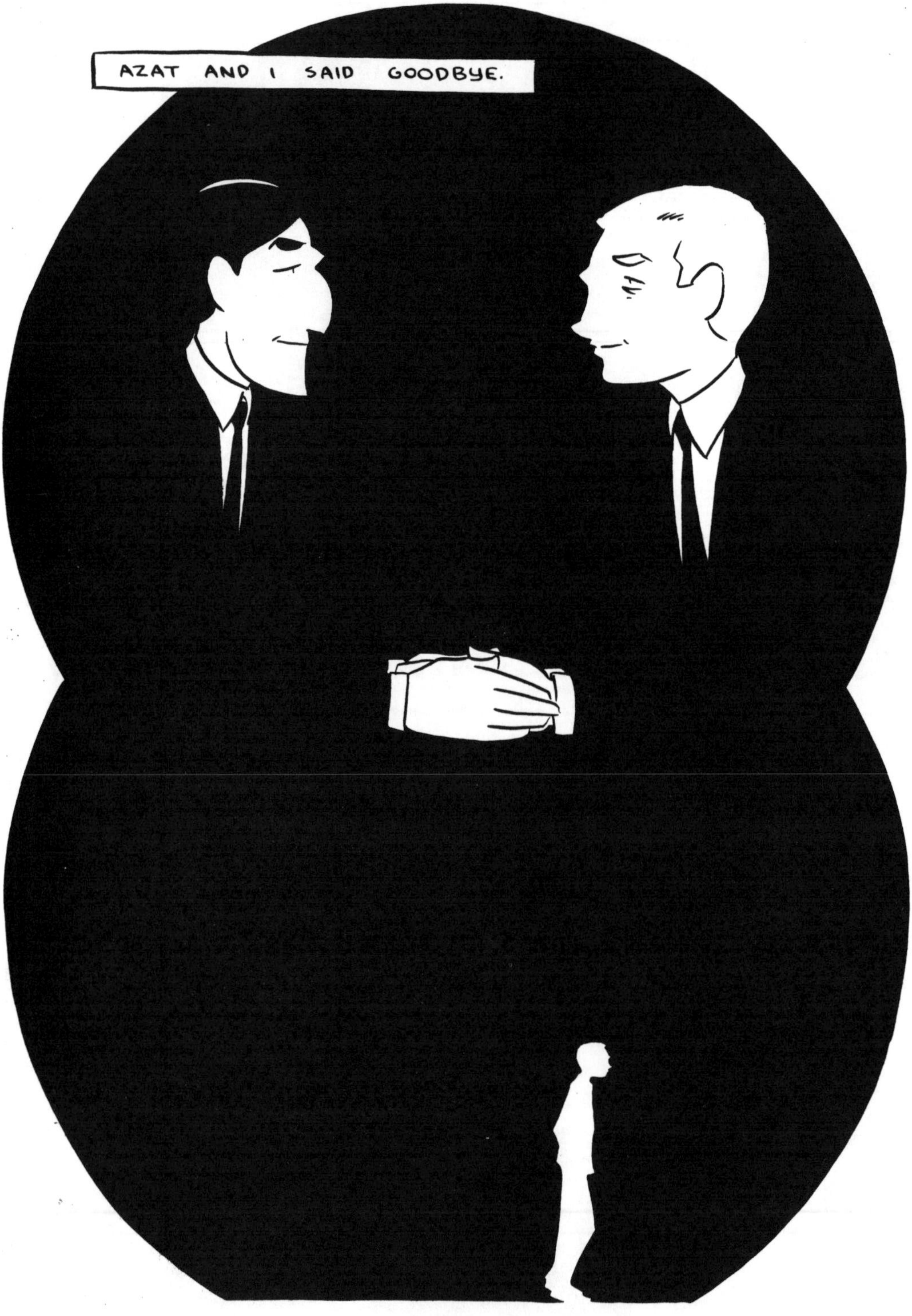
AZAT AND I SAID GOODBYE.
AND THAT WAS THE LAST I SAW OF HIM.

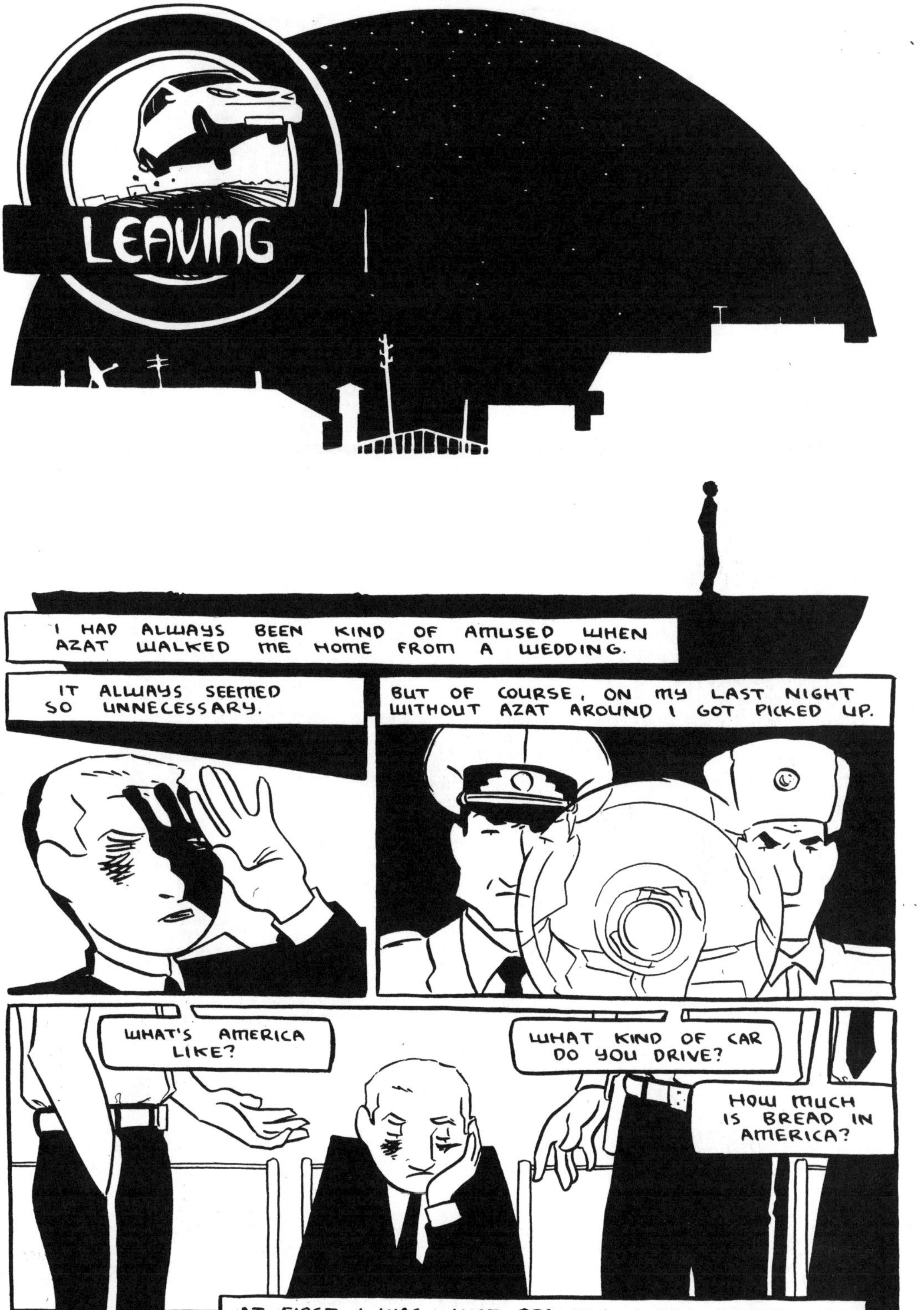
LEAVING
I HAD ALWAYS BEEN KIND OF AMUSED WHEN AZAT WALKED ME HOME FROM A WEDDING.
IT ALWAYS SEEMED SO UNNECESSARY.
BUT OF COURSE, ON MY LAST NIGHT WITHOUT AZAT AROUND I GOT PICKED UP.
WHAT'S AMERICA LIKE?
WHAT KIND OF CAR DO YOU DRIVE?
HOW MUCH IS BREAD IN AMERICA?
AT FIRST I WAS JUST DEALING WITH UNDERLINGS WHO HAD NO IDEA WHAT TO DO WITH ME.

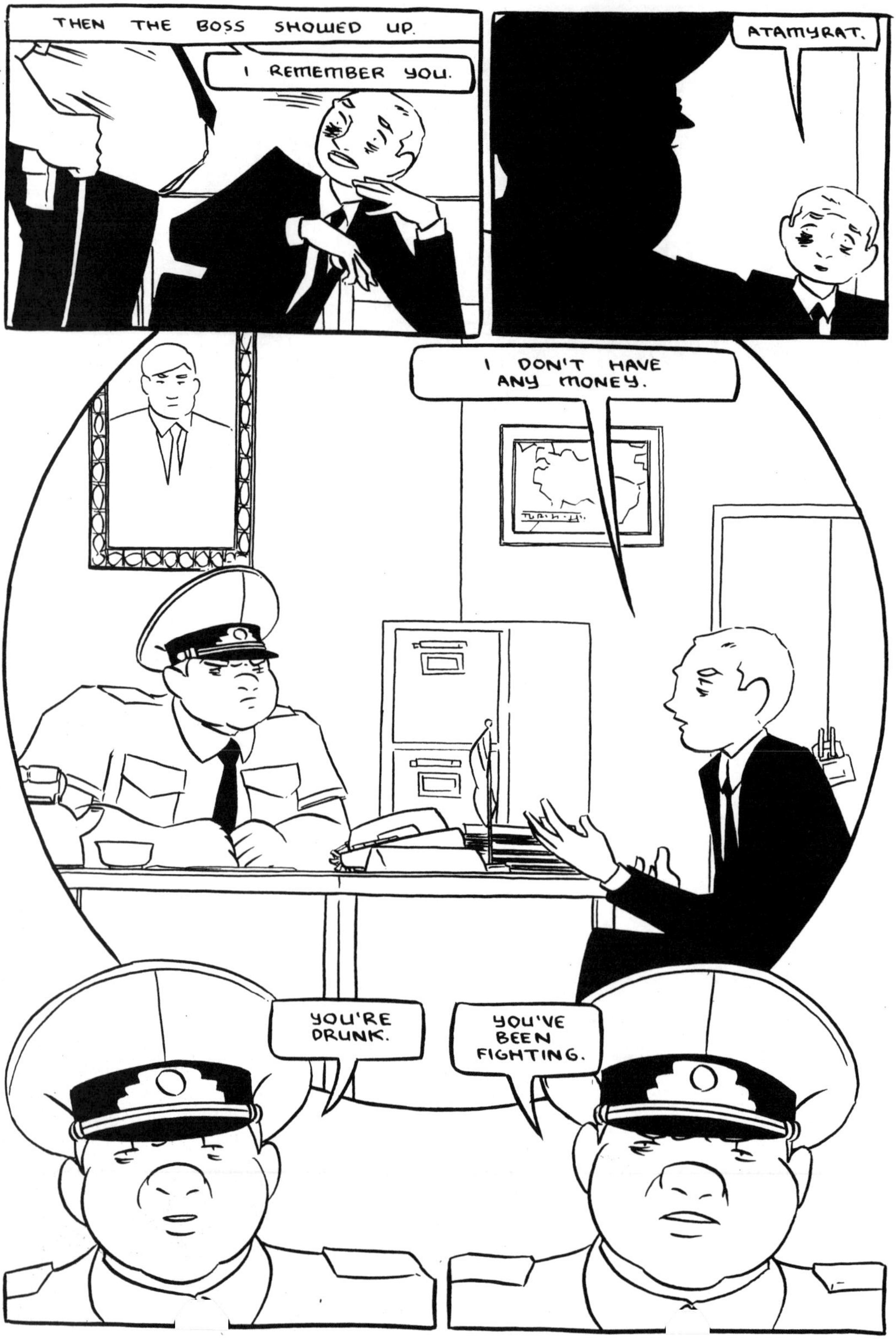
THEN THE BOSS SHOWED UP.
I REMEMBER YOU.
ATAMYRAT.
I DON'T HAVE ANY MONEY.
YOU'RE DRUNK.
YOU'VE BEEN FIGHTING.

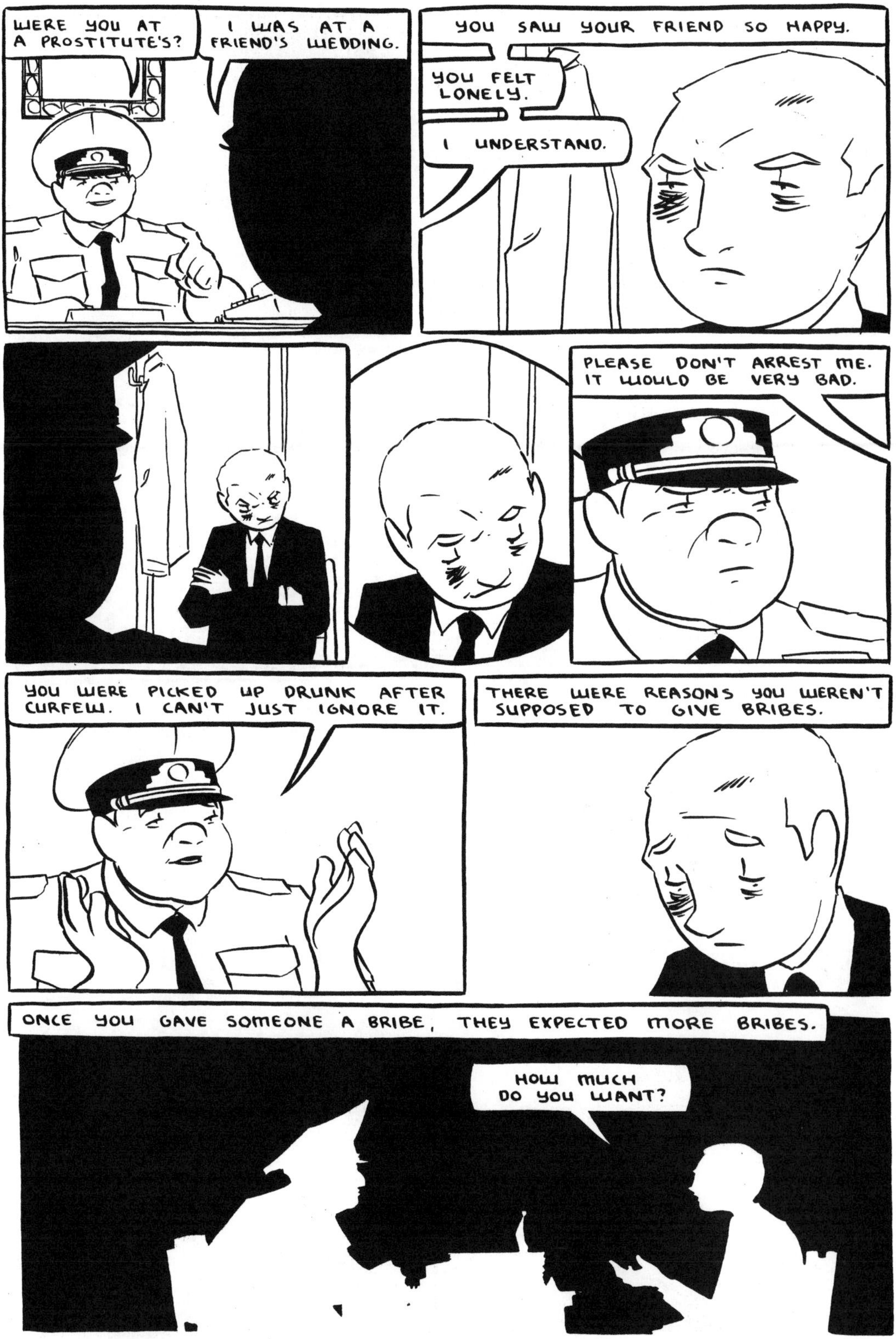
WERE YOU AT A PROSTITUTE'S?
I WAS AT A FRIEND'S WEDDING.
YOU SAW YOUR FRIEND SO HAPPY.
YOU FELT LONELY.
I UNDERSTAND.
PLEASE DON'T ARREST ME. IT WOULD BE VERY BAD.
YOU WERE PICKED UP DRUNK AFTER CURFEW. I CAN'T JUST IGNORE IT.
THERE WERE REASONS YOU WEREN'T SUPPOSED TO GIVE BRIBES.
ONCE YOU GAVE SOMEONE A BRIBE, THEY EXPECTED MORE BRIBES.
HOW MUCH DO YOU WANT?

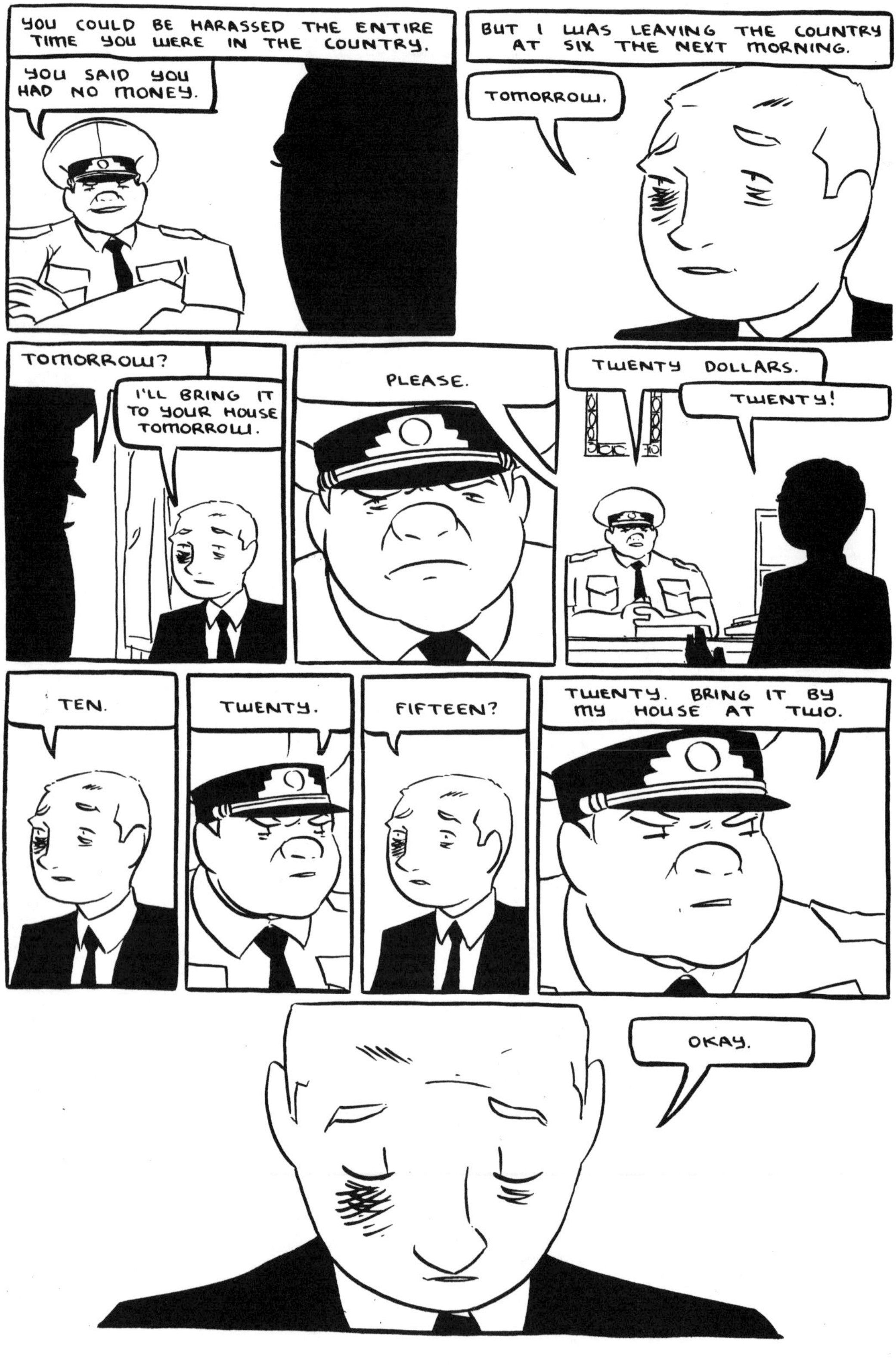
YOU COULD BE HARASSED THE ENTIRE TIME YOU WERE IN THE COUNTRY.
YOU SAID YOU HAD NO MONEY.
BUT I WAS LEAVING THE COUNTRY AT SIX THE NEXT MORNING.
TOMORROW.
TOMORROW?
I'LL BRING IT TO YOUR HOUSE TOMORROW.
PLEASE.
TWENTY DOLLARS.
TWENTY!
TEN.
TWENTY.
FIFTEEN?
TWENTY. BRING IT BY MY HOUSE AT TWO.
OKAY.

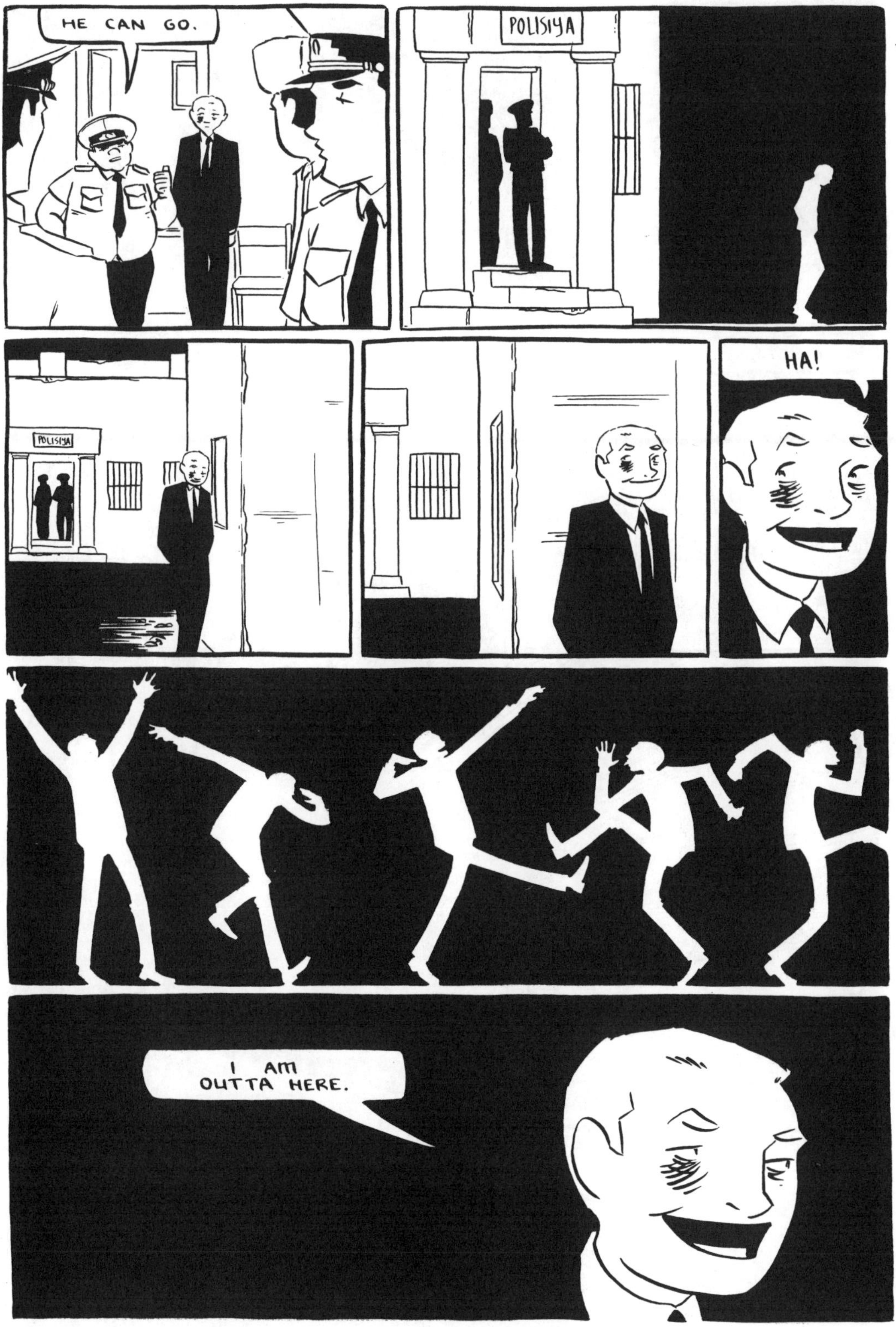
HE CAN GO.
POLISIYA
POLISIYA
HA!
I AM OUTTA HERE.

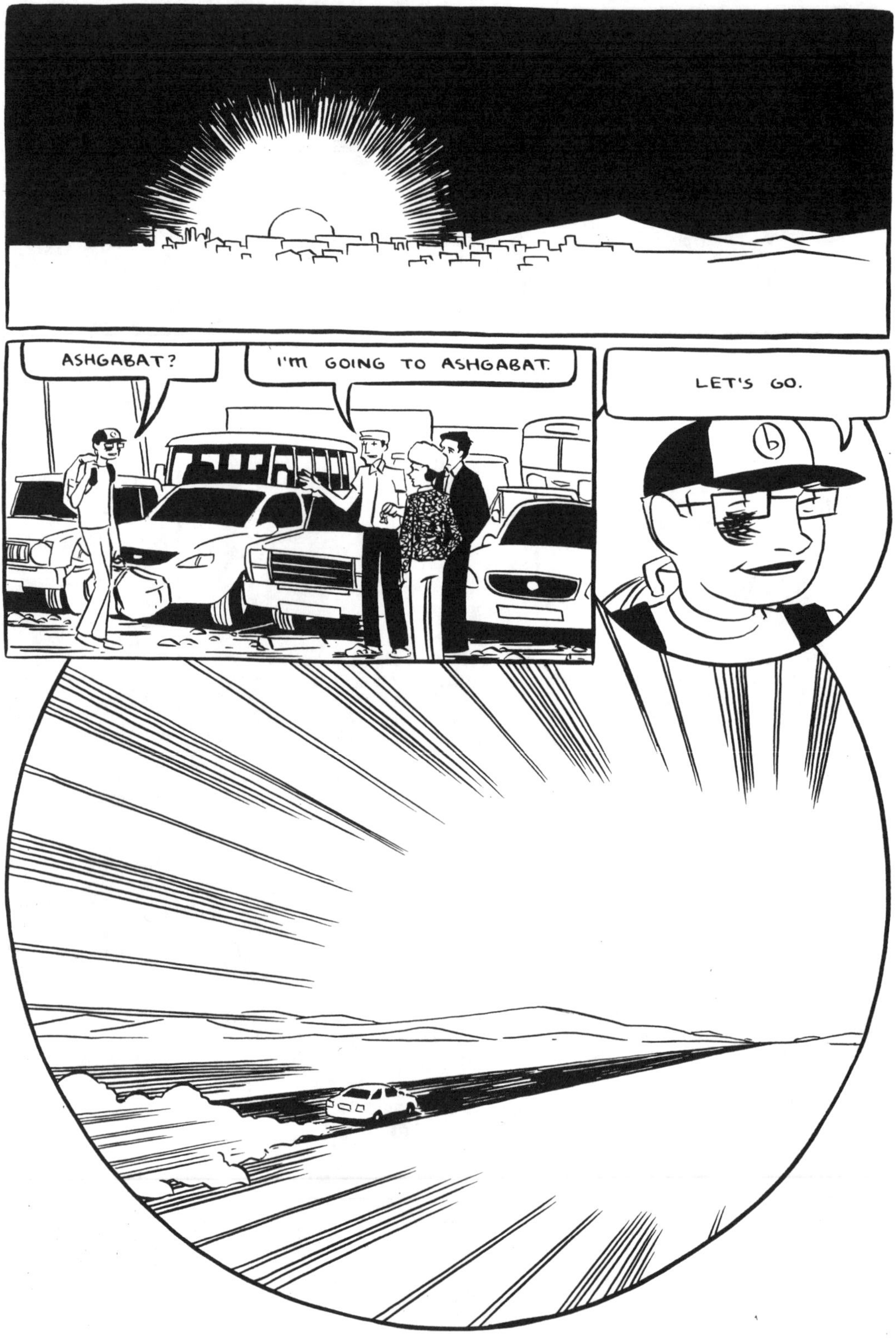
ASHGABAT?
I'M GOING TO ASHGABAT.
LET'S GO.

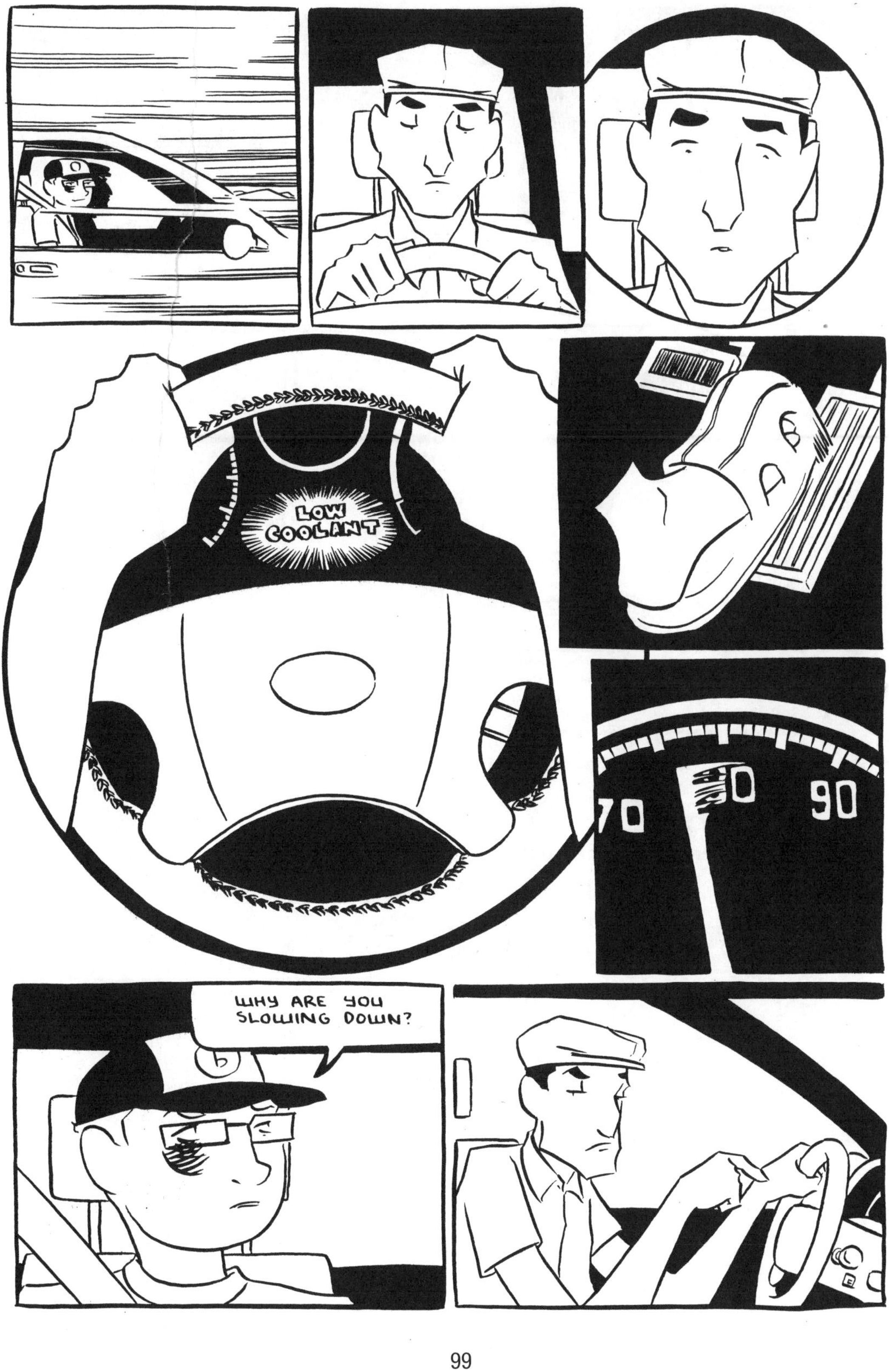
LOW COOLANT
70
90
WHY ARE YOU SLOWING DOWN?

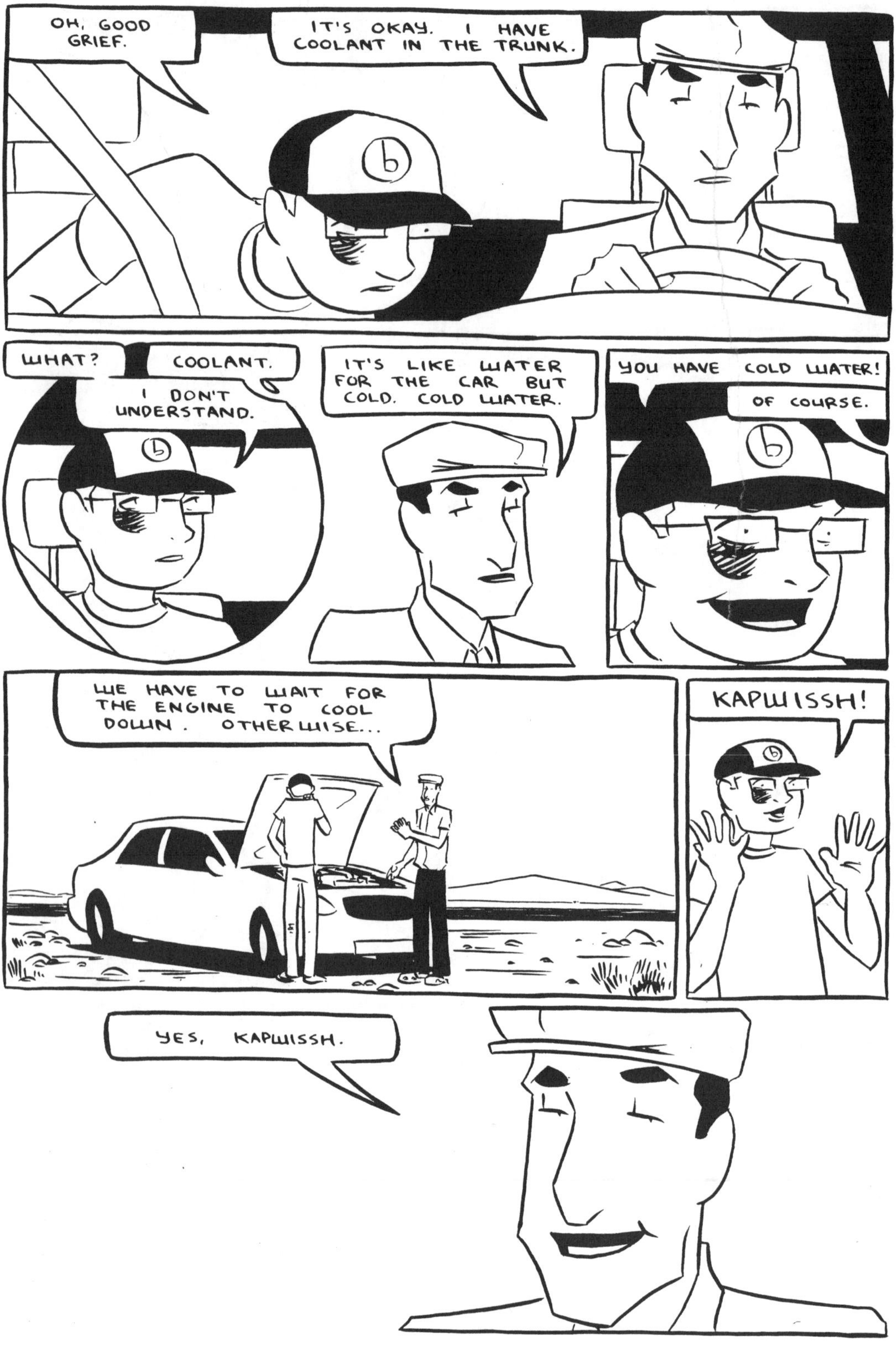
OH, GOOD GRIEF.
IT'S OKAY. I HAVE COOLANT IN THE TRUNK.
WHAT?
COOLANT.
I DON'T UNDERSTAND.
IT'S LIKE WATER FOR THE CAR BUT COLD. COLD WATER.
YOU HAVE COLD WATER!
OF COURSE.
WE HAVE TO WAIT FOR THE ENGINE TO COOL DOWN. OTHERWISE...
KAPWISSH!
YES, KAPWISSH.

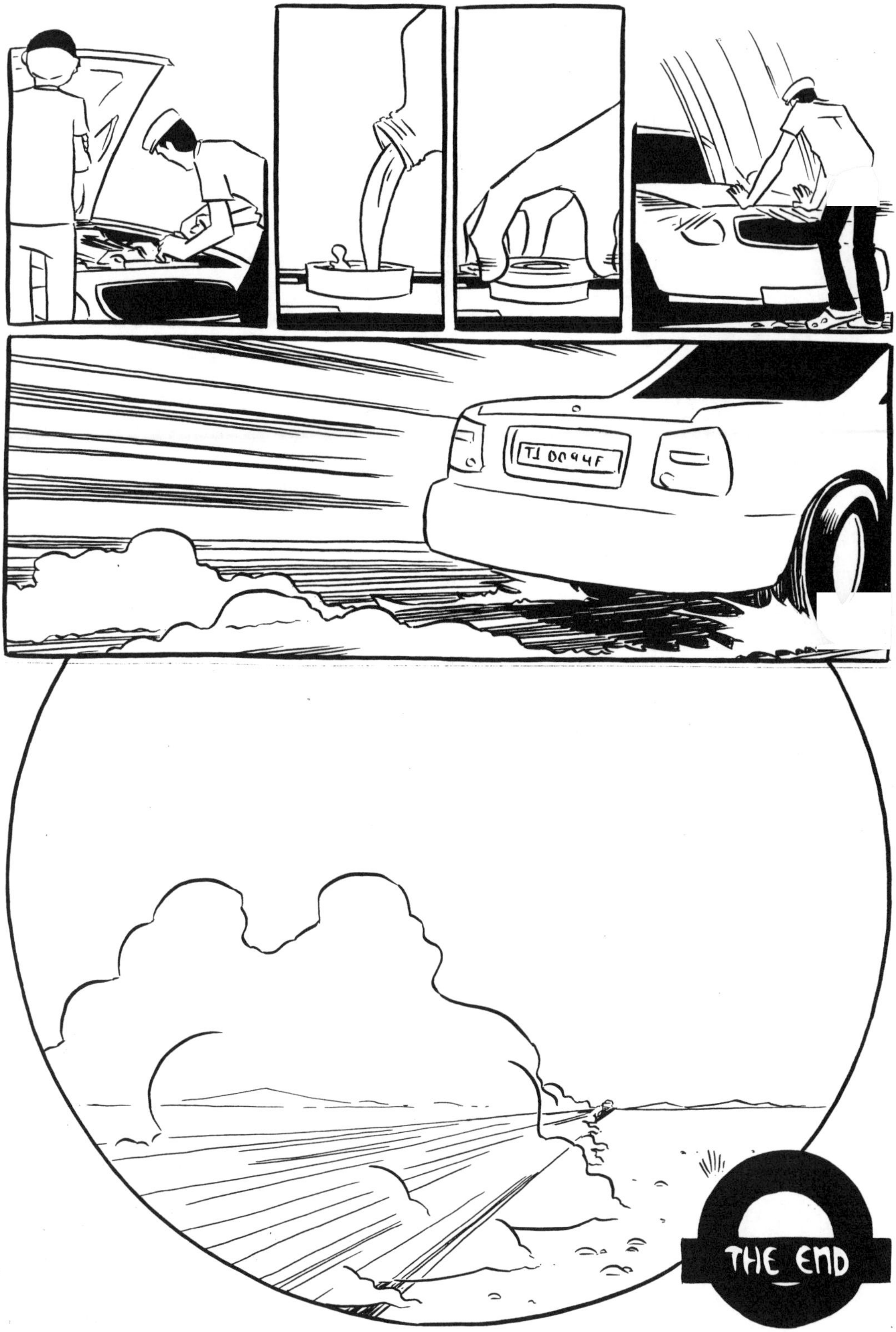
THE END